THE DEMON

Michael Tanner was born and educated in Oxford. After attending Littlemore Grammar School he went up to St Edmund Hall where in addition to taking his degree he represented the University numerous times on the rugby field. He was a schoolmaster for 18 years prior to becoming a critically acclaimed and award -nominated author specializing in sport and history. Besides contributing features across the print media, he has been involved with radio and television at both local and national level. The Demon *is his 27th book. He now lives in Lincolnshire.*

Also by Michael Tanner

Non Fiction
Crime & Murder in Victorian Leicestershire
My Friend Spanish Steps
The King George VI Steeplechase
Teleprompter & Co
The Champion Hurdle
Pretty Polly: An Edwardian Heroine
Great Racing Partnerships
Dessie: A Year in the Life of Desert Orchid
The Major: The Biography of Dick Hern
Great Jockeys of the Flat
Michael Roberts: A Champion's Story
Lester Piggott: Return to the Saddle
Ali in Britain
Branston Abby: Record Breaker
A Season in Stripes: Life with the Leicester Tigers
In Your Face: A Rugby Odyssey
The Champion Hurdle: From Blaris to Istabraq
Troubled Epic: On Location With *Ryan's Daughter*
The Legend of Mick the Miller
Gentleman George? The Contradictory Life of George Duffield
The Suffragette Derby
The Spotted Wonder
The Oxford Murder

Fiction
The Tinman's Farewell
The Black Bridge
Red Hand

Michael Tanner's Work

'Tanner enjoys the myths and separates them adroitly from the facts.' *The Times*

'As good as any Dick Francis novel.' *Mail on Sunday*

'Tanner writes with humour and authority.' *Irish Times*

'Candid and entertaining, full of biting observations.' *Daily Telegraph*

'Fittingly listed for the William Hill Sports Book of the Year.' *The Independent*

'A heart-warming, evocative book.' *Sunday Telegraph*

'Impeccably researched.' *The Spectator*

'Tanner's magnum opus.' *Sunday Times*

'Book of the year...infectious prose...the author's scholarship shines through.' *Racing Post*

'Brilliant – the definitive account.' *Books Ireland*

'Entertaining as it is informative.' *The Field*

'Book of the year...the style and panache of a true Oxford graduate.' *Horse & Hound*

'One of the sports books of the year.' *The Observer*

'The writing is sharp, the story well told.' *Irish Field*

'Barrow loads of passion and no shortage of incident.' *Pacemaker International*

'One of our top sports writers.' *Leicester Mercury*

'If you can afford only one racing book this year, look no farther.' *Raceform*

'A huge contribution to Turf literature, and a compulsive read.' *Blackpool Gazette*

'A fascinating blend of social history and sporting drama.' *Time Out*

'Blimey, what a book!' *Sky Sports*

'A book you will treasure. The closing passages turned me to blubber.' *Teletext*

THE DEMON

The Life of George Fordham

M<small>ICHAEL</small> T<small>ANNER</small>

authorHOUSE®

AuthorHouse™ UK
1663 Liberty Drive
Bloomington, IN 47403 USA
www.authorhouse.co.uk
Phone: 0800.197.4150

Published by AuthorHouse 05/09/2017

ISBN: 978-1-5246-8011-4 (sc)
ISBN: 978-1-5246-8019-0 (e)

Print information available on the last page.

CONTENTS

PREFACE

The finest jockey is not necessarily the most successful. Or the most celebrated. When legend becomes entangled with fact it's legend that tends to be perpetuated.

Nowhere is this truer than on the Victorian Turf. Fred Archer was the most successful and the most celebrated jockey. He attracted attention like a firecracker tossed through an open window. But George Fordham, 'The Demon', was the finest. He was a genius. And defining genius taxes conventional criteria; one may as well try to measure happiness with a slide-rule. A gift more precious than gold, frankincense and myrrh was brought to Fordham's crib. A talent only God bestows.

George Fordham unleashed that talent with successes in the Cambridgeshire and Chester Cup as a four-stone mite of 16 and became champion jockey at 18. Twenty years Archer's senior, his prolific career as a multiple champion overlapped that of his pale, lanky and brooding rival who was nicknamed 'The Tinman' owing to his insatiable pursuit of 'tin' - Victorian slang for money; indeed, there were traces of the inoffensive bank clerk in his countenance. 'The Demon' was the very antithesis of 'The Tinman'. Fordham was much shorter, his squat frame giving him a distinctly lower centre of gravity, while a rubicund face of the soil advertized a certain rustic affability. And if Archer rode like a man with the devil at his elbow, Fordham rode like a wizard with wand in hand; working gossamer reins with enough finesse to crook a marionette's finger.

The deposed 14-times champion fought a guerrilla campaign against the young pretender for more than a decade; and despite the inevitable loss of the war Fordham bested Archer in countless skirmishes. When the 'tyranny of the scales' eventually became too much for his fragile psyche and brittle constitution 'The Tinman' put a gun in his mouth and pulled the trigger. He was just 29 years-old. Thus are legends implanted in our sporting consciousness: books are written; laurels awarded.

Yet truth will out. Fordham was considered Archer's superior by the majority of contemporary jockeys, trainers, horsemen or scribes. Indeed, Fordham was the one jockey Archer feared and whose talents reduced him to utter frustration; 'The Demon' was the itch he couldn't scratch. But his death was far less Homeric. Thus are legends expunged from our sporting consciousness; books are not written; and laurels wither on the vine. *The Sporting Life* pronounced: 'If it had pleased providence to take him, as poor Archer was taken, in the heyday of his splendid career, what obsequies we should have witnessed.'

Thus, it is high time George Fordham received his due. Nobody can deny that the worth of any competitor is gauged by those he competes against, and the measure of George Fordham is the greatness of the jockey deigned his inferior. Archer is the Frazier to his Ali: the Mill House to his Arkle. Wherever loyalties lie one thing is indisputable. If

Fordham stands parity with the single 19th century jockey mentioned in the same breath as 20th century icons Steve Donoghue, Gordon Richards and Lester Piggott he surely merits equal deification.

In racing, as in all things, there are stars. Then there are real stars. And then there's genius.

Michael Tanner
Sleaford,
April 2017

THURSDAY, 10 MAY 1883:
SETTLING DAY

Newmarket racecourse is abuzz. The afternoon's run of the mill sport will be elevated by a match race. The two horses in this equine duel are of little account. But their partners are Fred Archer and George Fordham. And there's no love lost between 'The Tinman' and 'The Demon'.

The ruthless young champion can get away with bullying every other jockey in the weighing room, but not 'The Demon'. Fordham gets under his skin. The tempestuous rivalry between the two champions finds no edgier expression than match races. 'The Kidder', another Fordham alias, excels in any such battle of wits. And this particular match race is destined to be a corker.

It was made for £200 over the final five furlongs of the Rowley Mile. The duellists are Lord William Beresford's six-year-old Reputation and Leopold de Rothschild's five-year-old Brag. Archer was engaged for Reputation; Brag is in the hands of Fordham. It's the third day of the meeting. Fordham has already humbled Archer in one match on the Tuesday, forcing Tourist up to beat Indecision by a neck. 'That old devil always terrifies me in matches at Newmarket,' Archer told the Duke of Portland. 'Nobody knows what he is up to. They're about right when they call him the "Old Demon"'

Having carved up Thursday's opening three events between them, neither jockey is short of confidence. 'Mind the old man don't do you again!' a mischief-maker chafes as Archer passes on Reputation. The barb finds a nerve. That countenance redolent of a well kept grave hides a short-fused temperament. Archer wants to win this match as badly as a miser wants to own gold sovereigns. 'I will be half-way home this time,' he fires back instinctively, 'before the old gentleman knows where he is!'

Unfortunately for Archer this slight is overheard by Fordham's friend Henry Custance. Knowing Fordham is walking to post, he jumps on his hack, catches him up and reports Archer's threat. Fordham smiles inscrutably and says deadpan: 'All right, Cus.'

Fordham's smile is both measured and prescient. No man, before or since, has ridden Newmarket with greater mastery than he. He'd stockpiled knowledge of its every bump and divot as a banker hoards securities; and he'd more faith in his choosing the right moment to cash them than a saint has in Christ himself. He knew every blade of grass and possessed an uncanny awareness of where the winning line lay - and thus when to launch his famous 'rush' that collared an opponent in the final stride. So sure was he about the course taken by the winning line from one side of the wide Rowley Mile to the other that he once had the temerity to ask no less a personage than Lord Falmouth to point out to him where a jockey should aim to win. His lordship was astonished to find his estimate way off kilter when Fordham proceeded to show him.

The jockey had no intention of making his social superior appear foolish. But 'The Demon' sets out quite deliberately to make an utter fool of Archer in this match. Fordham is never the most articulate of men, yet mounted on a thoroughbred he becomes fluent in a language they both understand. He will tease and torment Archer throughout every yard of the five furlongs.

First of all he pulls Brag around at the start to the accompaniment of a few 'whoas', giving the impression his mount is being uncooperative. Then, when the flag falls, he takes a pull to endorse that recalcitrance. Duped into thinking he's stolen a march on an opponent who isn't in the mood to race, Archer feels he can afford to show his hand. He pushes Reputation clear. He's unaware Fordham has him on the rack.

The older Reputation is conceding a stone to Brag and ought to have been conserved for one short run at the death. But Fordham now has him where he wants him. He tucks in behind. He's holding back until the weight and the exertion begin to tell. Still he waits as Archer spurs a tiring Reputation down into the Dip for one final effort. The screw is tightening.

Experience tells Fordham that Archer must steal a peek at some point to ascertain his position and how well he is going. When Archer does just that, Fordham feigns distress. Once Archer turns his gaze back behind Reputation's mane, however, Fordham's elbows cease rowing and his habitual 'cluck-clucking' exhortation stills. There remains just one final turn of the screw.

On meeting the rising ground inside the final 100 yards Archer's partner falters, as Fordham knows it must. 'The Kidder' stops bluffing. No jockey keeps his powder dry quite like Fordham. Now he primes Brag and fires him at the line. This is the renowned Fordham 'rush': the deadly swoop of hawk impaling rabbit that is his trademark. Archer feels Brag's hot breath and hears the rhythmic snap of the whip stoking it. But he is helpless. Brag wins by a neck. Archer's chin slumps to his chest. He's been toyed with; used like a play-thing; and then tossed aside. He looks across at his personal Torquemada. Fordham's air of serenity leaves no doubt how deep his satisfaction goes; 'The Demon' lets a smile curl under his nose like a trail from his favourite cigar.

This second humiliation inside a week is too much for Archer. He storms into the weighing room, angrier than a wasp in a jam jar. He slings his saddle at his valet and utters the telling phrase: 'I can't beat that kidding bastard!'

Those six words settle the argument. Archer knew he was second best. Fordham was a jockey apart.

The diminutive Fordham perched atop his first winner – Hampton.

ONE

HONESTY IS THE BEST POLICY

His father was a groom and his mother was a Newmarket girl who nurtured an aspiration to be a school ma'am. That he grew up small determined he'd follow the path ordained by his father; but not to the detriment of that altruism inherent in his mother's good intentions.

The boy child destined to find fame as 'The Demon' took his first breath on Sunday 24 September 1837 in the Cambridge parish of Holy Trinity. The groves of academe within touching distance would never call him. Horses not books beckoned. He was born to ride not read. His calling lay on the Turf.

The boy's birth coincided with the dawn of a new age that became synonymous with the name of the queen who'd ascended the throne a few months earlier. The nation over which Victoria reigned was coming to terms with a recent General Election that returned the Whigs to power under Lord Melbourne while news of continued unrest in Cork and Limerick filtered across the Irish Sea. A number of aesthetes had just enjoyed listening to the pianist and composer Felix Mendelssohn performing a selection of Bach at the Birmingham Festival; but thousands more had attended Doncaster races and witnessed Mango win an eventful St Leger in which one runner was barged off the track into a ditch and another was felled by a large greyhound wandering into its path. There's no question which event would've most interested the horse-loving Fordhams.

The infant George would not be short of kith and kin. There were as many Fordhams along the Cambridgeshire-Hertfordshire border as one could throw a stick at. The surname was first recorded in the early 13th century and Fordhams had owned land hereabouts since Elizabethan times; and a village advertising that fact (Old English for a flat low-lying meadow by a stream) lies just outside Newmarket. A second child of the 19th century born in the locality blessed with the name of George Fordham would earn a knighthood following a distinguished career in public service that included the offices of Sheriff of Cambridgeshire and Chairman of the County Council.

However, the George Fordham who earned his honorary knighthood 'in the pigskin' hailed from humbler stock. The Cambridge residence of his 23-year-old mother Amelia is listed as White Hart Yard, home to a fishmonger and a plumber in addition to the parish workhouse. Amelia Wing had married James Fordham in 1835 and their first son, named after his father, was born the same year. The family swiftly multiplied with the addition of Amelia and Thomas and moved a few hundred yards to Hobson Street; and just as quickly plunged into dire circumstances when the birth of a fourth son, Charles, coincided with the death of his father in May 1845 from a diseased heart at the age of 36.

With seven-year-old George and four other young mouths to feed Amelia Fordham was left in a desperate plight. If the workhouse was to be avoided solutions had to be found quickly. The accommodation problem was solved by sharing a house in King Street with another family. Finding a source of income was more problematic. However, Amelia Fordham did not lack drive. By 1851 she'd begun working as a school mistress. Given that she couldn't sign her name on George's birth certificate this advancement suggests a woman of some tenacity. Quite possibly any latent aptitude for the classroom was brought forth by teaching her own children; certainly, there's no evidence of an education beyond the rudimentary to be found in her son George. In time he'd sign his name in a flowing copperplate that suggested a degree of untapped potential, but he could never claim to be learned. Amelia Fordham's career in the school room was short-lived. The most pragmatic course of action for her to pursue was seized in 1852: she remarried and resumed a life of domesticity. William Rayner was a local agricultural labourer who gave her three more children. Amelia never left Cambridge, dying there in 1885.

As soon as George was able-bodied he began making his small contribution to the family purse; he became a grocer's errand boy. The future for an undersized boy from the lower classes in the England of the 1840s was bleak. Beyond the dubious benefits arising from a life of crime, the main path someone of George Fordham's background might take toward bettering himself was through sporting prowess. At the time the prize ring or the back of a thoroughbred racehorse was the only home to the paid sportsman: emulating Bendigo or Frank Buckle was the boyhood dream. The young Fordham was too puny to make a pugilist. But the boy was the son of a groom and an affinity with horseflesh ran in the family. He'd have known his way round a horse at a tender age, soon put on the back of one by his father. He observed their ways and mannerisms. The seeds of horsemanship were sewn in his young brain.

As is often the case in the closed community of the Turf, the youngster would profit from a healthy dose of nepotism. His uncle Thomas Fordham was well placed to help. Capitalizing on the best schooling the Turf could offer at Robert Robson's Classic-winning Newmarket stable, he'd risen to the position of head lad in the yard of Richard Drewitt on Mickleham Downs, near Leatherhead in Surrey. The obvious step was for George to join elder brother James, who'd already exploited the family ties by moving to Mickleham; in time Thomas and Charles followed the same route. James and Thomas became proficient enough to get rides and often pitted their wits against George – with the outcome not always favouring George. James eventually assumed the position of Drewitt's head lad; Thomas would find notoriety as a 'tout'; while Charles became a newspaper tipster and huntsman.

To all intents and purposes George Fordham was born at the age of ten the day he accompanied his uncle Thomas back to Mickleham and entered the world of a racing stable. Removed from the bosom of one family he was thrust into another comprising the half dozen other tots with whom he shared a dormitory. It was not long before he was on the move again. Drewitt transferred to Upper House Stables in Lewes and took his nephews with him.

Dick Drewitt was the perfect type of individual to school the young Fordhams. He was a diligent, meticulous and capable stableman who'd been tutored by William Forth, trainer of the 1840 Derby winner Little Wonder. Moreover, Drewitt was scrupulously honest. He cared little about the science of handicapping and had no interest in betting. Once, having watched a favourable trial with Sir John Astley, the owner asked how much he would have on. Drewitt pulled his waistcoat down with both hands while contemplating an answer. 'Drat it!' he replied. 'I won't have anything, thank you. But if he wins, you will have to give the Missus a new bonnet.' As Mrs Drewitt tipped the scales at every ounce of 14 stone the cost of a bonnet was preferable to a dress. As for her husband, it was frequently said Dick Drewitt cared more for his Berkshire pigs as he did the racehorses in his care.

How the pint-sized George - he weighed 3st 7lb when his apprenticeship commenced - was treated is unknown. But shortly before his death Fordham penned a brief note to a friendly journalist at *The Morning Post* in which he stated: 'My early life was a dog one as I had to ride four stone in big races and heats.' The Drewitts were childless and we're told Penelope Drewitt warmed to Fordham more than most of the boys owing to his better behaviour - even though he was said to display 'an almost uncontrollable love of mischief.' Beyond that proviso he'd have been treated no differently than any other boy in Drewitt's yard. It's no exaggeration to say apprenticeships in a Victorian racing stable boasted curricula harsher than any Victorian school – which was brutal enough. The dawn-to-dusk seven-days-a-week life of unremitting toil and systemic bullying for scant reward would either make a man of a boy or break him. But it was preferable to being a chimney boy. 'Whatsoever thy hand findeth to do, do it with all thy might,' was the maxim. There was little time left for any social life or formal schooling.

The boys had to learn to ride before their weight reached four stone so they might be used on the 'feather' weights that dominated most races on a card. Any youngster who showed Drewitt promise would start his road to the racetrack by riding in trials on his master's gallops. If that test was passed he'd be given a ride in public; overcome that obstacle successfully and the boy might earn a retainer of £10 per annum – or even double that were he extremely promising. A top jockey might generate a retainer of £200 in addition to five guineas per ride and 'presents' from grateful winning owners – besides the 'unmentionable' hand-outs from bookmakers and hangers-on in return for inside information. However, the harsh facts of a jockey's life for nine months of the year were inescapable. *Baily's Magazine* set them out for all to read. Even if the young Fordham had neither time nor inclination to read them or they weren't spelled out to him by Drewitt, he'd quickly become aware of them.

> For the jockey lamb comes in at Easter in vain and he dare not dream of venison in September; salmon might as well remain in the Tweed as far as he is concerned. The life is not without charms. He is courted by all ranks of society, from the peer of the realm who fills his cigar case down to the licenced victualler who stands him a fiver in return for a good thing. He represents a class who exercise more potent influence on the destiny of mankind than is generally understood, and in whom at times noblemen and gentlemen repose as much confidence as they do in their family solicitor or physician. A jockey of the first class is in general a living advertisement of the gratitude of his friends and his residence is as much a museum of their favours; the liquids with which he washes down dinner will be tempting enough to make him relish a walrus. How quick lads are in catching the living manners as they rise and, having the opportunity of coming across the highest in the land they naturally form a standard of excellence of their own. He must have the courage to ride violent horses; coolness in difficulties; judgement with respect to pace; and a good head never to ill-use a horse when he is doing his best; and when we discuss the feats of a brilliant jockey, and the races he has pulled out of the fire, the most flattering episode we can add to his fame is that no money could tempt him to do wrong.

Not unsurprisingly Drewitt's nephew was one apprentice who displayed visible promise around thoroughbreds; certainly enough to invoke immediate tutoring in the fundamentals of horsemanship and jockeyship. These two qualities are not mutually inclusive. A fine horseman understands horses, empathizes with them, masters them, guides them and channels their energy to maximum effect. But he might not make a proficient jockey who depends more on his race-riding ability than any degree in horsemanship. He'd need to judge pace; know the gaps to seize and those to leave; and when to make his run. If Fordham could affect a successful marriage between these twin qualities his future in the saddle would be assured.

Month by month the boy gradually became accustomed to greeting each day from between the ears of a horse while listening to a dawn chorus of larks ascending and thumpety-thumping hooves. A month after his thirteenth birthday he was deemed ready. On Thursday 24 October 1850 Fordham got his first taste of race-riding aboard his master's Isabella in the Feather Plate, the opening race of a Brighton card. One can only imagine the eager teenager's anxiety on that day because racing was in jeopardy. This card should've been run the previous afternoon but torrential rain had reduced the course, tricky enough at the best of times owing to its curves, cambers and descents, to an 'unfavourable state' in the opinion of the Stewards. Fortunately for young George, the Stewards opted for a 24-hour postponement instead of abandonment.

Six opponents lay in wait for Isabella. The two-year-old bay daughter of Pantaloon had not run since mid June. If she reproduced that early season form Isabella would stand a grand chance. Her two starts had borne a win first time of asking at Hampton and a laudable second place at no less a venue than Ascot in the Windsor Town Plate. Then she'd carried the colours of the Duke of Richmond. Thereafter something must've gone wrong with her. There's no record of what that might've been, but her sale and subsequent four months on the sidelines suggests a problem – and contesting a Brighton Plate is a long way from the giddy heights of Ascot. The winner of this race was to be sold for £50, in return for which the two-year-old was allowed a 14lb allowance from her seniors.

Fordham rode her at home. And would have no bother making the 5st she was set to carry. Indeed, his body weight was increased to the necessary impost with heavy clothing and a large saddle. That tiny boys should ride in races was nothing new. They were a plentiful commodity in a Victorian society plagued by inadequate nutrition. The weight range in handicaps, for instance, reflected this fact of life. To see the majority of runners carrying less than 7st was routine. Five stone and lower was not uncommon. Obtaining the services of a proficient 'tiny' or 'feather' capable of controlling half a ton of thoroughbred horseflesh at speeds of 35 miles per hour was a constant source of worry for the Victorian trainer. Delays at the start resulting from these minute boys being incapable of controlling fractious beasts eager to get on with the job they were trained to do were daily occurrences. Spills were a fact of racecourse life. 'Runaways' were ten a penny. If Drewitt could make a jockey of Fordham he'd become a priceless asset. And compared to one or two, Fordham was positively gargantuan: Kitchener's body weight was only 2st 12lb when he won the Chester Cup on Red Deer in 1844.

The favourite for the Feather Plate was the three-year-old filly Handsome Doe. She won as a favourite should, by three lengths and unflustered. The future 'Demon' passed the post last of the sextet. The fledgling jockey's craving for a further dose of the exhilaration he'd felt was granted on 5 November when he went to Epsom to ride Cora. The chestnut filly was another 'cast-off' from a bigger yard. Earlier that season she'd represented Lord Exeter in the One Thousand Guineas and Oaks; though unplaced in both Classics, Cora had won at Newmarket, Ascot (a walk over) and Goodwood besides finishing second in Ascot's competitive sprint handicap, the Wokingham Stakes. In Drewitt's care she'd toured minor southern tracks to no avail, and this day she gave Fordham no hope of success on his first experience of a racecourse that would become something of a bogey to him. By the time Fordham returned to Brighton in October 1851 he'd had one further mount, Don Pedro in a two-mile event at Hampton in June. They finished third of seven. But now, at the fourth time of asking, Fordham would ride his first winner.

The horse was Hampton, a two-year-old chestnut colt by Slane, winner of the Oxford Cup and second in the Gold Cup at Ascot. Unfortunately, in the words of 'The Druid', alias Henry Hall Dixon of *The Sporting Life*, Slane had 'a sad aptitude for getting animals whose chief speciality was to be game and slow.' Drewitt had purchased Hampton for the specific purpose of being Fordham's equine tutor. However, it was surprising, mindful of Dixon's reservations, to see Hampton pitched into a sprint race, Brighton's Trial Stakes on 9 October. It would be his sixth race of the season, a second place at the Brighton August meeting being his best effort. Fordham, once more aided by plenty of padding, weighed out at 4st 11lb. Among the eight he and Hampton faced was his nemesis of last year, Handsome Doe – set to give her younger rival a hefty 2st 6lb. Drewitt knew what he was doing. Hampton defied his parentage, and The Druid's disparagement, to win by two lengths; thereby initiating his sale for 55 sovereigns. He was turned out the next day for the Feather Plate, but the concession of 7lb to Venison proved one length too much for the colt and his young partner. Fordham subsequently trod the same path to Epsom the following month as he had in 1850, riding Hampton in a race over a mile – with the same disappointing outcome as the previous year.

Fordham would not ride another winner for two years. Drewitt's aim was to give him experience rather than a stream of winners; to become acquainted with the minor tracks that provided the bread and butter of Victorian racing while still finding him opportunities in the Turf's premier handicaps. With this end in mind Fordham entered the orbit of Edward 'Ned' Smith whose varied racecourse involvement was conducted under the *nom de course* of 'Mr Mellish'. Smith was as shrewd as they come in matters of the Turf and good company to boot. The young Fordham had found himself another 'uncle' who could give his career a leg-up.

His education gradually gained pace. At one end of the spectrum he rides at King's Lynn, Rochester, Northampton, Warwick and Tunbridge; at the other he gets a mount at Ascot, finishing third, and experiences the amphitheatre that is Chester's 'Roodee' for the first time by riding Benita in the 1852 Tradesman's Cup (later, of course, better known as the Chester Cup). Surviving two circuits of this cramped racetrack in the midst of 43 runners could not have done Fordham anything but good. The next day he finished second on a horse belonging to Lord Clifden. Later on York's Great Ebor Handicap offered him a second opportunity to advertise his wares in the highest company during 1852. Establishing contacts with prominent owners like Lord Clifden was as crucial as gaining experience of England's racecourses. On 12 August, for example, he finished second on a horse called Freetrader at King's Lynn owned by a certain 'Mr Howard'. This was one *nom de course* of Henry Padwick, moneylender to the rich and an acolyte of the powerful 'Danebury Confederacy' overseen by the Day family. It would not be long before Fordham and Danebury became synonymous.

Fordham's fourth season replicated its predecessor. He partnered lightweights in major handicaps such as the City and Suburban and Great Metropolitan at Epsom, the Chester Cup, and the Stewards Cup at Goodwood. More significantly, he participated in his first 'match' of sorts. This came at Tunbridge on 18 August 1853. Some races were still settled in heats. In the three heats that decided a routine Seller, Fordham took the first heat but lost the next two. The following month Fordham did manage to record that vital second career victory, gaining Rochester's Medway Stakes by a head on Luxurious. Fordham was now just a heartbeat away from seeing his name up in lights.

Drewitt's yard housed another son of Slane called Little David. He was an outsider for the 1853 Cambridgeshire, whose prize of £2,115 (£360,000 in today's money) made it one of the most valuable, and thus most keenly-contested, handicaps in the calendar: even Classics such as the Two Thousand Guineas and St Leger only paid £1,940 and £2,035 respectively. No fewer than 64 horses featured on the racecard of whom 39 (including the French mare Hervine and the German raider Seahorse) would face the starter. Like all the country's great handicaps the race was a potential red letter day for the 'tinies' or 'feathers' because low weights predominated – 22 horses carried less than 7st. Little David was handicapped at 5st 10lb, humping 26lb of lead in his saddlecloth as Fordham still only weighed 3st 12lb stripped; just one rival carried less weight. The plan was to make that pay. Fordham's orders were simple: let the horse loose. Drewitt drew confidence from the fact that Haco, one of the favourites having just won the Cesarewitch, was once in his yard and Little David had been tried to be 9lb his superior. Yet Haco was set to give Little David 9lb in the second leg of the Autumn Double instead of receiving it.

Little David's owner owner was a Mr Hutchinson, a wealthy and mildly eccentric tanner, who raced under the imaginative *nom de course* of 'Mr W Smith'. A successful ship-owner (until ruined by the Crimean War), it was said he only read three books in his life – the Holy Bible, the Sporting Calendar and the Duke of Wellington's Despatches – from which he selected names for his horses. As the Cambridgeshire was one of the major betting mediums of the season

Hutchinson was keen to profit from his knowledge of a 'good thing' before the price was stolen. 'For God's sake,' he implored Drewitt on the way to Newmarket, 'let us get through London quietly!'

The journey was completed without disclosure: Little David went off at 33 to 1. Were he to win, it would not only be a staggering result but, more importantly, it would be a huge feather in Fordham's cap. Packed train after packed train arrived at Newmarket station on a balmy autumn day to create an atmosphere far exceeding that of Cesarewitch day. *The Times* paints the backdrop to the forerunner of many momentous race days in Fordham's career:

> The Cambridgeshire was marked by its familiar and distinguishing characteristics of eager excitement and businesslike proceedings. The weather was propitious, and the attendance of professional Turfites and pleasure folk was unusually numerous. Indeed, just before the decision of the great event of the day the long line of horsemen that stretched from the top of the Stand to way down the course presented a scene which no other country than England could parallel.

Fordham was geed up. In his eagerness, he twice anticipated the start. But he judged the third accurately and soon took up the running – or, at least, Little David did. The extent to which his young pilot was a mere passenger must remain a moot point as a dazzling low sun ruined visibility from the enclosures. Doubtless clinging on for dear life, all he had to do was keep Little David pointing down the straight green sward of the Rowley Mile – a stretch of turf on which he'd eventually be without peer. The partnership reached the Bushes, two furlongs out, with a comfortable lead and kept on extending its advantage, which had grown to ten lengths by the winning post. *Bell's Life* recorded the teenager's breakthrough success thus:

The cavalry charge that was the start of the 1853 Cambridgeshire.

> A more runaway race was never seen, the winner having jumped off with a clear lead lead at starting and held it throughout. All attempts to catch him proved futile. Little David hung toward the lower ground on the stands side very much all the way through the final furlong but he was so full of racing that he galloped almost into the town before his clever little jockey could pull him up – which will account for his being the last to weigh in.

Victory was indeed a textbook example of a successful 'runaway'. Said Fordham: 'He was a good horse and I couldn't stop him!' Even so, some reckoned they'd identified something in the boy's seat and method that hinted at greatness to come. Hutchinson's worries came to nought. 'Little David was backed by friends of his trainer only and the investments on him were not considerably heavy,' reported *The Times*. Some measure of the colossal amounts at stake in the betting ring during this period may be gleaned from the fact that Hutchinson's winnings of £2,000 – roughly *£340,000* in today's currency – was not regarded as noteworthy. Drewitt was rewarded with £300 (*£51,000*); and the young jockey was presented with a Bible, a tie pin, and a gold-headed whip inscribed: 'Honesty is the best policy'.

Little David was in the form of his life. He started at even money a week later in Epsom's Autumn Handicap, and even the 7lb penalty failed to prevent him from giving a two-length beating to no less than Jouvence, winner of both the French Derby (Prix du Jockey Club) and French Oaks (Prix de Diane). 'Little David followed up his Newmarket success,' said *The Times*, 'by carrying off the chief handicap sweepstakes with a degree of ease which materially added to his reputation.'

It's highly improbable Fordham employed his new whip at Epsom. But who knows just how many times the boy examined that handsome gift and pondered its sentiment in the months and years to come. Since jockeys of any age seldom received personal mementos, this first present, like a first love, may have resonated. How prescient that inscription would turn out. As 'Thormanby', W Willmott Dixon, wrote: 'At all events, he ever afterwards adopted it for his motto, and acted up to it with scrupulous fidelity.'

Fordham's well-being and progress were closely monitored by Drewitt who ensured his earnings were not squandered: one of his owners with knowledge of the investment market, Mr JS Douglas, was entrusted with investing most of it so that 'there was no fear of its being improperly employed or the young jockey being left without rescources in the evening of his life.' Nevertheless, Drewitt couldn't wrap the boy in cotton wool. Accidents happen. And one befell Fordham which nearly cost him his life, and certainly scarred him for life. He was exercising an old 'schoolma'am' of Drewitt's called Miss Nipper in the straw-yard when the mare threw him and, his foot slipping through the iron, he was suspended by the knee. Miss Nipper panicked, and dragged Fordham round the yard, trying to kick him as she went, before Drewitt could effect rescue. The accident had profound ramifications. Fordham sported an enlarged knee joint until his dying day – an encumbrance that restricted his ability to control his weight by the accepted method in the years before the advent of Turkish baths, which was walking considerable distances in heavy clothing. There was but one option– as Fordham later recalled:

> I only weighed 3st 7lb when I began to ride – feather weights they were in those days – and when I got 4st 3lb they wanted me to get down to 4st. Then I got 4st 7lb and they wanted me to do 4st 5lb, and so they kept on at me. When I commenced riding for Jaxon and Barber, I had to begin 'physic' to keep under 5st, through partly being a cripple because of my knee.

Prolonged usage of 'physic' as a purgative could damage a man's constitution – and in Fordham's case it would. Lastly, and perhaps more importantly, this sickening experience in Drewitt's straw-yard may have brought home to him the perils of recklessness in the company of equines that found permanent expression in his safety-first policy when running the gauntlet that was Epsom's Tattenham Hill during the every-man-for-himself anarchy of a Derby.

Fordham's physique continued to serve as a bonus rather than a liability. At this time weights went down to 4st; it was some years before the Jockey Club raised minimum weights to 5st 7lb. And whatever his lowest weight every jockey was encouraged to 'boil' himself down to an even lower one: the 8st veteran would try manfully to reduce his weight to that of a young man; the 7st youngster would eye the weight of a boy; and a boy like Fordham would be forced to replicate a babe in arms - especially if the objective was to win a prize like the Chester Cup. In 1852 he'd almost matched Kitchener's feat on the scales by riding Benita at 4st – one of 26 in a field of 43 that carried less than 7st; they finished fourth. The following season he rode Rosalba at 4st 10lb. Finally, in 1854, he emulated Kitchener by winning the Cup.

Chester's spring meeting was one of the beacons in the English racing calendar. Newmarket, home to the Jockey Club and the best part of a thousand horses in training, was the headquarters of English racing, but every provincial racecourse had its day – or, to be more accurate, its days. The growing presence of railways had transformed many of these country meetings into suburban meetings or, at very least, vast gatherings – nowhere more noticeably than in the North. However, railways were only just beginning to be adopted for travelling racehorses. Thus it made sense for meetings to last a day or two, and longer still for major venues. When hosting Classics, for instance, the meetings at Epsom and Doncaster lasted four days. Four days also suited Ascot and Goodwood, which were important social as well as sporting events; Newmarket's Houghton meeting in October lasted the five days of Monday to Friday. The racing year had settled into a round of provincial highlights where, from Liverpool and Manchester to Stockbridge and Brighton, sport and entertainment were married on a broader scale. Racing was as much a part of the country faire as the carousels, side shows and 'bearded ladies' that entertained well into the night. Chester's attendances during its three-day faire would see 35,000 people passing through its beleaguered railway station en route to the Roodee, the cramped saucer of ground wedged between the city walls and the River Dee that hosted the sport.

> *Away to Chester's ancient walls!*
> *A thousand screaming trains have started;*
> *'Tis neck or nothing – Pleasure calls.*

The Cup constituted one of the season's prime betting markets. Wagering on the outcome had been conducted for months. It was fertile ground to propagate chicanery. The raging ante post favourite for the 1854 renewal of the Cup was the three-year-old filly Virago. She was trained by John Bahram Day at Michel Grove, high up on the Sussex Downs near Worthing, and owned by Henry Padwick. At this time there was no rule insisting horses must've won or run three times before they could contest a handicap. Reputation and word of mouth often played a key part in deciding an unexposed animal's handicap mark. Thus, Day and Padwick planned to hide Virago's potential from the prying eyes of Chester's handicapper, Edward Topham, by running her only once as a juvenile, in a back-end seller at Shrewsbury, with no intention other than making her appear next to useless. Day even ordered his head lad, William Goater, to hold her at the start and not release the filly until the rest were underway. With publication of the Chester Cup weights still two months away Padwick proceeded to snap up any fancy prices. But Topham was a wise old bird. He'd detected the whiff of deceit, and weighted Virago accordingly – burdening her with 20lb more than Day and Padwick had envisaged. The two conspirators were not amused. Virago was scratched. Instead she went to Epsom's spring fixture where she was weighted more to their liking. Virago carried 6st 4lb to win the City & Suburban Handicap over ten furlongs and 5st 9lb to win the Great Metropolitan Handicap over almost twice as far – all in the space of one hour. The filly went on to add the One Thousand Guineas and, among others, the Goodwood and Doncaster Cups. She was frequently referred to as the finest mare of the 19th century.

Virago's defection proved heaven sent for the remainder of the 1854 Chester Cup field whom her subsequent form suggested she'd had beaten hollow. The race now had an open feel to it. Over half the record 216 entry accepted Topham's handicapping and 24 eventually faced the starter for the £2,555 (*£434,000*) prize. *Bell's Life* captured the betting mood:

> Business in the Ring was conducted with the same boisterous spirit that of late has characterized proceedings of that body, which has degenerated to such an extent that the old stagers and respectable portion thereof begin to look with horror upon the 'roughs' who have lately embraced the profession of bookmaking.

Even Fordham's mount, the three-year-old chestnut gelding Epaminondas, was given the squeak of a chance with just 4st 10lb on his back (one of 11 carrying five stone or less) in spite of having met defeat in the previous day's Grosvenor Stakes. That, however, was over a sprint distance and may well have tuned him up. At any rate his price shortened 10 points to 25 to 1 in the hours before flag-fall. The classiest horse in the race was six-year-old Newminster, victor of the 1851 St Leger; the handsome son of the legendary racemare Beeswing shouldered top weight of 8st 2lb. But he wasn't favourite, the honour going to Dr O'Toole at 6 to 1.

Riding Chester and winning the Cup over two and a half miles posed Fordham totally different problems than riding Newmarket and winning the Cambridgeshire over a straight nine furlongs. A 'runaway' on Newmarket's open spaces might yield a few hairy moments for the feather on board but it was as nothing compared to riding in a big field round Chester's tight track that, barely one mile in circumference, kept horses constantly turning left-handed for almost three circuits. Fordham would need to deploy a blend of strength and balance to keep Epaminondas on his left lead throughout the race. Equally, he'd need to be alert to the possibility of early bunching as the field dashed for the first bend that came soon after the start. Then he'd to watch out for anything that had gone off too fast beginning to tire and fall back onto horses trying to launch a race-winning challenge. The chances of buffeting or clipping heels were high. Chester was notorious for its falls. For Epaminondas to be in contention, his rider's previous experience of riding in the Cup would need to belie his youth and size.

It was just as well Fordham was a quick learner – and that the Fates were on his side. He and Epaminondas enjoyed a trouble-free run. Following the best start to the Cup for years the race was soon confined to just half a dozen led by Baalbec, Acrobat and Epaminondas. Then a second stroke of luck came Fordham's way. With a half mile of the two and a half remaining, Newminster was going like a winner behind the three leaders when he suddenly broke down. Then, as if Fordham's cup was not already overflowing, Dr O'Toole came down just as he was poised to lock horns. This left the single challenger to Epaminondas in the short finishing straight as Indian Warrior. Fordham held him at bay to win cleverly by a length.

Bell's Life reported: 'The winner's success was hailed with tremendous cheering from the Ring, generally uproarious at the triumph of the outsider.' The result was a 'skinner' for the bookmakers. Even the horse's owner, Captain Douglas Lane, had backed him to win just a measly £80. So assured was the 16-year-old jockey, however, that he earned a striking plaudit from bookmaker William Davies, renowned as 'The Leviathan' on account of the magnitude of his transactions: 'That lad's the best lightweight I have ever seen.' This was some accolade given the fashion for lightweight jockeys in this era. Lord Howth went further, describing Fordham as 'The most wonderful lightweight that ever got into a saddle.'

It's possible neither observer had any idea who the 'lad' was in the first instance because Epaminondas had been omitted from the race-card. When the Judge, Richard Johnson, hoisted his number, he was instantly besieged by people yelling 'Hi! Mister Judge, there's nae such horse in the race as that number!' Some minutes elapsed before the row ceased and the vast crowd could make out which horse had prevailed. Fordham still required one more slice of good fortune. There was the possibility of an objection. *Bell's Life* explained:

> From a belief that little Fordham, who, be it said, rode remarkably well, had declared 2lb overweight beforehand, a slight misunderstanding arose at the scales owing to his inability to draw the 2lb. But it being satisfactorily proved to be a mistake, the owners of Indian Warrior – who stood to win a great stake – immediately admitted there was no ground whatever for an objection to the winner.

Back-to-back successes in two of the calendar's most competitive handicaps had entrenched Fordham's name in the minds of connections eager to secure the priceless services of a feather capable of landing a gamble in lucrative betting markets. The young rider's progress gathered momentum. In the words of *Baily's Magazine*, 'Drewitt found him almost a gold mine and far more profitable than many of the horses he trained, despite Fordham's abilities not being as fully appreciated as they ought to have been.' He rode three winners at Stamford's July meeting, two of them aboard El Dorado, in the Burghley Stakes and the feature event, the Stamford Cup. The race for the Burghley Stakes was especially prophetic. It resulted in a dead heat with Cock Pheasant ridden by the reigning champion jockey, John Wells. In the run-off Fordham revealed the guile that would win him endless match races by snatching the decision by a short head. Greater things awaited him at York. As soon as the weights were published for the Great Ebor Handicap he was snapped up for the mount on Grand Inquisitor by one of the canniest trainers in the business, Tom Parr of Wantage. Thus did Fordham go on to win a third of the Turf's great handicaps inside 12 months.

But it was two races in the dying embers of the 1854 season that announced George Fordham's coming of age. At Newmarket, on 27 October, still only a month past his seventeenth birthday, Fordham fought his first head-to-head duel with Nat Flatman, seven times leading jockey and supreme master of the 'match' race and the Newmarket track. Though Fordham and Jessamine had to give best to Flatman and Orson (the 6 to 5 on favourite) by a neck, it gave Fordham a priceless tutorial in the wiles he needed to perfect if he were ever to replace Flatman as lord of Newmarket Heath. The following week, in Epsom's Autumn Handicap, he was involved in a second desperate finish. It was yet another with John Wells. And the verdict went Fordham's way - as it had at Stamford.

Fordham dismounted from Mishap in the sure knowledge he had it in him to assume the mantle of king of the weighing room.

TWO

HEIR APPARENT

The weighing room entered by the 13-year-old Fordham in 1850 had contained only one champion jockey. Since totals were first logged annually in 1846 there'd only been one champion: Elnathan Flatman.

'Nat' Flatman was modest, dependable, honest and discreet – a jockey 'whom no bribe could corrupt' according to a contemporary writer. These constituted a clutch of attributes rare among early 19th century jockeys whose usual modus operandi went along the lines of 'win, tie or wrangle.' In 1846 these qualities made him eminently suitable to become the first officially recognized champion jockey with 81 winners. He retained the title for the next seven years, achieving his highest total of 104 in 1848. He was a worthy role model for the teenage Fordham.

Unlike many of his nefarious and venal contemporaries there was nothing flash or ostentatious about Flatman. Indeed, the very fact he was not popular with his fellow jockeys stands as more of an accolade than a brickbat. So strictly did he adhere to his personal code of honour that he steadfastly refused to disclose the outcome of trials in which he'd participated and refused to accept any retainer greater than £50. Remarked the The Druid: 'We should call him rather a good jockey by profession, than a great horseman by intuition. He seldom did anything brilliant but his good head and fine patience served him, and he rarely made a mistake as regards measure in the last few strides. A tremendous finish, when a horse had to be ridden home from below the distance, was not his forte; and it put him all aboard if he had to make the running. His thighs were so short that he hadn't sufficient purchase from the knee to use a sluggish horse and if he had a free goer he was a little apt to overdo it.'

Flatman's ace card was his weight: a natural lightweight, he was barely 11lb heavier at 50 than he was at 20. However, this only worked in his favour once he'd carved a reputation because owners and trainers did not regard 'tinies', 'feathers' or 'bantams' worth the extra lead in the saddlecloth. He had no ride in public until he turned 19, and his star only began waxing after the filly Pickle landed an almighty gamble in Ascot's Albany Stakes of 1834. There was only one Derby success on his escutcheon - and that aboard Orlando only materialized following the disqualification of the four-year-old 'ringer' Running Rein in 1844. He was, however, associated with a Derby winner of greater renown in the form of Voltigeur, whom he partnered to victory over The Flying Dutchman in the celebrated match for the 1850 Doncaster Cup; the following year saw the places reversed in the eagerly awaited re-match at York. Despite a marked lack of success at Epsom (he failed to win even one Oaks), Flatman was the trailblazer when it came to Newmarket jockeys gaining a foothold in the North, where he won three St Legers. All told his Classic tally reached 10 before his career was terminated in 1859 by a horrific injury sustained following a match at Newmarket. As he dismounted from Golden Pippin the filly lashed out and struck him a fearful blow in the body. He never regained his health and died a year later aged 50, leaving a tidy sum of £12,000. The whiter-than-white Flatman wore the laurel of champion jockey with pride and established a worthy template. Yet with his large saucer eyes and long broken nose suggesting the visage of a clown, he lacked the charisma often associated with a champion sportsman.

In 1853 Flatman was succeeded by John Wells. 'Brusher' Wells was an altogether different specimen to Nat Flatman – on and off a horse. Unlike his predecessor he courted celebrity. He was a dandy. Prior to a St Leger he exercised his mount on Doncaster's Town Moor wearing an Alpine hat adorned with several feathers, a suit made from Gordon tartan and a pair of red morocco slippers. 'My tailor makes my clothes for nothing,' the unabashed Wells informed those who mocked. 'It is not often he comes across a figure like mine to fit them on.' On other days he'd sport a tall hat with an exaggerated curl to its brim or a cream-coloured one with a deep black band. 'You would like to know,' he answered Henry Custance's query about the source of his hats, 'so that you could get on like it? Wells didn't bat an eye when his fellow jockey replied: 'If I did, I would be complete and get a monkey and an organ with it!'

His patrons cared not a jot about his flamboyant dress sense because Wells could certainly ride, even if, as *Baily's* remarked, 'he was more resolute and determined than finished and artistic.' Custance described him thus: 'He was a very strong man on a horse and used to lap his long legs round them at the finish. He always sat well back in his saddle, kept fast hold of the horse's head, and he was a very resolute finisher. Take him altogether I think he was a good jockey.' He got his chance to ride good horses on Tom Parr's Weathegage in the 1852 Cesarewitch and John Bahram Day's superlative Classic-winning filly of 1854 Virago. Wells was fearless around Epsom and secured three Derbies. 'Not one jockey out of 50 who cared a straw for life would have dashed through the mob of horses that shut him in as he did,' said one observer of the ugly finish to the 1859 renewal Wells won on Musjid. Wells collected eight Classics and headed the jockeys list a second time in 1854. He took care of his money, investing in a Birmingham pen factory and buying a brewery for his father. He swore by the good fortune deriving from the potato that he always carried in his pocket – no bigger than a pea and as hard as a stone – given him by a supposed witch. But his luck ran out. The jockey nicknamed 'Tiny' who could do 6st stone during his first championship season soon struggled to make 8st 7lb. His death aged 39 in 1873 came as no great shock. There was much the young Fordham might learn from 'Brusher' Wells – not least the one vital quality he shared with Nat Flatman. He was dead honest.

These were the two great jockeys from whom Fordham learnt the value of probity and against whom he'd to measure himself as the 1855 season commenced. The lowest total with which either had secured the championship was 78 – by Flatman in 1851. Fordham had barely two dozen wins to his name in a brief four-season career. And yet, at the tender age of 18, George Fordham would become champion jockey in 1855 with a total of 70 winners, three ahead of John Wells. It was an indication of the comparitively low esteem in which jockeys were generally held that while the Turf Press listed the leading owners and horses it denied like exposure to the 'knights of the pigskin'.

The highlights of this initial championship came at Ascot in June. Fordham won three races: the Trial Stakes on Coroner; the Royal Hunt Cup on the filly Chalice; and a division of the Wokingham Stakes (then run in two parts) on the 2 to1 favourite Palmerston. Success in the Turf's greatest prizes, the Classics, however, proved elusive. Indeed, he'd not yet had so much as a ride in one. Most owners were reluctant to use 'tinies' in elite events where weights were higher. In such circumstances even a 'tiny' as good as Fordham might be carrying two or three stone of 'dead' weight – an inert liability compared to the dynamic force brought to bear by the muscle and sinew of a genuinely heavier jockey.

However, three-year-olds did receive stacks of weight from their elders in races like the Goodwood Cup. The Goodwood Festival in Sussex – 'Ascot-on-Sea' in the eyes of many – was held annually in the last week of July. The race to win was the Cup, the centrepiece of the fixture, as most Cup races were on Victorian race-cards. The two and a half miles up, over and round the Sussex Downs always attracted a strong field. The French, for instance, had been taking an increasing interest in the event.

It was symptomatic of the era that French-bred horses were considered sufficiently inferior as to warrant generous weight concessions – in direct contrast to the treatment meted out to English-bred horses in France where they were barred from the principal races. Two years previously the filly Jouvence, trained at Epsom by Ralph Sherwood, had won both the French Oaks and Derby before profiting from the advantages of English training and the allowances of being a "foreigner"' to win the Goodwood Cup under just 5st 8lb – thereby making history as the first French-bred to carry off an English trophy. *The Times* stressed: 'When it is remembered that some of the best blood of our Turf celebrities is now in France and that the two nations are now so clearly joined by steam communication, it will be at once perceived that the distinction between French and English horses is now materially lessened.'

In the 1855 renewal of the Cup it was Baron Nathaniel de Rothschild's three-year-old Baroncino, second in the Prix du Jockey Club, who reaped the benefit of just 5st 13lb on his back. And it was the champion jockey in waiting that was entrusted with the ride. The partnership went off favourites at 5 to 4 and beat John Wells and the Padwick-owned Oulston, fresh from victory in Ascot's Gold Vase, by one and a half lengths, 'very cleverly.'

But of all those 70 victories securing George Fordham top spot in the jockeys list for the first time perhaps the most illuminating came at the midlands backwater of Warwick on 4 September.

The pace-setter in Baroncino's Goodwood Cup was a filly belonging to the Irish courtier Lord Clifden called Homily. The three-year-old chestnut daughter of Surplice was just caught on the line by Rataplan and finished fourth. Fordham had ridden her in the past – without success. She was still a maiden and was sent to Warwick with a view to competing for the three-mile Cup on 5 September, but as Lord Clifden was not present her trainer, Isaac Day, decided to let her take her chance in the Leamington Stakes over two miles on the first day of the meeting. Fordham, who was due to partner another runner, switched to Homily. He'd already taken the opening two races on the card when he weighed out at 5st 8lb to ride the 20 to 1 outsider in a field of 11. The Chicken, at 7 to 2, was regarded 'a real good thing' in the words of *Bell's Life*.

The pace was very fast. Fordham instinctively settled Homily at the back as The Chicken disputed the lead with four others in the certain knowledge they'd cut their own throats by such bravado. Fordham saved every inch he could by sticking to the inside rail all the way round. There he anchored Homily until 'after several disappointments he at last got "free" and took Homily to the front', plunging her through a gap on the inside at the half-mile pole. The favourite, now in hot pursuit, was obliged to forfeit ground by giving chase on her outside. By the time The Chicken drew alongside he was so exhausted he hung in toward her. Fordham shrugged him off and went away to win by one and a half lengths. 'After disappointing her friends on previous occasions when entrusted with their money,' reported *Bell's Life*, 'Homily obtained her maiden triumph in a manner which must prove equally mortifying to them, the more not having been backed for a shilling today, except by two or three bookmakers to whom the price was too tempting, especially with Fordham up.'

The young Fordham, still three weeks shy of his eighteenth birthday, had barely enough hair on his chin to warrant shaving. Yet he'd bamboozled the cream of the weighing room - Tom Ashmall, Luke Snowden and the great Nat Flatman - with a faultless exhibition of pace judgement and tactical acumen. Although the crowd who witnessed this feat of arms in the flesh was minimal, the evidence of its eyes was soon relayed throughout the small world that constitutes the Turf fraternity. This bravura display came to be regarded as the first of four rides during Fordham's career that defined his peerless jockeyship. Some might argue he surpassed this ride the following day with a second on Homily – this time in defeat. They lined up for the three-mile Warwick Cup against their Goodwood adversary Rataplan. This tough customer had won a Gold Vase and Manchester Cup, run fourth in a Derby and third in a St Leger, and had won no fewer than 19 of his 29 starts in 1854. By some magic Fordham got the filly to within a short head of the five-year-old. *The Morning Post* gushed: 'For a lightweight like Fordham to make the running for three miles required no ordinary power, and never did a jockey, either "feather" or top weight, ride steadier. The mere outline of Rataplan's head won the day.'

As the seasons rolled past, many of Fordham's outstanding displays came at minor tracks on unheralded animals. In the spring of 1856 he won a paltry juvenile seller at Northampton on The Roman in such brilliant style by a head as to strike every observer present they'd witnessed a Turf miracle. And it was at the same meeting two years later that he gained a notable victory on Drewitt's Borderer in the Great Northamptonshire Stakes after being virtually tailed-off. So far behind was Borderer after three-quarters of the two miles had been covered that a thousand pounds to to half a sovereign were offered against his mount. Fordham gained the day by a neck. This was one of nine successes the partnership gained that season which also included the Stamford Gold Cup and a septet of Queen's Plates – the last three on a memorable excursion to the Curragh's three-day June fixture.

***

Since its very inception the 'Sport of Kings' had played host to as many knaves and jades as those fired with noble intentions. Fordham had no realistic hope of giving the former a totally wide berth. There were too many; and many occupied positions of considerable influence. The best he could hope for as he consolidated his status as champion jockey was to steer a clever course that kept him close, but clear, of the rocks that could wreck his career. That he managed to do so speaks highly of an innate wisdom which, in the parlance of later years, would see him dubbed 'street-wise.' And there were no craggier rocks than the Days.

The hegemony of the Day family at this point in English Turf history demanded it used the best jockeys. It was only a matter of time before Fordham began riding for Drewitt's near neighbours instead of against them. In 1856 he returned to Goodwood with another live contender for the Cup in Rogerthorpe, a three-year-old carrying 7st 2lb. The colt was trained by John Day junior, the current custodian of Danebury.

The renowned 'Danebury Confederacy' had squeezed a fortune from the Turf in the first half of the 19th century; at its heart were the Days. Its fiefdom lay in Hampshire, a few miles north-west of Stockbridge on the flanks of the 470 feet Danebury Hill and its Iron Age ring fort, where over 100 people were employed at Danebury Stables by the time Fordham made its acquaintance in the 1850s. The first John Day, thick of waistline, fond of brandy but gloomy in disposition, had left his native Somerset to set up stables on Houghton Down around the turn of the century. 'Gloomy' John Day was a confidante of the Prince Regent and encouraged the future George IV to patronize Stockbridge races. The next two generations raised the family profile as jockeys and trainers to unprecedented levels of achievement. Between 1821 and 1869 the dynasty would train or ride the winners of more than 50 Classics courtesy of 'Gloomy' John's two sons Sam and John Bahram and the latter's sons John, William, Sam and Alfred.

John Bahram Day assumed control of Danebury following 'Gloomy' John's death in 1828. Unlike his 22-stone father, John Bahram was small and wiry enough to ride, and sufficiently talented to win 16 Classics. Indeed, his stock was so high he became the principal Royal jockey and earned for himself the soubriquet, noteworthy during an age of endemic corruption, of 'Honest' John. He set to work establishing Danebury as the premier training yard in the South. To this end he augmented the few existing buildings and laid out a new racecourse adjoining the yard where he acted as Clerk. Few trainers led a harder life than John Bahram Day. He was, in the awed words of *Baily's Magazine*, 'no ordinary man.' He began training with £10 in his pocket and averred he 'never had a coat on my back or a glass of wine in my house.' He was said to get up and down with the sun; on a summer morn he was abroad by four; his charges were back in their boxes by eight whereupon he breakfasted on tea and bread and butter. Then he went for a mile walk, invariably swinging the umbrella that seldom left his side. His training methods were equally harsh: 'I think Danebury Hill will be a little too much for that one,' was one of his stock phrases. He preferred horses laden with stamina than speedsters. Yet, provided they stood this preparation, his horses went to post superbly fit – whatever their size. 'They look big,' observed *The Times* after one such had trotted up in a prestigious handicap, 'but are fit to run for their lives.'

Thanks to his career as a trainer many have concluded the moniker 'Honest' John was bestowed either through ignorance or sarcasm; even in an age when chicanery was taken for granted Day was associated with enough shady episodes to embarrass even the most arrant blackguard. For instance, his Northern counterpart, John Scott, 'The Wizard of Whitewall', was equally successful but was never tainted by scandal on the same scale as 'Honest' John. Day, like almost every trainer and jockey, bet heavily and was a dab-hand at deceiving owners, bookmakers and public alike. Many of his traits typified the diversity of the Victorian character. He abhorred swearing and smoking, attended church twice of a Sunday and afterwards held bible classes for his stable lads – when his whip would chastise any who dozed off while he read aloud. He was popular with Lords Derby and Palmerston – especially the latter, which gave rise to the tale of Day's visit to the House of Commons in furtherance of a position for his son Henry. He was informed by a functionary that he could not see the Prime Minister. 'Tell him,' said the trainer, 'John Bahram Day is here to see him.' The functionary disappeared; Lord Palmerston soon appeared. The son got his position.

Yet seldom was there a racing scandal or *causes celebres* on the Victorian Turf without the involvement of Day or one of his family, notably his sons John junior and William whom he helped establish as trainers – albeit not before both had been warned off as jockeys. John, who'd trained as a veterinary surgeon in Oxford, assumed control of Danebury in 1846 following a row with his father and brother William; John Bahram moved to Michel Grove in neighbouring Sussex to act as private trainer to Henry Padwick while William set up at Woodyates in Wiltshire. It's fair to say that John Day junior trained and behaved to his father's template. Success followed success – a Guineas and Derby soon materialized in 1847; and controversies were never far behind. But the statistics do not lie. The figures compiled on Danebury's behalf for the period 1832 to 1865 speak of 1,175 ½ wins accumulating £362,998 in prizemoney (the equivalent of around £72 *million* today); and in 1867 Day sent out the winners of 146 races, a seasonal record that stood for 120 years.

If the Days were the instruments of the Confederacy its arch schemers were Harry Hill, John Gully and Henry Padwick. This unholy trinity encompassed bookmaking, moneylending and betting. They'd court aristocratic gamblers, lend them the money to bet on races and then manipulate the odds so that their 'marks' invariably wound up in debt – and thus be forced to borrow more money or else hand over such property and possessions they'd put up as security. The picture was completed, naturally, by the co-operation of jockeys being sought and financially secured. When Gully's Pyrrhus the First won the 1846 Derby, Hill pocketed a large sum; as did Gully when Hill's Cymba (1848) and Mincepie (1856) won their Oaks – all three trained by the Days.

Hill was a Mancunian who'd acted as Lord George Bentinck's commission agent when he'd been a prominent Danebury patron. A former boot-black and bookmaker, he was the biggest bettor of his time on the Derby and the master of the 'Yearling Book' where he'd lay £10,000 to £150 about any unfashionably bred colt. Coarse in speech and dress, he was prone to 'cracking his sides with laughter at his own personal and ill-timed gibes, not being ashamed to utter what others would blush to hear.' *The Satirist's* description of him continued as a model of character assassination: 'Tall, gaunt and grisly, he can at periods be as rigid as a pump-handle, chained by the parish beadle. He became familiar with a horde of touts, robbers, and other moral pestilences, and through them also he progressively cultivated the confidence of jockeys and trainers. For men who profess to keep their escutcheon unstained, he did the work of darkness.' This 'Prince of Darkness' eventually accumulated enough capital to acquire his own gentleman's residence in the form of Winchester's Marwell Hall.

Gully, unlike Hill, was a man of many parts, albeit many of them questionable. He was, stated *Baily's Magazine* kindly, 'a striking instance of what may be accomplished in this country when industry is united with integrity and sharpened with the constant intercourse of the keenest set of men in the world.' He came to Danebury when Bentinck departed. In the year of Rogerthorpe's Goodwood Cup he was 73 years of age, a little past the peak of his influence but a leading light nonetheless.

The methods by which Gully had advanced to such wealth and giddy heights tested close scrutiny – even in the 19th century. Born in 1785, he was the son of a pub landlord-cum-butcher whose failed pursuit of the latter occupation soon landed him in debtor's jail. Gully was a big powerful six-footer of a man, described later as 'finely formed, full of strength and grace, his face coarse and with a bad expression, his head set well on his shoulders, and remarkably graceful and dignified in his actions.' More significantly, at this stage of his life Gully proved handy with his fists. While incarcerated in the Fleet Prison he was persuaded by the prize-fighter Henry 'Hen' Pearce, known as 'The Game Chicken', to enter the ring against him. The bout was made for 1,000 guineas. Gully was retired after surviving 64 rounds over 70 minutes. But he'd acquitted himself well. 'Thou'rt the best man I've ever fowt,' Pearce declared; and when he retired shortly thereafter the title of champion was offered to Gully and gratefully accepted. Following two defences of the title against the lumbering Lancastrian ex steamboat captain Bob Gregson, Gully relinquished his title and took a public house in London's Carey Street where he operated as a bookmaker. Clearly, no one was going to mess with this bruiser and his star waxed rapidly. In 1832 he was elected MP for Pontefract without opposition (a victory doubtless aided by his placing barrels of beer in the streets) and he proved he could use his tongue with the same crushing effect as his fists. Some of his increasing wealth was channelled into the acquisition of collieries and a country mansion that epitomized an assumed gentility. He even managed the time to father 24 children. The only occasion it seemed he might have taken a wrong turning was when he fell foul of the noted duellist Squire Osbaldeston. Some averred that common sense prevailed and the hostile meeting never came off. The popular version of events, however, had the Squire sending a bullet through Gully's hat – whereupon Gully was heard to mutter: 'Better my hat than my head!'

Needless to say the Turf readily welcomed a moneybags like Gully as an owner. In 1827 he bought that year's Derby winner, Mameluke, and backed him to win thousands in the St Leger. However, there was a conspiracy to stop Mameluke from winning. The starter was bribed and, after a series of false starts, Mameluke was left the best part of 100 yards – he still caught Matilda but was too exhausted to ward off her renewed effort and succumbed by a length. Gully lost £45,000 on the race. He was not financially embarrassed for long. He entered into a partnership with Robert Ridsdale, another character of charm and acquired taste who'd risen from boot-boy to country squire despite a dubious moral compass. Gully pocketed £60,000 (*£13.8 million*) when Ridsdale's St Giles won the 1832 Derby; it was said that with the sole exception of Perion, every one of the 22 horses who started ran in the interest of Ridsdale and Gully. He pocketed another £40,000 when Margrave added the St Leger. The latter, running in Gully's name, was trained by John Scott. Thereafter, Gully joined forces with Hill, and his Turf activities centred on Danebury, first with John Bahram Day and then John Day junior. Father and son delivered him seven Classics.

The final member of this gang of knaves and chisellers was Henry Padwick - of whom one casual acquaintance said: 'That man makes me believe in Hell.' He'd been on the fringe of the Confederacy when John Gully was its moving force and had learnt much at the feet of the master. He was the son of a Horsham butcher. Short and stocky and now in his mid-forties, he'd enjoyed a decent education, possessed a suave and plausible manner and considerable financial ability; at one point he was an aide to no less a personage than Prince Albert and, through a scarcely credible shot from Cupid's bow, his son married a niece of the Director of the Bank of England. The legal profession for which he'd been trained did not appeal to him for very long, and Padwick established himself as a money-lender, first in Davies Street and then at 2 Hill Street, off Berkeley Square (by a richly ironic coincidence, Admiral Rous, that bastion of Turf integrity, lived just round the corner at 13 Berkeley Square).

Padwick prospered. Both banks and individuals would place at his disposal large sums of money: he borrowed at 2% and loaned at 20% to his 'friends', 60% to strangers and a whopping 500% to undesirables. He was clever and sophisticated, very much a man of the world. The Turf was the ground on which he was most likely to meet the rich young bloods he marked for his victims. He hired the best cook and kept a fine cellar with which to entice them. He'd pamper their egos and offer paternal sympathy when finances were low; a loan would be arranged without demure. If repayment proved arduous and the debtor had assets such as race-horses, 'Old Masters' or land, Padwick was perfectly satisfied with taking them in lieu of cash. Soon 'Mr Howard', 'Mr Henry' and 'Mr Bruton', as he styled himself on the racecourse, began to attract notice as the owner of some 40 thoroughbreds.

Two Iagos as John Bahram Day and Henry Padwick were destined to fall out at some stage. The parting of the ways came about following the St Hubert-Lord of the Isles affair. Both colts had genuine Classic credentials in 1855. Day trained the former for Padwick; son William trained the latter for James Merry at Woodyates. Racecourse gossip insisted that father and son had reached a deal: Lord of the Isles would be given 'a clear course' in the Two Thousand Guineas with St Hubert being similarly accommodated in the Derby. However, if this pact was made, Padwick knew nothing of it, and when he learnt St Hubert had been sparkling on the gallops he backed him accordingly for the Guineas. St Hubert started at 7 to 4 on, with only Lord of the Isles (5 to 2) backed to beat him. And beat him he did – by a neck.

Once Padwick got wind of the rumours he severed all relations with John Bahram Day (as did Merry with William Day) and sent his horses to be trained in a new yard at Findon, appointing Day's head lad, William Goater, to be his private trainer.

These, then, were the stamp of men with whom Fordham was obliged to mix and on whom his rise very much depended. That his name was untainted by their sleight of hand bore witness to just how seriously he took the sentiment on the whip presented to him by Smith. The proximity of Danebury and Findon to Goodwood ensured Fordham any number of choice mounts at the meeting. The majority were for Goater's roguish patron and Day's coterie of 'plungers'. Rogerthorpe was the first.

Rogerthorpe ran in Hill's name. Tom Parr's Fisherman – off a winning streak of 12 that included the Gold Vase and in the midst of the seasonal total of 23 that wrote him into the record books – was the favourite for the 1856 Goodwood Cup. Another from the same generation and gingering the mix was Yellow Jack, who sported the Padwick colours. He'd to give 'Little Roger' 8lb. From France came the crack four-year-old Monarque, victor of the previous year's Prix du Jockey Club, from whom Rogerthorpe received a valuable 13lb. Compromising his chances was the fact he'd run 24 hours earlier in the six-furlong Stewards' Cup, finishing third; unless, that is, the sprint was designed to prime him for a late burst of speed. Of the remainder Muscovite's ability to stay the marathon was taken for granted because he'd won a Cesarewitch over almost as far. But with 9st 2lb on his back (that included Nat Flatman) he was giving weight to every one of the other nine competitors. As the runners circled at the start Rogerthorpe was being 'backed with considerable spirit by his stable' in the words of *Bell's Life*.

Anyone who grumbles about the English summer being nothing more than winter painted green should've attended this particular Cup day. The heat was intense and a broad unclouded sunshine lit up the picturesque scenery unique to this course. 'The multitude of elegantly dressed gentlemen and elegantly attired ladies,' commented *The Times*, 'were indications of the undiminished glories of Goodwood.' A paragraph of two-dozen lines was needed to list the luminaries – the Prussian princes and English aristocrats - present in the Grand Stand. Snootily it continued: 'An absence of all crowding and rioting to which Cockney pleasure-folk are accustomed at Epsom and Ascot is one of the pleasantest characteristics of the gathering.'

Fordham set about capitalizing on his mount's feather weight by pushing Rogerthorpe straight into the lead. There he stayed, up hill and down dale, until Monarque was inexplicably urged alongside him with a mile yet to run. Completing a punishing half mile at this critical stage of the marathon contest shattered Monarque and rounding the final bend he was left looking as if 'stood still'. Muscovite now made his covering move, seeming to be galloping better than anything. Then, in the blink of an eye, the race was settled. Entering the final furlong Muscovite broke down. Rogerthorpe maintained his gallop, 'game as a pebble' according to *Bell's Life*, and a late thrust from Yellow Jack was foiled by three-quarters of a length. Poor Yellow Jack had caught a severe dose of 'seconditis'; this narrow defeat was part of an unenviable streak numbering losses by a head or a neck in the Two Thousand Guineas, Derby, Chester Cup and Ascot Derby. For years afterwards a horse that was habitually second was referred to as 'a regular Yellow Jack'.

One cloud did emerge to blot the purity of that clear Goodwood sky. In view of the brainstorm suffered by Monarque's jockey and Hill's capacity to influence a result through buying a jockey's co-operation, it's worth adding that *Bell's Life* asserted Hill was so confident of Rogerthorpe's victory that he'd already promised the winner's trophy to an 'old and esteemed friends some days previously.'

That possibility notwithstanding, the 1856 Goodwood Cup left the elder statesmen of the weighing room like Flatman and Wells facing the uncomfortable realization that eventually confronts all ageing sportsmen: a new star was in the firmament.

Richard Ten Broeck

THREE

WILL YOU PUT FORDHAM UP?

Fordham had gone from strength to strength - and very quickly. What manner of champion would he be? What kind of role model would he present? What image of the Turf would he parade before the public?

At the mid point of the 19th century horse-racing was a far more significant sport than it was to be a century or so later. Horses were, of course, a common sight in country and town. The Victorian populace understood the equine more than subsequent generations and was quick to appreciate the merits of a good horse. To watch horses race and to bet on the outcome was second nature. Such opportunities were boundless. There was not a corner of the realm that did not possess a racetrack. From Bodmin and Weymouth to Morpeth and Paisley via Holywell and Hednesford race-tracks abounded. The leading jockeys assumed idolatory status. Their only rivals for the affection of the sporting public were the bare-knuckle pugilists of the prize ring such as Bendigo and Tom Sayers. Consequently, 18-year-old George Fordham had a significant role to fill, knowing his public would be scrutinizing his every action for flaws. Would he grow too big for his boots and bend the rules to his own ends like Sam Chifney, a self-proclaimed 'Genius Genuine' but a stranger to integrity; or perhaps he was destined to turn into a venal booze-sodden scallywag like Bill Scott? On the other hand, might he choose to follow the straight and narrow path trod by Frank Buckle, Jem Robinson and Nat Flatman? The Danebury Confederacy, for instance, had helped propel him to the top of the greasy pole – yet it might just as easily bring him sliding back down again on the back of its intrigue. That Danebury did not reduce the teenage champion into a Chifney or a Scott was in part owing to the youngster's inherent honesty and in part to the support of other patrons.

One particular fan was the American Richard Ten Broeck. The American invasion led by Ten Broeck did not bring with it the unsavoury baggage of crooks and alchemists that accompanied 'Tod' Sloan and the Reiffs toward the end of the century. That of 1856 included Ten Broeck's private trainer, DD Palmer, two jockeys, Littlefield and Gil Patrick (allegedly America's finest jockey), and a posse of negro stable hands. More importantly, Ten Broeck shipped a select team of stayers primed to carry his patriotic colours of 'red and white striped jacket, blue stars and blue cap' with distinction.

Ten Broeck's 'Enterprise of England' had been 12 months in the planning. Almost overnight it imposed a degree of Yankee glamour on the English Turf that the Establishment found refreshing, if not downright eccentric. 'The toilette of the jockeys,' said one paddock observer, 'was unexceptionable, except that Littlefield's high military heels seemed as strange on a jockey as Patrick's genuine Yankee beard.' Ten Broeck himself appeared to have stepped from the pages of a Mark Twain novel, resembling most people's idea of the Mississippi river gambler – which he had been at one point. Indeed, glaring out from the heavily bearded face were two chips of blue ice for eyes that would make the devil himself throw in his hand without drawing a card.

Ten Broeck was 45 years-old. He belonged to an old and distinguished Dutch family with military connections from Albany, in upstate New York; his maternal grandfather having fought alongside George Washington. It was, therefore, perfectly natural for Ten Broeck to enter the US Military Academy at West Point, which he did in the same intake as Robert E Lee. However, he soon left in circumstances sufficiently questionable for his family to disown him. He either resigned or was expelled. The story went that he challenged one of his instructors to a duel after claiming to have been insulted. Some said the instructor was killed: a charge which Ten Broeck did nothing to dispel. The upshot was Ten Broeck left West Point in a hurry. 'I spent several years in the South,' he'd admit, 'where my racing career began in earnest.'

He'd caught the racing bug after being taken at the age of 11 to see the famous match between American Eclipse (representing the North) and Henry (carrying the standard of the South) which drew 60,000 Americans to the Union Course on Long Island in May 1823 – the largest crowd of Americans ever assembled up to that date. Ten Broeck served his Turf 'apprenticeship' chugging back and forth on the Mississippi for the best part of ten years, racing and betting at every port of call. Then, in 1843, he took a string of racehorses from New Orleans to the Valdez racetrack in Havana. The Cubans were unimpressed: they made it plain they'd rather see locomotives race than horses. Ten Broeck switched his attention to the Canadian border. But the purses in Montreal and Ottawa were meager; more importantly, the betting market was moribund. By 1847 he was back in the South, operating the tracks of Bingaman and Bascombe around New Orleans, and four years later he assumed control of the Metairie racecourse. He soon proved himself to be a racing promoter *par excellance*, raising the track's profile by the inauguaration of the Great State Post Stakes that brought together the best horses from Kentucky, Maryland, Virginia, Missouri and Louisiana, whilst refurbishing the Grand Stand with an eye to attracting both the gentlemen and the ladies of the South's highest society.

Ten Broeck also proved he had an eye for a horse. He put together a syndicate to buy a colt called Darley for $5,000. Renamed Lexington, his purchase became a great racer and a champion sire. He lost just one of his seven races and, ridden by Patrick, knocked more than six seconds off Lecompte's record for four miles to land Ten Broeck a bet of $10,000. That same year of 1855 Lexington beat Lecompte twice. Ten Broeck sold Lexington for three times what he'd paid for him. And left for England: 'An idea grew upon me continually till I carried it out, an ambition to beard the English lion in his den.'

Arriving in 1856 armed with an introduction to at least one member of the nobility, Ten Broeck was soon rubbing shoulders with plenty of others. He was the Duke of Richmond's guest at Goodwood during the races; was entertained at Badminton by the Duke of Beaufort; and was elected a member of the Coffee-Room at Newmarket thanks to Admiral Rous – whose friendship he tactfully courted since he'd be handicapping his horses. 'Such lavish hospitality and kindliness as I had never seen before,' said the American visitor. And, within a year, 'Tenny', as his society chums soon tagged him, had married a rich widow, Patricia Duncan Anderson. 'Unlike his countrymen, Mr Ten Broeck is free from the besetting fault of curiosity,' stated *Baily's Magazine*, 'and one secret of his popularity is that while he minds his own business, he does not interfere with that of other people.'

However, although considered an astute racing man and a fearless punter when he'd made up his mind about a horse, 'Tenny' was not regarded an especially clever man - which only went to render him more appealing. Henry Custance put it succinctly: 'He fancied himself too much at any game.' One such 'game' involved match races. 'Match-making has always been a peculiar hobby of mine,' he maintained, 'and through my acquaintance with many of the racing magnates I was enabled to arrange a considerable number.' He calculated on winning three out of every four.

Unfortunately, Ten Broeck didn't restrict himself to merely making and betting on these matches. He rather fancied himself as a rider. At the Houghton meeting of 1858 he challenged Count Batthyany to a match of 100 sovereigns a side over the Ditch Mile, each to ride one of his own horses. Ten Broeck rode Barbarity, a 14-race winner, whom he bought while in England. They easily accounted for Batthyany on Olympus. Match-racing, however, did not always run so smoothly. Custance records him riding in one at Warwick 'looking more like riding in the park or hacking about Newmarket than racing...dressed in a pair of large worsted cord breeches, black jack-boots, a racing-jacket cut very low in front, like a dress waistcoat' - complete with a large cigar lodged in the corner of his mouth. He had backed himself heavily, got left six or eight lengths at flag-fall and came with a mighty rush when the race was all but done: 'Well, I guess he had the foot of me all the way,' he explained to his commission agent, George Payne. The later replied: 'Well, my advice is, Ten Broeck, never ride again. I never saw such a mess in my life as you made of it.' Payne later confided to Custance:

'Had not I put him £800 on, I should have sworn he had pulled the horse!'

Ten Broeck would bet on almost anything – which ensured he was one of the victims of the notorious 'Reindeer' bet while a guest at Sir Lydston Newman's country house, Mamhead, near Exeter. En route to Exeter races two Army officers, Colonel Edwyn Burnaby, of the Grenadier Guards, and the Hon Captain Randolph Stewart, of the 43rd Royal Highlanders (the Black Watch), discussed the possibility of renaming one of their horses 'Reindeer' which led to a disagreement regarding the correct spelling of the word. Burnaby declared he was an awful speller and always carried a Johnson's *Dictionary* to assist him in letter writing. He insisted that 'Reindeer' should be spelt with an 'a'; viz 'Raindeer'. Stewart thought it should be with an 'e'. They entered into a light-hearted bet of £5 on the outcome. The subject was raised over dinner and heavy bets were made with Johnson's *Dictionary* to serve as the arbiter. Ten Broeck bet Stewart £100 to £1 that the word was spelt with an 'e'. Burnaby and Stewart, however, were in cahoots. They'd already consulted the authority and knew this was the one dictionary spelling the word with an 'a'; and planned to split the £100 between them. Their initial disagreement had been a 'bubble bet', Victorian parlance for the deliberate ploy of invoking bets when possessing prior knowledge of the result; a subterfuge known as 'duffing' or 'skittle-sharping' when practiced by the sharks frequenting fairs and race meetings. The outcome of this particular 'duffing' provoked a great deal of 'unpleasant discussion'. Stewart was reported to have owned up to the fact that the bet was 'fictitious'. Ten Broeck refused to pay up; and communicated the facts to his friend Admiral Rous at the Jockey Club (to rub it in he named one of his horses Reindeer with an 'e' that Fordham would ride it to victory in Goodwood's Cowdray Stakes). But the Turf Establishment neither forgave nor forgot. The affair would resurface a few years later and aired in public amid acrimony from all parties.

Ten Broeck's English expedition was backed by the successful breeder Francis Morris of Throgg's Neck Farm in Westchester County, New York. The best of the horses Ten Broeck brought with him was Lexington's former adversary Lecompte, winner of 11 from 17 starts and the only horse to beat Lexington, whom he had bought out of its stud career with the intention of mopping up the English staying races. Lecompte was a fine-looking chestnut with no lumber about him yet seemingly capable of carrying 14st to hounds. Unfortunately, he developed leg problems and then became ill, dying of colic in early 1857 - which, given the future performances of his siblings, was a considerable blow to Ten Broeck.

Initial reaction from the training fraternity to the arrival of the Yankees was ridicule. America's organized equine sport had only latterly moved away from the trotting track, a form of racing evolved as a compromise owing to the opposition shown by the Puritan community to horse-racing. It was dominated by long-distance races of three or four miles contested in heats. Consequently, Palmer (and his successors, Brown, Miner and Pryor) trained Ten Broeck's horses in the American style, which amounted to lots of walking, long slow work and a great deal of 'sweating' - exercise under heavy clothing. Sometimes the horses would be galloped two-three miles twice a day – even if they were being prepared for races as short as a mile. Xenophobia was rampant and these seemingly bizarre methods of training drew scorn from the cognoscenti who kept watch over the Houghton Downs yard, near Stockbridge, where the string was initially stabled. The injection of funds from his marriage enabled Ten Broeck to move his string to Primrose Cottage Stables in Newmarket. The braying of the 'know-alls' grew louder. However, as William Allison, long-time 'Special Commissioner with *The Sportsman*, was at pains to point out: 'Americans are not readily understood by people in this country, who are slower of thought and imagination.'

Ten Broeck's great ambition was to win the Goodwood Cup whose distance of two and a half miles offered the best chance of his long-distance stayers hitting the bullseye. He recognized that the odds on him winning an English Classic with horses bred and trained to run four miles were remote to the point of non existant. With Lecompte out of the equation, Ten Broeck's hopes lay with his younger half sister Prioress. Their dam, Reel, was the product of English breeding, and been lauded as 'Louisiana Champion'. Her daughter Prioress was by the English-bred Sovereign, a direct descendant of Eclipse. The chestnut filly had won both heats of the Equus Stakes at Metairie on her debut as a juvenile, and followed up over a mile at the same track a week later. Ten Broeck bought her in a job lot with Lecompte. The four-year-old filly made no show in the 1857 Goodwood Cup, being hampered in an incident that saw four animals fall. Nor did their jockeys wow the English critics; Ten Broeck soon put Littlechild and Patrick back on a ship to the United States. Prioress did little to advertise her potential immediately after Goodwood, finishing well beaten at Lewes and Chester. But Ten Broeck had seen the light. Both times she was ridden by George Fordham.

Admiral Rous allotted Prioress 6st 9lb in the Cesarewitch in which she'd be ridden by Ten Broeck's latest Yankee recruit, a young lad called Tankesley, since Fordham partnered St Giles for William Day. Thirty-four went to post. The class horse in the race was Fisherman; Rous had virtually handicapped him out of the contest with a top weight of 9st 3lb. M Dopler was favourite at 4 to1; Prioress could be backed at 100 to1. Ten Broeck was broke. His stable had yet to get off the mark. He was on the verge of quitting England. After settling his bills in Newmarket he rode to the track with no intention of backing Prioress. But when he discovered her odds he invested his last £10 note.

The outcome proved an outstanding piece of handicapping by Rous: the rarity of a triple dead-heat involving Prioress, El Hakim (6st 9lb) and Queen Bee (4st10lb) after an epic struggle from the Bushes. 'Between the three,' reported *Bell's Life*, 'the final struggle was one of the most exciting ever witnessed, and the judge awarded one of the fairest dead-heats ever seen. The scene which followed can be better imagined than described.'

Ten Broeck reckoned Prioress ought to have won. The American jockeys had impressed the locals even less than the trainers and Tankesley carried the can. 'One would have had to travel far and look hard to find such specimens of all in horsemanship that was indifferent,' said George Hodgman. The owner and bookmaker continued: 'They were, in truth, about as bad as anybody could make them, riding with the reins twisted round their wrists.' Hodgman thought Prioress should've won by a couple of lengths; when Tankesley brought her to win the race on the wide outside she'd swerved with him. The run-off was arranged for after the last race. In the meantime Ten Broeck pondered a new jockey. Switching jockeys before a run-off was nothing unusual; indeed, El Hakim also had a new rider. And the champion jockey was now available.

Hodgman was a canny individual, endlessly chewing over the possibilities of making a bob or two as he sucked on the trademark twig that invariably resided in the left corner of his mouth. He immediately put £100 on Prioress before hurriedly seeking out Ten Broeck.

Fordham and Prioress prevail in the run-off for the Cesarewitch.

'Will you put Fordham up?' asked the breathless Hodgman when he found Ten Broeck at the paddock entrance.

'Can I get him?' replied the American.

'Yes. He told me he should have liked to have ridden for you this morning.'

'Get him then.'

Hodgman soon found Fordham and engaged him forthwith.

The revised market put in the Great Ebor winner El Hakim at 5 to 4, Prioress at 2 to1 and Queen Bess the 3 to1 outsider. Given her record in multiple four-mile heats in one afternoon, this run-off would be a piece of cake for Prioress. Ten Broeck took no chances. As the late autumn temperature dropped he gave his filly a three-mile sweat and ordered the rugs to stay in place until just before the off. He also reckoned a thunderstorm was brewing, and ordered lard to be packed into his filly's hooves to prevent balling dirt. Then, after giving his filly a slug of whiskey, Prioress was ready.

It was five o'clock when the three horses reached the starting post and so dark that they couldn't be seen with the naked eye until they were half a mile from home. El Hakim, apparently, led from flag-fall until Fordham allowed the hard-pulling Prioress to assume command after some 50 yards. He humoured her for a while; and then dropped away last, some three lengths adrift. Stop-start were the usual tactics over a distance of ground – the more so in a small field. Concealment – the art of 'The Kid' – was paramount. Was a horse genuinely tired or galloping flat out? Or was its jockey 'kidding'? No jockey ever perfected this ruse better than Fordham. The first nickname bestowed on him spoke as much: 'The Kidder'.

'The Kidder' was indeed at work. Now he had his rivals in plain sight. Queen Bee made her move and was still clear at the Bushes. Now Fordham got down to business. Prioress quickened. Again she hung to the left. When Fordham was seen with his whip up there was a cry of 'the American's beat'. But he'd only drawn his whip to straighten the filly. Fordham may not have weighed any more than Tankesley, but he had the hands and the strength to balance Prioress without loss of momentum. They tore up the hill to put one and a half lengths between them and the exhausted El Hakim, with Queen Bess a head further back. Fordham had saved Ten Broeck's bacon. 'Winning the Cesarewitch,' said the American, 'gave me renewed hope and courage.'

A fortnight later Prioress, reunited with Tankesley, ran down the field in the Cambridgeshire, which Fordham won on Odd Trick for Fisherman's trainer Tom Parr. Nevertheless, Ten Broeck had achieved his aim: the first English race to fall to a horse bred, owned and trained by Americans. Prioress ran unplaced in the 1858 Cesarewitch, but she and Fordham added a Great Yorkshire Handicap at Doncaster plus several Queen's Plates and match races (including one under her owner) before the mare was retired to Sir Lydston Newman's stud where she died foaling.

The association between Ten Broeck and Fordham blossomed. And it was on Prioress's younger half brother Starke that Fordham helped Ten Broeck achieve his greatest ambition.

Starke was described as a 'mealy chestnut of 15.3 hands'. He was a son of Wagner (a great grandson of Derby winner Diomed) who blazed a winning trail through Kentucky in 1838; in all the long-necked Wagner won 14 of his 20 races. Starke had been purchased by Ten Broeck for $7,500 after winning his debut at Metairie. Touted as a champion before being shipped across the Atlantic, he was six years-old when Fordham rode him in the Goodwood Cup of 1861 against the 1860 Derby winner Thormanby and The Wizard, second in that Derby and winner of the Two Thousand Guineas. It seemed as if John 'The Pusher' Osborne had the Cup in safe keeping on The

Wizard when he inexplicably raised his hands to ease him. *Baily's Magazine* picked up the story:

> The Wizard was steaming on like the Great Eastern without an engineer when Fordham, who had almost hopelessly persevered with his horse, pounced on him and won by a head. Of Starke, Mr Ten Broeck may really be proud, as he is a real genuine horse, and bore his flogging like a sailor going round the fleet.

The Morning Post could not overlook the role played by Starke's partner, applauding the 'best piece of jockeyship Fordham has ever shown.' Starke endorsed this view by adding the Bentinck Memorial, the Brighton Stakes and the Warwick Cup. Ten Broeck added to his winnings over the Goodwood Cup when the two-year-old Umpire (one of the few offspring got by the deceased Lecompte) won the valuable Nursery in Fordham's hands; indeed, so impressively, some immediately claimed he was a three-year-old, a slur just as quickly confounded by the veterinary surgeon. The following year Umpire ran fifth in the Derby. Had Umpire prevailed, Ten Broeck would've collected £150,000 (a barely credible *£18 million*) from the Ring - the largest sum ever taken by one individual over one race.

The Anglo-American alliance flowered with Optimist, who provided Ten Broeck with an inaugural Ascot winner in the two and a half-mile Ascot Stakes of 1861. The four-year-old son of Lexington had run third to Starke in the Goodwood Cup, and was only third best in the market at 6 to1, but he steadily wore down the favourite, the feather-weighted Weatherproof, up the straight to record a comfortable two-length success. The shorter Classics, as Ten Broeck had anticipated, always remained beyond reach - although Paris and Fordham were beaten only a length by General Peel in the Two Thousand Guineas of 1864.

Ten Broeck had one crucial, endearing, trait not often found in owners who gambled on a grand scale: he was capable of treating triumph and disaster just the same. When Fordham landed him a winner he was suitably rewarded; a four-figure 'present' was not uncommon. Not everyone took a kindly view of such largesse. William Day was one such – though his opinion of Ten Broeck was likely jaundiced by the bad blood that came between them when Day later trained for James Keene. To Day's irritation, Ten Broeck acted as unofficial advisor to his friend and compatriot - and his input was decidedly unwelcome. 'Mr Ten Broeck was the first gentleman to introduce the ruinous practice of giving large presents to his jockeys, which soon spoiled them, did himself no good, and discredited the Turf. He was looked upon as a modern Croesus and as prodigal with his money as Timon of Athens. The thousands and thousands he gave Fordham for riding at different times seem positively incredible. This ostentatious liberality which scatters bounty but confers no benefits, and buys flattery but not friendship, is to be condemned.'

There were no recriminations, however, when things went wrong – as they did spectacularly at Newmarket on 1 October 1862. Ten Broeck owned a four-year-old filly called Amy. Although she and Fordham had won a couple of match races at Newmarket and the Durdans Handicap at Epsom, Ten Broeck decided her time was up. He chose to mark her departure with a spectacular wager in a two-mile seller (after which the winner was to be sold for 300 sovereigns). Amy's opening odds in a field of six was 10 to 1. After Ten Broeck had waded in she wound up displacing Wild Rose as favourite at 6 to 4 and, *Baily's* contended, 'was considered a real sweetmeat.' The owner's winnings seemed secure for all bar 50 yards of the two miles. Fordham had made the running and, knowing himself well clear, steadied Amy up the hill to the line. Suddenly, Sam Rogers conjured a burst of speed from Wild Rose and she shot forward as Amy dropped to a walk. Fordham was half asleep – and was caught on the post. 'The laughter from the Ring can only be compared to the one which greets Clown and Pantaloon when they make their first bow in a Drury Lane pantomime.'

On an otherwise dull card the outcome attracted all the Press attention: 'A sensation such as the oldest Turfite cannot remember,' commented *The Times*. 'It was a stolen race to no little surprise of the rider of Amy.' *The Morning Post* went to town:

> A profound sensation. Amy had all her opponents safe, and they actually ceased to persevere. Fordham was so mortified he left the Heath for some time. The Ring shouted like Ojibbeway Indians and Fordham would not be comforted, fancying the cheering of the bookmakers was aimed at him. But one would have the heart of Pharaoh not to feel sorry for him after the contrition he felt for the serious consequences he had entailed upon Mr Ten Broeck and his friends for this act of carelessness. Even Sam Rogers was chagrined at the result, and in a manly and good-natured way assured Fordham that he exceedingly regretted the occasion. Although Mr Ten Broeck had backed his animal heavily he was the first to assure Fordham that he had no other feeling than that it was the kind of accident which might happen to any jockey.

Fordham's gloom plumbed depths as spectacular as his patron's losses. 'This was gall and wormwood to Fordham,' opined *Baily's*, 'who is not yet sufficiently thick-skinned to put up with adverse criticism.' That night he returned to his lodgings and went straight to bed where he cried like a child. He offered to pay Ten Broeck's bets out of his own pocket as well as re-purchasing the filly. However, Ten Broeck wouldn't hear of it. He bore no grudge. He wrote his jockey a kindly letter, telling him to put this solitary mistake out of his mind: he was 'perfectly satisfied, as was everybody else, it was an accident' and, furthermore, he was certain the jockey had won him a great many races he 'ought not to have done.'

Fordham's close association with Ten Broeck diminished after 1865 when he accepted a £500 (£60,000) retainer from the Duke of Beaufort. But Fordham rode for the American at every possibility until he returned to America in 1867. And the two would eventually reunite to particular effect in 1881 through the medium of Foxhall.

***

A second larger than life figure who helped the young Fordham stay atop the greasy pole was Tom Parr of Letcombe Regis.

Parr had risen from itinerant tea peddler hawking his wares, first on foot and then with a horse and trap, round the remote villages of Devon and Cornwall to the station of superb trainer of thoroughbred racehorses. He began training in 1843 and struggled to make ends meet until he laid out 60 guineas for Weathergage nine years later. Then Parr demonstrated how he could work wonders with a horse. In a few weeks he transformed the three-year-old from a horse unable to win a seller at Northampton to one of the best of his age. After winning the Goodwood Plate (Stakes), the ensuing ten weeks saw him add four small prizes and then the Cesarewitch.

Although Parr could convert base metal into gold, he'd no like talent for holding on to his money. Many a day was spent hiding in his hay-loft while creditors banged on his front door to be informed by head lad George Hall that the guv'nor' was 200 miles away at a distant race meeting. The guv'nor was caught unawares on one trip to York, however, having forgotten he'd omitted to pay his hotel bill on a previous visit. He was arrested and incarcerated. The horse he'd brought to run at York duly won, and the bet secured on borrowed money proved enough to gain his release. Parr's horses were dispatched all over the country, often being grazed on some grassy verge, when he was truly hard up, as he walked them from one place to another. Mostly they raced for trifling stakes of £15. In spite of his major successes, this penchant for 'little fish' ensured he was never able to make ends meet for long. But he was never happier than when his off-the-cuff approach to making a living obliged him to go out and unearth another hidden gem.

The list of hidden gems Parr turned into money-spinners is lengthy. He won a St Leger with Saucebox and Manchester (Tradesmen's) Cups with Rataplan and Saucebox; plus successive Ascot Gold Cups with the 'iron horse' that was Fisherman. This son of Heron, whom Parr owned at one point as well as trained, epitomized his preference for quantity over quality and a training regimen tailored to suit that end. Parr loved to tell how he humoured the horse 'either with a long gallop or a short one but never left him long without work.' Fisherman didn't win a single race as a two-year-old but thereafter displayed the durability Parr's methods had instilled by winning no fewer than 23 races in 1856 from 34 outings between 12 February and 30 October. Excluding three walk-overs, Fisherman covered something like 49 miles on tracks as far afield as Plymouth and Carlisle and won on 16 different ones. On three occasions he won twice in two days and at the St Leger meeting turned out three times. He won over distances as disparate as six furlongs at Stamford and three miles at Bedford. The following season he added a further 22; and then surpassed himself by numbering the Ascot Gold Cup among the 21 victories of 1858 – reappearing the following day to win the Queen's Plate in a canter. Even these herculean labours failed to awe Parr. This accolade only grudgingly materialized later in the season after Fisherman gave 65lb and a head beating to Misty Morn, the winner of a dozen races that year. In 1859 Fisherman repeated his Ascot double. In all, Fisherman accumulated 69 victories from 119 starts; 26 of those wins came in Queen's Plates – a record haul. Parr's methods did not sit favourably with everyone. The *Pall Mall Gazette* printed this stinging rebuke: 'Parr did not deserve to have a good horse when we recall how he hacked poor Fisherman up and down England – night journeys in a draughty horse-box, clothing forgotten (or pawned) and the old horse sent again to the post the next day.'

Like the majority of his training contemporaries, Parr set his sights on the prestigious handicaps, winning successive Cambridgeshires in addition to the Cesarewitch. A shrewder punter than Parr would've collected thousands by punting on the likes of Weathergage, Fisherman, Rataplan and Saucebox. But so long as he went home from a meeting with his expenses covered, Parr was perfectly content. Needless to say, Parr's attitude to money ensured he died in poverty and obscurity, paralyzed with old age, in January 1880.

But not before Fordham had benefited greatly from the canny trainer's touch. When Parr needed a bantam to ride Saucebox at 5st 12lb in the Lincoln Spring Handicap of 1855 (forerunner of the Lincolnshire Handicap) he turned to Fordham, resulting in a cosy half-length victory. Later on it was Parr's Coroner that gave Fordham his first Ascot success, the Trial Stakes of 1855; and given that Saucebox would go on to win the St Leger, the bay colt was a good thing for the 1855 Manchester Cup under 5st 10lb. John Wells was Parr's regular jockey of choice, but that weight was beyond him. Parr knew he could call on a rider who was disputing leadership of the jockeys list with Wells, and Fordham booted Saucebox to another prestigious win. The following June, Fordham won the two and a quarter mile contest a second time, aboard Mr Jemmy Barber's Pretty Boy, another lowly weighted three-year-old. Fordham put up

3lb overweight at 5st 4lb and still beat the Nat Flatman-ridden and odds-on favourite, Typee, 'cleverly'. Later that same afternoon Pretty Boy defeated Typee a second time to carry off the Salford Borough Cup; and a month afterwards he and Fordham inflicted a third defeat on Typee to add the Liverpool Summer Cup.

Two years after Saucebox's Manchester Cup success Parr faced a similar jockey predicament before the 1857 Cambridgeshire. He knew what it took to win the race, having taken it 12 months earlier with Malacca. His three-year-old Odd Trick had a fighting chance with 7st 4lb. He approached Fordham – who thus found himself in a dilemma because his victorious Cesarewitch partner Prioress was also engaged. Ten Broeck understood the situation: Parr and Fordham had the longer association. The start was a war zone: the 39 runners were kept wheeling and turning for 40 minutes, during which pandemonium the favourite, El Hakim, was kicked in the head. From the moment Fordham drove Odd Trick into the lead approaching the Dip, spectators knew the identity of the winner. Odd Trick won by a cosy couple of lengths at odds of 13 to 1: Fordham got a present of £200 (£24,000). He had achieved the rare distinction of winning both legs of the 'Autumn Double' in the same season.

***

The Days continued to provide Fordham with a torrent of winners – and the occasional kerfuffle. Fordham's status as champion was reinforced by more opportunities coming his way in stakes races. At the Ascot meeting of 1856, in front of Queen Victoria, he recorded a breakthrough victory in the New Stakes, the premier event for two-year-olds during the week and one of the most prestigious in the calendar. Unfortunately his all-the-way victory on the unnamed filly, soon to be christened Zaidee, did not pass without controversy. She wasn't even quoted in the betting and her success by a neck scuppered an almighty 'plunge' on Padwick's odds-on favourite Goldfinch. Padwick took the reverse sourly, and objected to the winner on the grounds that she was 'not of proper age.' An examination of the horse's mouth the following day disproved its case. Fordham then thwarted another Padwick gamble when Termagant landed the Chesterfield Cup at Goodwood.

Padwick may have been piqued by these setbacks but was not so stupid as to bear a grudge when it came to getting his preferred jockey. Fordham won successive runnings of Ascot's Gold Vase in 1857 and 1858 for him aboard Arsenal and Sedbury respectively. Arsenal ran through pelting rain to upset the odds-on favourite Strathnaver by a length. Sedbury was Padwick's best animal in 1858, one of three horses he'd run unsuccessfully in the Derby; the two miles of the Vase was a recovery mission. The race offered favourable weight allowances similar to the Goodwood Cup. Sedbury carried 7st 3lb compared to the gallant Fisherman's 9st 7lb. Only Tom Parr's evergreen horse (6 to 5 on) was backed to beat Sedbury (5 to 1). But at these weights Fisherman wasn't up to the task. In glorious weather, before a rather quiet first-day crowd in the absence of any Royal patronage, Fordham brought Sedbury up to Fisherman's quarters inside the distance and 'beat him cleverly by a neck'.

Readers were becoming used to seeing the term 'cleverly' associated with a Fordham win. At the end of the 1856 season he rode a filly belonging to one of his first patrons, Lord Exeter, to win the Criterion Stakes, one of the Newmarket 'back-end' events for juveniles that pinpointed a future Classic prospect. Beechnut missed the Guineas but proved her quality by easily winning the Coronation Stakes at Ascot and the Nassau at Goodwood. The latter was one of three notable successes for Fordham at the meeting. He won the Stewards' Cup by a head on Tournament ('after a rousing set-to' according to *The Times*) and the Chesterfield Cup on Padwick's 10 to 1 shot Comquot. What with this success being book-ended by wins on Adamas in Epsom's City and Suburban and the Autumn Double triumphs of Prioress and Odd Trick, Fordham could have no complaints about his luck in the calendar's premier handicaps in 1857.

By now Fordham's fame had spread to Ireland. In June 1858 he was invited to ride at a three-day meeting at the Curragh. He received a warm welcome and won five races: a hat-trick of Queen's Plates on Borderer; the Challenge of the Kirwans on Altro; and the Stewards Plate on Buckstone – 'a win cleverly achieved by Fordham brought the afternoon of sport to a most successful issue,' reported *Bell's Life*. At the September meeting he won the Scurry Stakes on Sobieski. He'd cross the Irish Sea again in 1860 to win four more races at the Curragh and one at Howth and Balydoyle.

Fordham was a young man in demand and a young man in a hurry. That same summer of 1860 he rode Pierrefonds to finish third in the Prix du Jockey Club on 20 May in between riding at Harpenden on the 18th and Epsom on the 22nd. *The Sporting Life* calculated that on the racecourse alone he must've walked, cantered and galloped upwards of 300 miles during the season.

Thanks in no small measure to his alliance with the Days, Padwick and a pair of Turf eccentrics, the young tyro had built on his initial championship success of 1855 to retain his title through the next three seasons with totals of 108 (surpassing Nat Flatman's record of 104), 84 and 91. Dubbed 'The Demon' on account of his penchant for a devilishly executed late 'rush', he'd rapidly attracted a 'blind' following among punters: Army officers about to serve abroad, for example, were wont to leave commissions to back every horse he rode for a tenner.

There seemed no limit to Fordham's talent. Or the heights to which he might aspire. But there was still one peak he'd not conquered.

Formosa

FOUR

CLASSIC BREAKTHROUGH

By the opening of the 1859 season George Fordham was still only 22 years of age. He'd been champion for four years. He'd proved his success was no flash in the pan. His pre-eminence was now plain for all to see. Yet his status as top dog was undermined by one glaring omission from his curriculum vitae: he'd not yet won a Classic.

Fordham's young hide was thin and tender. If he'd not actually overheard the tittle-tattle he'd heard it in his mind: Fordham can ride winners in the bread-and-butter races; he's unstoppable round Egham and Bedford; but in the Classics it's men like Flatman and Wells, the jockeys with proven records, that connections seek out. Fordham itched for a Classic victory. With the continued support of Padwick and the Days, and the forging of alliances with any number of other powerful patrons, it became only a matter of when that initial

Classic victory would arrive – then, and only then, might Fordham stop scratching.

Quantity was all that mattered to become champion jockey; during the next dozen seasons, for instance, Fordham would lose and regain his title without ever being in danger of relinquishing his crown as the foremost 'knight of the pigskin'. Success in major handicaps multiplied – and proved lucrative. But Fordham was no different to any other jockey. He craved something more. He yearned for success in the Classics.

By the time he won his first jockeys championship in 1855 the five great races of the English Turf confined to three-year-olds and run over diverse distances and tracks at widely separated points of the season had come to be known by that term. After 1853, when West Australian won all three of the Classics open to colts (and geldings too until the early 1900s), the Two Thousand Guineas at Newmarket in the spring (first run in 1809), the Derby at Epsom in high summer (1780) and the St Leger at Doncaster in early autumn (1776), another term was coined: the Triple Crown. In addition to competing for this Triple Crown with a sex allowance, fillies had another confined to their own sex: the One Thousand Guineas (dating from 1814) and the Oaks (1779) in addition to the St Leger. The two races for the Guineas were initially considered much inferior. The Derby swiftly became the most coveted and carried the most prestige – the 'Blue Riband' of the Turf in the words of Disraeli. But to a great many the St Leger was the more venerated – a view passionately championed by the Tykes of its Yorkshire homeland who were wont to say: 'The fittest horse wins the Guineas. The luckiest horse wins the Derby. But the best horse wins the Leger.'

What proved a boon in handicaps served to hamstring Fordham in the Classics: his weight. The usual weight carried in the Classics during the 1850s was 8st 7lb (fillies carried 3-5lb less when competing against the colts) and 'live' weight in the saddle was considered more useful than the three stone of 'dead' weight that Fordham would be obliged to carry in his saddlecloth. However successful the 'feather', this was the prejudice 'tinies' had to overcome. Furthermore, Drewitt rarely had a Classic horse let alone a prime contender; and Alfred Day, brother of John and William, 'King Alfred' to racegoers, was ahead of Fordham in the pecking order for any of the Danebury and Woodyates Classic mounts.

Fordham was champion for two years before making his debut in a Classic. It turned out an inauspicious start. The colt Apathy lived up to his name in the 1857 Two Thousand Guineas, and Tricolor did likewise in both the One Thousand and the Oaks. Tournament at least put up fighting displays in the Derby and St Leger. He was sent off 4 to 1 favourite at Epsom, only to finish fourth behind Blink Bonny; at Doncaster he came third to another filly in Imperieuse after taking the lead half way up the straight.

The next season proved no better – and in a sense proved worse. In the Two Thousand Guineas Fordham partnered The Happy Land on whom he'd won the Criterion, the traditional contest for juveniles holding Classic pretensions. The colt was trained at Woodyates by William Day for the Lancastrian Lord Ribblesdale, a man whose delicate health ensured he spent most of his time abroad. He ate and drank sparingly but wagered extravagently. The previous spring he'd stood to win £20,000 if his two colts St Giles and The Happy Land won at Northampton with Fordham in the plate. St Giles obliged, but later in the afternoon Fordham got beat on The Happy Land, thanks, in the opinion of Day, to the jockey being caught dozing at the start and missing the break. The Happy Land went off at 7 to 1for the 1858 Two Thousand Guineas carrying wads of

Ribblesdale's cash. However, the owner communicated to his jockey that he'd received an anonymous letter stating Fordham intended to prevent his horse from winning. Fordham broke down in tears at this slur: he was the champion jockey; his integrity he held sacrosanct. He determined to show the horse being put into the race. He set a scalding pace and was soon clear, and still three lengths to the good passing the Bushes. But as they met the rising ground coming out of the Dip, Wells had stirred Fitz Roland from a sheltered position at the rear of the pack. They came at The Happy Land with a rare rattle. Then 'the little black rolled like a ship in a gale at the final incline,' according to the *Pall Mall Gazette*, and Fordham was beaten a length and a half.

Day's fingers were as burned as Ribblesdale's, and as a means of placating the owner he cast aspersions on the way Fordham had ridden his colt. 'If', he said, 'I train a horse to win a race and a jockey doesn't second my efforts, is it my fault, my lord?' Fordham may've been a mere 20-year-old who should mind his manners in the presence of his elders and betters. But he was the champion jockey; he'd his status to protect. Reduced to tears a second time, he was called before the Stewards to explain his riding and promptly reported what Ribblesdale and Day had said. He refused to ride for William Day again – besides maintaining a watchful eye on the racecourse performances of Day's horses for anything untoward.

The 1859 season was therefore a significant one in Fordham's career, for it heralded a Classic breakthrough for the multiple champion. And he won not one but two. Both came courtesy of fillies. Both were trained by Tom Taylor.

Mayonaise was an attractive daughter of Teddington who'd used his odd-sized feet to good effect when winning the Derby, Gold Cup and Doncaster Cup. Her mealy bay coat was offset by a beautiful head and neck and strong hind quarters. The latter she'd deployed to good effect by recording five wins as a juvenile, including the decent prizes of Liverpool's Great Lancashire Produce Stakes, the Ham Stakes at Goodwood and the Bretby Stakes at Newmarket – all in the hands of John Wells. Nevertheless, Mayonaise drifted out in the Guineas betting to 9 to 2 in a four-horse field dominated by 9 to 4 on favourite Ariadne; there have only been three smaller fields in the race's history. Quite possibly her walk in the market had something to do with Wells being on the sidelines following a five-horse pile-up at Chester (riding Summerside in the Dee Stakes) - and Fordham taking over in the saddle. Would Fordham prove a 'Jonah'?

He did not. Ariadne proved a damp squib and Mayonaise was kicked clear by Fordham below the distance to romp home by 20 lengths – a record margin of victory unequalled to this day. 'The defeat of the favourite created a sensation,' reported *The Times*, 'and imparted an unexpected importance to the proceedings.' The newspaper damned the Classic with faint praise: 'It does not boast the great features of the Two Thousand Guineas. Indeed, it is rarely mentioned in the racing world until the evening before its decision.' *The Sporting Life* concentrated on the attributes of the winner: 'She struck us as the finest mare we had seen for many a day, with wonderful quarters and an action like a greyhound. All over a long way from home for Mayonaise could have galloped away from the favourite at any time.'

Fordham had settled the 'Doubting Thomases' by adding the kudos of Classic victory to his name. Moreover, this Guineas established a precedent: he'd eventually ride seven winners of the One Thousand Guineas (from 21 rides), a record that still stands. The owner of this first was William Stirling Crawfurd. This was also the first Classic success for the 40-year-old Scot who came from an old and well-heeled family. Known as 'Craw' to his friends, the various pies in which his fingers prospered included property and coal mines – one colliery alone brought him £30,000 per annum. Consequently, 'Craw' endured no obstacles to making a juicy punt or purchasing any bloodstock that tickled his fancy. There were many of both. Success and failure visited in equal measure; but there was never any trouble financing a winter sojourn in Cannes. He was a docile, some might aver servile, member of the Jockey Club whose deference to Admiral Rous was more in keeping with the character of Uriah Heep than a shrewd owner attempting to curry favour with the handicapper. In time, Crawfurd's friend from the hunting field, Lord Chesterfield, encouraged him to put his horses with Tom Taylor's son, 'Grim Old Alec' Taylor, which led to 'Craw' part funding the foundation of the Manton training centre in Wiltshire. 'Fortress' Manton was organized to resist any siege from touts. Somewhat awkwardly it transpired that the head of one tout summarily punished with a clout from a hefty stick belonged to Thomas Fordham, the champion jockey's younger brother. This potentially lethal blood-tie did not dissuade 'Craw' from ultimately offering Fordham a retainer of £1,000.

Taylor held a strong hand for the Oaks. Wells was fit to partner Mayonaise and Fordham, after being set to ride an outsider, was engaged for Summerside. A half sister to the 1856 Derby winner Ellington, she was a low lengthy daughter of the first - and, thus far, the only - Triple Crown winner, West Australian. Possessed of good shoulders, back and loins, muscular quarters and a blood-like head and neck, the brown filly had a switch tail and a distinctive white star on her forehead and one white heel behind. Summerside's juvenile career had ended with victory in a Doncaster sweepstakes after unplaced efforts in classier contests: the Convivial Stakes at York and the Champagne Stakes at Doncaster. *The Life* noted that Summerside had grown over the winter; she'd been reserved for this Classic; and, the paper added, she represented different interests to the favourite. She belonged to Lord Londesborough, a keen yachtsman, a former Liberal MP for Canterbury and latterly a diplomat upon his elevation to the peerage in 1850. Money poured on Mayonaise, forcing her to odds on. But the Guineas winner, regarded a far better specimen of her sex than the mighty Virago or Derby winner Blink Bonny by *The Sporting Life*, was this day 'foamed and fretted with not a dry spot on her.' Summerside, by contrast, looked surprisingly well considering her nasty Chester experience, and was well supported at 4 to 1.

Taylor's two fillies could just be made out through the summer haze holding positions mid-field as Schism led the 15 runners round Tattenham Corner. When Mayonaise made her move shortly thereafter she was shadowed by Summerside who, 'responding gallantly the instant she was called upon by Fordham', quickly took her measure. The favourite fell away to finish fourth as Fordham and Summerside passed the post with half a length to spare over their nearest pursuer. Though the first of five Oaks winners for Fordham (from 22 rides), Summerside was Londesborough's only Classic winner; her victory arrived in the nick of time because he died the following year at the early age of 55. He rewarded Fordham with a cheque for £300.

Neither Mayonaise nor Summerside especially distinguished themselves thereafter. Summerside won a small race at Newmarket as a four-year-old before running unplaced in the Cambridgeshire under top weight. Mayonaise did rather better. Fordham steered her to comfortable successes in the Gratwicke at Goodwood and a Biennial at Brighton before Wells got back on her in the autumn. The Gratwicke provided one of those race-riding instances where a jockey's luck can go either way. Chapeller decided to fly open mouthed at the nearest opponent, which happened to be Mayonaise. But she missed her, and caught the filly standing next to Mayonaise. Thus, instead of Fordham being left with a badly lacerated leg, this misfortune was visited on Tom Ashmall.

The 1860s proved a profitable decade for Fordham in the Classics. He won six. Nemesis struck first, in the One Thousand Guineas of 1861. The bay daughter of Newminster was trained by William Harlock for George Hilton, who often raced his horses under the name 'Fleming' from his place of residence in Essex. Of a straightforward and excitable disposition, he was apt to take the blackest view of his jockeys and if he caught wind of any criticism levelled at them the culprit was destined to be 'button-held' and treated with scorn. Nemesis had only an indifferent juvenile career to commend her. She'd needed six outings to break her maiden, but after Fordham had managed a second place on her at Goodwood, she won at Lewes, Egham (twice) and Warwick. Her Classic prep outing was inauspicious to say the least: she finished fourth of four at Newmarket and could be readily backed at 20 to 1 the night before the Guineas. Optimists pointed out that the Guineas favourite, Brown Duchess, was behind Nemesis in Goodwood's Findon Stakes, and that she'd been in season at Newmarket. Even so, her starting price of 10 to 1, only sixth best in a nine-runner field, was not unjust.

For the second time in the week the bells of Newmarket's churches would ring out in celebration of a local Guineas winner. Nemesis drew inspiration from the success of Diophantus in the Two Thousand by making virtually every yard. Taking up the running some way from the finish, nothing was capable of running her down and Fordham held Fairwater at bay by a length with Brown Duchess a head back in third. She was the third leg of a Fordham treble. Nemesis subsequently started favourite for the Oaks in which Fordham was claimed for Vergiss-mein-nicht; neither filly featured as Brown Duchess reversed the Guineas form over the longer trip. Nemesis continued to visit the racecourse but only as a lesser light. She managed one more win, at Epsom as a four-year-old. On one occasion, at Lincoln, she was reduced to contesting a three-mile steeplechase under 12st.

Four years later it was Siberia's turn to win the One Thousand. Trained by John Day, she sported the blue-and-white hooped jacket of one of Danebury's most aristocratic patrons, the Duke of Beaufort. The 8th Duke had first sent horses to Danebury in 1855 and was one of the most popular men on the Turf. *Baily's Magazine* summarized the reasons thus: 'He is a popular nobleman not because he doesn't tell his jockeys to "pull" his horses, or because he doesn't pay his debts of honour when he owes them, but because he is a generous and industrious supporter of all sports which England regard as national.' His was a kind spirit – not that he was above demanding two reporters be ejected from the Ascot Grand Stand because they'd criticized his late withdrawal of Rustic from the 1866 St Leger. More typical was his treatment of the touts lurking in the Danebury woods awaiting Rustic's pre- Derby trial. He had them rounded up and coached to a Stockbridge inn where they were given a sumptuous breakfast at his expense. 'As I have let you have possession of the ground for some months,' he told them, 'perhaps you'd be kind enough to let me have it for an hour.' The source of the Duke's generous nature may be deduced from the tale he was fond of recounting about the thrashing he received from his first headmaster for 'ending a pentameter with a three-syllable word.' The beating lasted three minutes and 'was repeated the following morning after prayers because two thrashings would be remembered better than one.' Rather than bullying begetting a bully, his case quite possibly saw any endemic aristocratic nastiness beaten out of him. After Eton he'd served with the Life Guards (acting as Wellington's ADC) and the 7th Hussars, albeit regretting the lack of active service, and sat as a Conservative MP for East Gloucestershire until inheriting his title and the family seat at Badminton in 1853. He flung himself wholeheartedly into the role, patronizing local shows with his cattle and sheep and, in 1855, assuming active control of the Beaufort Hunt's field operations. Known as 'the Blue Duke' from the colour of the coats worn by members of the Hunt, he preferred chasing 'Reynard' than racing (seldom having fewer than 45 hunters in his stables); when a recession in the iron industry hit his Monmouthshire estates hard he gave up the Turf temporarily in 1867 in order to divert all available funds toward maintaining his hounds. He was also a master at driving a four-in-hand and a devoted angler. His enduring gift to the Turf was the Badminton Library, a series of 28 volumes (a further five were added in due course) he co-edited - and some of which he part wrote - detailing various British sports and pastimes. 'There is no modern encyclopaedia to which the inexperienced man who seeks guidance can turn for information,' the Duke explained. The first five volumes covered Hunting, Fishing, Racing and Shooting; others included volumes on Billiards, Yachting; number 26, somewhat prophetically, put the spotlight on Dancing.

Siberia was brown filly by the Cesarewitch winner Muscovite out of Figtree. She'd proved herself an exceptionally sturdy individual, for Day subjected her to the typically robust Danebury juvenile campaign. She visited the racecourse 13 times, starting at Newmarket on 25 April when running third. Fordham won a two-horse event on her at Ascot, small races at Stamford and York, and a match at the Houghton meeting. Her best form probably surfaced in five placed efforts: principally when splitting the two colts Bedminster and Gladiateur in what *The Times* described as 'a slashing race' for the Prendergast Stakes at Newmarket in late October. Gladiateur would advertise that form by going on to become the second winner of the Triple Crown.

Siberia's preparation for the One Thousand Guineas went smoothly via a 20-length win over course and distance at the Craven meeting. The gales recently hammering Newmarket had thankfully subsided, and squally showers settled the dust that had rendered the Heath 'a perfect Sahara' in the opinion of *The Times*. The betting suggested the Guineas was a two-horse race: the bookies calling '10 to 1 bar two!' Gardevisure went off at 6 to 4 with Siberia at 3 to 1. However, after leading for six furlongs, the favourite suddenly crumbled. Siberia and White Duck swept past. Fordham took up the running at the distance and soon shook off the attentions of White Duck. Then a roar alerted Fordham to another danger. Harry Grimshaw had rousted La Fortune. But Fordham, in the words of *The Life*, 'answered instantly when he saw the late rush get La Fortune to White Duck' and won by a length and a half and a head.

An outbreak of influenza at Danebury failed to dampen public support for Siberia in the Oaks. On the day she looked tucked-up and was joined as favourite by Wild Agnes. Siberia never looked to be in the contest in which Regalia made virtually all. Put back to a mile Siberia won the Coronation Stakes at Ascot before finding one too good for her over the longer trip of the Yorkshire Oaks; and in another over no less than four and a quarter miles at Stamford. She ran six times as a four-year-old (with Tom Cannon aboard) to no success before being reunited with Fordham for the swansong of a walk-over at Goodwood.

The Fordham-Beaufort-Day triumverate struck again in the One Thousand Guineas of 1869 with Scottish Queen. By the Derby and Leger winner Blair Athol, she was a handsome chestnut with good arms and thighs, though somewhat 'shelly' in her frame. The previous October she'd had put up a highly promising display to divide the colts Pero Gomez (giving her 3lb) and Pretender (conceding 10lb) in the Middle Park Plate. It was just the third running of the richest race in the calendar for two year olds which was already being dubbed the 'Second Derby.' *The Times* strove to be more accurate: 'It would be more correct to say it was a Derby trial as some of the best of the year are supposed to contest for the honour of being first favourite for the Epsom event, besides the line it gives to the running of others who are absentees.' On this occasion it certainly proved to be the case. Pero Gomez went on to win the St Leger while Pretender took the Two Thousand Guineas and Derby. Scottish Queen got to within half a length of Pero Gomez and was well clear of Pretender. On dismounting Fordham assured the Duke that his filly was 'a real beauty.'

Throughout the early weeks of 1869 the local correspondent of *The Sportsman* was besotted with Scottish Queen: 'The "Queen", if she keeps doing as well as she is now will win both the One Thousand Guineas and the Oaks.' He was proved half right. He was unaware Scottish Queen was touched in her wind. Eventually this defect would catch up with her – but not before she'd won the One Thousand Guineas. The John Porter-trained Morna was favourite at 100 to 60 on the strength of her juvenile prowess in winning the Champagne Stakes; she was pursued in the market by Stirling Crawfurd's Heather Belle; Scottish Queen was easy to back at 10 to 1 once news leaked out from Danebury that she'd lost her trial despite her greatest fan in *The Sportsman* reporting that 'she greatly pleased everyone in cantering by her beautiful style of going.'

The anticipated two-horse race did not materialize. Heather Belle, considered a 'certainty' by 'Craw', failed to stay the distance and Morna was soon overhauled by the patiently-ridden Scottish Queen a furlong out. Fordham was not taxed in winning 'cleverly' by three-quarters of a length. 'Fordham's luck in this race is quite remarkable,' declared *The Sportsman*. The trade paper was wide of the mark. By 1869 Fordham's expertise on the Rowley Mile was priceless and worth at least 2-3lb over any other jockey riding.

Despite this loss Morna remained Oaks favourite at 2 to 1 with her Guineas conqueror at 7 to 2. By the day of the race Scottish Queen's odds had drifted out to 5 to 1. She was now a confirmed 'roarer'. The race was run in the immediate aftermath of a thunderstorm of biblical proportions that had reduced conditions underfoot to a quagmire. The pace was wretched; the race took just short of three minutes to complete. The survival of the fittest ultimately reduced the contest to a duel between the two fillies who had chased Scottish Queen in the Guineas, with Brigantine proving stronger than Morna. Ploughing through heavy ground exposed Scottish Queen's breathing problems and she struggled past the post in sixth place. Ascot and Goodwood brought further failures.

Fordham's achievements with the aforementioned quintet of Classic-winning fillies were put in the shade by the exploits of Formosa in 1868. Not only did she achieve the first Fillies Triple Crown she added the Two Thousand Guineas to make an unprecedented four - a feat equalled by Sceptre in 1902 but by no other. Fordham steered her to three of them. By rights he should've been aboard her for all four. That he was not owed more to his judgement of humans than equines.

Formosa was trained at Beckhampton by Wiltshire-born Henry Woolcott, 'as chubby as a cherub on a tombstone' to use the highly descriptive phraseology of a contemporary. Woolcott had learnt his trade at the knee of a master practitioner: John Bahram Day. He'd spent 10 years with Day, the last four as head lad. In 1866 Beckhampton had been acquired by William Graham, head of gin distillers Nicholson's, who promptly invited Woolcott to be his private trainer. Graham's background was as intoxicating as his liquor. His original claim to fame was as a Cumberland wrestler. In a career boasting 19 victories it was said: 'In vain did his opponents try to throw him off his balance. He stood as if rooted to the earth.' Having started out in the liquor trade as Nicholson's northern representative, he was fast-tracked to head office and then a partnership. Graham, who'd enjoyed a horse or two in training in Malton, then began taking a serious interest in the Turf. But as a 'self-made man' he viewed the ways of the Turf and its aristocratic natives with a degree of suspicion. He adopted a number of race-card aliases – Jones, Keswick, Brown, Hessey – in an effort to keep his equine lights under a bushel which caused *Baily's Magazine* to refer to him as 'Messrs Graham'. Graham's reputation survived more or less unscathed. 'He is neither a blackleg nor a defaulter, nor a purloiner of stable secrets through the mediums of touts and stable boys,' declared *The Sporting Life* as if that was the criteria of a Turf worthy.

Graham paid 690 guineas for the dark chestnut yearling he was to christen Formosa. After failing to get the filly at that price in the ring at the Doncaster Sales he acquired her from County Durham breeder James Cookson over his breakfast egg the following morning. She was the pick of Cookson's draft of eight Buccaneer yearlings, the average of which was a mere 266 guineas. Her dam, Eller, was closely related to the dam of Derby winner Ellington and Fordham's Oaks winner Summerside, to whom she finished sixth at Epsom. In a nod to her sire Formosa was named after the island in the China Sea that served as a notorious haven for pirates. Formosa came from the few crops Buccaneer sired before his export to the Kisber Imperial Stud of Austria-Hungary once he'd become an untrustworthy 'savage'. On the track Buccaneer had been dubbed a 'quitter'. However, it wasn't so much lack of resolution as lack of stamina that ruined his Classic season. He'd run down the field in both Derby and St Leger. Two days after the Leger he was put back to a mile and easily won the Don Stakes by three lengths; at four he'd add the Royal Hunt Cup. Speed was his forte; he'd won the July, the Molecomb and the Drawing Room Stakes at two.

Formosa was as busy a juvenile as her sire. She ran nine times, winning at Stockbridge, Newmarket (the Chesterfield Stakes) and Abingdon. Given the Danebury schooling shared by Fordham and Woolcott it was obvious who would ride her whenever he was available. When it came to the Middle Park Plate in the autumn, however, Fordham was committed to riding the year's juvenile star. Fordham had partnered Lady Elizabeth to a dozen straight wins. She was the darling of the public and he could not desert her. Jem Adams thus rode Formosa.

A filly would win the Middle Park. But it was neither hot favourite Lady Elizabeth nor Formosa. The honour fell to Green Sleeve, in receipt of 10lb from the favourite. John Porter's filly pipped his colt Rosicrucian for the £4,410 prize by a head; Lady Coventry was two lengths behind in third; Formosa, trounced by Lady Elizabeth at Bath earlier in the year, stole fourth place from her by a head.

The decision as to who rode Formosa in the Two Thousand Guineas the following spring was thus far from straightforward. Fordham was due to ride the John Day-trained See-Saw but, when

Lord Wilton's colt dropped out, negotiations began for him to replace Adams. The latter was regarded as 'a model feather' but no more than that. He and Fordham were retained by Graham on the same terms. The owner left the decision to the two jockeys. Fordham paid Adams £50 for the ride.

On a chilly April day Formosa attempted to turn the tables on Green Sleeve and Rosicrucian in the Two Thousand Guineas. She looked ready. *Bells Life* purred: 'She was brought out by Henry Woolcott in first rate fettle. She has grown a little, but is nice and compact, with a sweet, pretty head and neck and big powerful quarters.' The two fillies went off joint favourites at 5 to 2 for what was usually a dog fight between males. A large crowd gathering round the 14 runners at the start made Tom McGeorge's task of getting the field away evenly and on time virtually impossible. After 15 minutes delay he finally achieved an acceptable line. The pace was moderate and no animal seemed to hold an advantage for 50 yards or more until Moslem, the 100 to 8 Manton outsider in the Stirling Crawford colours, drew ahead of the group on the right while Formosa could be spied leading the division on the left. On reaching the Bushes the effort of Porter's two representatives fizzled out, leaving Moslem and Formosa to indulge in a ding-dong battle to the line. Formosa appeared to gain the upper hand when Moslem swerved off a true line, but Tom Chaloner rallied his mount and regained a slender advantage running up the hill. *The Sporting Life* recorded Fordham's response: 'Fordham rode the mare very tenderly, in a most artistic manner, closing on Moslem inch by inch within a few strides of the chair. A finer display of horsemanship has seldom been witnessed.' *The Sportsman* agreed with its fellow trade paper: 'Twenty strides from the Chair they were locked together. The most artistic riding on either side could gain no advantage, and they passed the post so evenly that most persons who were in a position to form an opinion could tell it was a dead-heat. But for Fordham's wonderful riding Moslem must have won. Both Fordham and Chaloner were greeted with loud cheers on returning to weigh in, and certainly a more brilliant piece of horsemanship on both sides was never seen.' Their reports might've pointed out Fordham had ridden the filly without the aid of whip or spurs.

A run-off was proposed for 15 minutes after the last race, but following some deliberation Woolcott and Graham declined and the stake was divided. 'The Formosa party exercised a sound discretion in agreeing to a division having an eye on the One Thousand Guineas, so giving the mare every possible chance of landing that event also.' However, Formosa's supporters who'd made her favourite for the decider were not enamoured of the decision.

It's quite possible the Press assertion that Formosa was being saved for the One Thousand Guineas 48 hours later was correct because on the day she was backed to win £20,000 (*£2.4 million*). The opposition was weak. Only eight opposed the 6 to 5 on favourite. Lady Coventry would line up but the other Lady – Elizabeth – was a contentious absentee. In her stead Danebury fielded Athena, a decent filly but pounds inferior to her illustrious stable-mate. 'The race was won so easily,' reported *The Times*, 'that it needs little description. Athena and Lady Coventry made most of the running but Formosa came out and won in a canter when Fordham dropped his hands. A much easier affair has scarcely been seen.' The official distance to Athena was three lengths; Lady Coventry was a further three adrift.

The formbook threw a dampener on Formosa's feat of replicating the twin Guineas victories of Crucifix back in 1840. It suggested she might not have beaten an awful lot. Moslem, 'a wear-and-tear sort' according to *Bell's Life*, had justified his 570-guineas price tag as a yearling by failing to win a race of any description at two, and merely two and four-runner events at Croxton Park and Newmarket before the Two Thousand; afterwards his sole success was a walk-over at Goodwood. And with the real Lady Elizabeth out of the equation the three-year-old fillies were easy pickings.

Graham was not always entirely happy with the attention his filly brought. 'Every man who buys a drop of gin at the place,' he lamented, 'thinks he has the right to come and pester me about the horses.' How unfortunate for the ungrateful owner that he was obliged to watch Formosa's record-breaking caravan move on to Epsom and the Oaks where she might at last put the 'talking horse' that was Lady Elizabeth in her place. She scared off all bar eight fillies, one of whom was only running to give her a lead. Graham was so confident he wrote Fordham a cheque for £500 (*£60,000*) before the race; equally bullish was his bookmaker associate, John Stephenson, who'd assumed the mantle of Davis and John Jackson as the leading bookmaker in the Ring. 'Stevey' was both a fearsome bully and bettor, who became so excitable during a race on which he stood to win or lose a bundle that, in the colourful phrase of *Baily's Magazine,* 'the veins on his face swell to the size of leaden pipes.' He was also prone to bouts of epilepsy which ultimately prompted him cut his own throat from ear to ear at the age of 45. For the Oaks he offered the special bet of 'an even £5,000 (*£600,000*) Formosa to beat Lady Elizabeth.' Those who took the bet must've wept when all the adverse rumours concerning Lady Elizabeth's well-being were confirmed by her appalling display in the Derby. Even if Lady Elizabeth turned out again for the Oaks she was in no condition to confirm her juvenile form with Formosa. Compared to a Lady Elizabeth described by the Press as 'worn to a scarecrow and a bag of bones', Formosa 'looked the beau ideal of a thoroughbred...her muscles stood out as hard as nails and her coat was bright and smooth as a piece of velvet.'

As it transpired the Oaks was fortunate to be run. Shortly before racing commenced so did an almighty thunderstorm which saw parts of the course under water. Thunder roared and lightning flashed. A cottage was demolished; lives lost – equine and human. A three-foot deep pond blocked one approach road over which a number of quick-witted Jack-the-lads imposed a toll for carrying pedestrians across on their shoulders. Fortunately the elements had settled down by the time the nine fillies were inspected by the members of the fourth estate. Formosa proceeded to be mobbed by dozens of her supporters at whom Graham glowered and Woolcott had difficulty removing. Once again *The Times* drooled over Formosa: 'She was brought to the post in beautiful condition, handsome to the eye, but not big, and altogether the best-looking mare in the race. Judged by her inches she is but a little one, for she reaches no higher than 15 hands one and a half. But she is capitally furnished and full of muscular power. She has a pleasing head, with a good breadth of forehead, and a strongly crested neck, reminding one more of a colt than a filly. She has strong shoulders, a good middle, famously-shaped quarters, and unexceptionable legs, on which she stands as firm as a rock. With her head well up and her bold carriage, she walked away with Fordham a very picture – and even then it looked to be all over.'

In spite of Lady Elizabeth's pitiful condition, she looked 'as narrow as a rail and bathed in perspiration' according to *The Sportsman*, she still held some worshippers in thrall to her former glories and she found backers at 9 to 2 to upset the 11 to 8 on favourite. Their prayers were in vain. Formosa's pacemaker Janet Rawcliffe took the field along until the mile post on sufferance whereupon Fordham decided to rely on his own resources. A shout went up as Lady Elizabeth momentarily inspired Tom Cannon with hope by running into her bridle. But the hope was short-lived. She fell away descending Tattenham Hill and Formosa strode up the straight like the queen of all she surveyed. Half way up the straight Fordham was seen to 'indulge Formosa with a pull' and play to the gallery by looking round with a big smile on his face. Never forced out of three-parts speed, Formosa passed the winning post ten lengths ahead of Lady Coventry; Lady Elizabeth crawled over the line in company with the pacemaker, 'made to look no more than a common plater.'

It was beginning to look as if Formosa was unbeatable. Yet she met defeat in both of her outings leading up to the St Leger. Her pretensions to staying the Leger trip were tested in Ascot's Prince of Wales' Stakes over one mile five furlongs. In view of what later transpired at Doncaster her dismal performance here must be attributed to the ordeal of Epsom's dire conditions a fortnight earlier - plus her 12lb penalty. In a race won by the Derby runner-up King Alfred she trailed home sixth, ahead of Lady Elizabeth but some way adrift of Moslem in third. Her run at Goodwood back at a mile was equally uninspiring: she succumbed by a length in a four-horse race for the Triennial.

With the St Leger looming Fordham must've felt a certain anxiety. And more so after hearing that Formosa had picked up a stone on the gallops and was reportedly lame. Her price drifted two points. Another report from the gallops planted further doubt in his mind. His friend George Hodgman told him how his own Leger candidate Paul Jones had demolished his 'tackle' in a trial. Fordham took Hodgman at his word and on the morning of the race begged off Formosa to ride Paul Jones. One can imagine Fordham's feelings replicating those of *The Times* when he caught sight of the allegedly infirm Formosa before the Classic: 'The Oaks victrix was brought to the post in the perfection of blooming condition. The fine sweeping action she displayed in her preliminary canter conclusively refuted the canard which had been so industriously put about during the morning that she was suffering from lameness.' Though Hodgman had assessed the chances of his 100 to 15 shot correctly, Paul Jones proved no match for Formosa who went past him like a rocket to win by a couple of lengths. Formosa's connections could celebrate her monumental achievements. She was the first to secure the Fillies Triple Crown and the first of only two ever to win four Classics. Fordham did not join in the party. He left the track immediately after the race.

Evidently Graham did not hold Fordham's apparent slight to his record-setting filly against him. Fordham was re-united with Formosa to win the Newmarket Oaks 'hard held'; and they began the 1869 season where they left off: a 'hands down' victory at Bath. But her fortunes waned. She failed in Cups at Ascot and Stockbridge and was burdened with win-stopping top weight in handicaps like the Chester Cup, Great Yorkshire and Liverpool Autumn Cup. Amid these disappointments was one final success in Fordham's caress – which constituted more of a hoot than a hurrah.

Goodwood's Bentinck Memorial over two miles on 29 July 1869 was reduced to a match between Formosa and Blueskin, ridden by Charlie Maidment. The market went 5 to 1 on Formosa. She won all right. But only at the conclusion of a race *The Times* described as 'a burlesque upon racing.' The two horses left the post at a walk. The walk eventually took them to the top of the hill. At this point they stopped. The pair stood looking at each other for fully 20 minutes. Fordham eyed Maidment; Formosa stared at Blueskin. Eventually Blueskin's owner, Henry Savile, hurried from the Grand Stand, ordering Maidment to curtail the farce by going on. Alas, Blueskin had grown accustomed to his spot of turf and refused to budge from it. Then Woolcott arrived on the scene. He instructed Fordham to get a move on. At last there was meaningful action. Fordham gave Formosa a kick in the belly. Away she went to win without coming out of a canter by the best part of a furlong. *The Times* was both agitated and concerned. It called for both jockeys to be severely dealt with because this was a shambles waiting to happen in distance races habitually run at a crawl for most of their length: 'This was an exhibition which ought to call for the intervention of the Jockey Club if they really desire to see long races in the calendar.' The Club sat on its hands.

Formosa's career ended under an even sorrier cloud in the 1870 Gold Vase and a Queen's Plate at Newmarket. She was, according to the *Sporting Review*, 'being hacked about all over the country and losing her reputation by being beaten for paltry prizes.' At Newmarket she was thrashed 10 lengths by the five-year-old mare Mysotia whom she'd have carried in their Classic season. A fickle Press that had once adored her now observed: 'Mr Graham must be considered a very fortunate owner to have won the Oaks with such a moderate animal.' Bearing in mind Formosa won him £21,253 (£2.5 *million*) in prize-money alone William Graham surely did feel he was a lucky man. Formosa's misfortune continued in the paddocks. She produced six foals before her death in 1881 – by which time she'd passed into the stud of aspiring French *Turfiste* Christopher Joachim Lefevre for the sum of 1,000 guineas. None of her progeny cut any especial dash. The filly White Poppy ran in the 1879 St Leger; her last foal, another filly called Formalite, won La Coupe at Longchamp.

Graham did not have to wait long before another of the female gender bore his green and black-belted jacket to Classic victory. In

1870 Gamos won the Oaks with Fordham again doing the steering. She was bred by Lord Falmouth and bought as a yearling for 220 guineas. Graham had taken to giving his horses classically Greek or Latin names and chose the Greek word for marriage for this daughter of Saunterer - once the property of that other self-made man from humble northern beginnings, bookmaker John Jackson. Unlike her handsome sire, Gamos wasn't much to look at. A tall filly, very straight in front with decidedly curby hocks, she possessed a plain head not particularly well set on a thin neck – altogether lacking, stated a disparaging Press, 'the character of a great race winner.'

Nonetheless, appearances do not win races. Gamos proved herself to be a decent juvenile by winning all bar two of her eight races, albeit gaining most of them in small fields. The brown filly's cramped odds of 8 to 1 for the Oaks through the winter looked ridiculous when Gamos was made to look a complete mug by the runaway Guineas winner Macgregor in Bath's Biennial barely a week before her Epsom target. Woolcott reckoned he'd never had her fitter and promised she'd 'stretch the favourite's neck'; but, in the words of *The Sportsman*, 'Gamos was so completely beaten that she could not make the necessary effort to get past the Judge who had quitted his box before she passed the post. She has no chance in the Oaks.'

The scribe must've regretted that final comment on Oaks afternoon because Gamos and Fordham won the Classic more easily than their one-length margin over Sunshine suggests. Only seven fillies went to post, the smallest field since 1821. The race was destined to be a 'dull' affair in the opinion of the Press: defeat for the One Thousand Guineas winner, Hester, would be a bigger shock than the Fordham-ridden Macgregor's in the Derby. Gamos was freely available at 100 to 8, since, *The Times* reported, 'the general public would have none of her, as she was so disgracefully beaten at Bath.' Other scribes insisted her forelegs would never cope with Epsom's undulations. Nevertheless, she was backed by 'persons who, in the slang of the Turf, are supposed to know "something".' That 'something' amounted to the discovery that the filly's deplorable display at Bath, where her tail had whirled like a demented windmill, was due to her being 'in season'. Graham was reported in the Press to have invested a mere 'pony' on his filly, but it's hard to think other than John Stephenson executing a significant commission on his behalf.

The race left bitter salt. Hester was beaten before Tattenham Corner. Rumours quickly circulated to the effect she'd been 'got at'. This left the way clear for Sunshine, a good filly belonging to James Merry, who'd won six races as a two-year-old – some of them aided by Fordham. An Oaks victory would compensate Merry for Macgregor's Derby defeat under Fordham. But Fordham was to disappoint Merry once again. However ineffective a race he rode on Macgregor, no-one could say he didn't excel on Gamos. He waited on Sunshine till meeting the rising ground and swept past to a mighty roar from the Ring to whom she was guardian angel and saviour combined. 'Such an unexpected result was quite overwhelming,' exclaimed *The Times*. 'That a mare who was beaten out of sight at Bath should have improved about two stone six days afterwards seems extraordinary. We cannot but look upon her running then and now as requiring some explanation, which there is no doubt Mr Graham will be able to give.' *The Daily Telegraph* devoted a lead article to wondering how Gamos had improved five stone since Bath. *The Morning Post* also pulled no punches: 'It is most fortunate that Mr Graham bears such an unexceptionable character for honesty of purpose, as does his trainer and jockey, otherwise the gravest suspicion would attach to the running of Gamos at Bath, but as Fordham was in the saddle on that occasion no one can insinuate that anything was done inappropriately. All must have had a high opinion of her to have started against Macgregor, then in the zenith of his prime.'

Letters subsequently appeared in the Press endorsing the latter. No explanation was offered by Graham who openly denounced the Press during Ascot – where he ruffled more feathers by declining to meet the Prince of Wales after his Sabinus had won the Gold Cup. What he did offer was £500 to anyone who could prove he'd acted in an underhand manner: this was the Press and Turf establishment ganging up on him again. *Baily's Magazine* provided the sweetest riposte to that charge: 'More individuals are likely to be poisoned with the liquid he distils than by writing in the Press. Repeated success, owing to lucky purchases, by no means entitle Mr Graham to become censor of the Press.' The ease of Gamos's victory, however, was aided by Sunshine being lame and Hester, allegedly, being 'nobbled'. Although Fordham subsequently won Newmarket's Grand Duke Michael Stakes at the end of the season on Gamos, she'd met defeat at Goodwood (Bentinck Memorial), York (Yorkshire Oaks) and Doncaster (Park Hill Stakes) in the interim. *Baily's* reached a derisory judgement: 'The mare of many headaches. About the most moderate Oaks winner that has appeared for some time. How she won at Epsom is a mystery.' Perhaps Graham sensed she'd used up all her luck because he soon sold her for 1000 guineas. If so, he was psychic because despite dropping 15 foals Gamos proved a failure in the paddocks and eventually changed hands for 15 guineas. She was the last of Graham's good animals. He died in January 1876.

***

Fordham had a way with fillies because 13 of his 16 Classic wins came courtesy of the female sex. His record in the One Thousand Guineas, for instance, remains second to none despite the passage of well over a hundred years. He collected seven - one more than his nearest challenger Frank Buckle – and missed an eighth, Repulse in 1866, owing to illness. This record also reflected his absolute mastery of the Rowley Mile – where he also added three renewals of the Two Thousand Guineas (from 22 rides). The first of these was Vauban in 1867.

Vauban was a brown colt by Muscovite belonging to the Duke of Beaufort. He'd not the best of joints, being dreadfully upright in front, but he was a fine topped colt with rare shoulders, a nice short back and grand, powerful quarters. Little as his forelegs looked like standing much strain, Vauban proved sufficiently hardy to win seven of his 15 races as a juvenile. They did not include any of the calendar's major prizes which were more or less mopped up by the marvellous filly Achievement, who trounced Vauban in the July Stakes and went on to win the One Thousand Guineas and St Leger. And at Stockbridge he'd twice been obliged to follow in the slipstream of Hermit – an adversary who'd continue to dog his fortunes in 1867. His best performance came in the Troy Stakes, at the Houghton meeting, in which he gave 3lb and a neck beating to Julius, with decent animals like Lady Hester, Bismarck and Marksman behind. However, Vauban wintered well and was successfully tried (beating the five year old Lord Ronald over a mile at level weights) before scrambling home by a head on his seasonal debut in a Biennial at the Craven Meeting.

Vauban

Fine weather drew a large crowd to the Heath for the Guineas which included the Prince of Wales who arrived on his grey hack. Vauban's principal rivals in the ante post market had been Julius and Plaudit, but the latter's condition – he appeared too hefty in the view of some paddock watchers – saw his price lengthened accordingly while that of Vauban hardened to 5 to 2 favourite. The market proved correct. Plaudit was beaten by half way (the outcome, it was said, of a 'pinched foot' while being shoed), whereas Vauban was in the van from start to finish. Initially Fordham kept him in the slipstream of his pacemaker and stable-mate Uncas. Passing the Bushes a line of three comprising Vauban, Marksman and Julius matched strides, but Fordham had his two opponents covered. He pushed Vauban clear going into the Dip and readily countered the late thrust of Knight of the Garter up the hill to win by two lengths. Marksman was a head back in third. 'This was as brilliant a piece of horsemanship as is conceivable,' said *The Sporting Life*. The Duke of Beaufort just shook his head in wonder: 'One piece of riding like that more than repays the extravagant salary such a jockey is entitled to receive.'

In *The Sportsman* resident poet 'Rolando' joined in:

> *Saw we not Plaudit! Yes, but then I find*
> *He won't be able, with his 'nobbled' feet,*
> *To come to Vauban's mark, for like the wind*
> *Muscovite's noble son will rush along the street*
> *Of crowded and excited faces, and repeat*
> *What the Bay Middleton did in days of yore!*

Two of the paper's other scribes, however, found themselves at loggerheads. 'Vigilant' (the highly respected John Corlett, later to own and edit *The Sporting Times*) had 'advocated the claims of Vauban through good and evil reports alike' and had tipped him to win. 'The Special Commissioner' (the equally regarded Fred Taylor) had been in Plaudit's camp and now picked a bone to gnaw: 'The public form of last season has been upset in the most astonishing and perplexing manner; in fact all reliance on public form and good looks would appear to be a complete farce in estimating the chances of a horse to win any race in the present "sensational" times.' Taylor finished his gripe by prophesying that Vauban would not win the Derby because 'his straight pasterns in front will prevent him from descending Tattenham Hill.'

In this regard 'The Special Commissioner' enjoyed the last laugh. The Guineas was one of nine successes in a row for Vauban during 1867 that were interrupted by just the one setback. But that single reverse for him and Fordham came in the Derby.

Ascot

FIVE

KINGPIN

The 1860s saw George Fordham in his pomp. He was the unquestioned king of the weighing room. He knew it and so did the fellow jockeys who were his minions. And this title was never wrested from him even though he twice forfeited his position at the head of the list.

When God sat down to design the perfect body for a jockey he might've had Fordham in mind. About to turn 23 as the decade opened, he still cut a diminutive figure at not much above five feet, but any lingering puppy fat had long since been burned off; his stocky frame was all muscle, gristle and sinew that raised his minimum riding weight from 7st 7lb to 8st by the end of the decade. However, any advantages lost through gaining weight were more than offset by the accumulation of tactical acumen and the confidence to put it into practice. The champion's status was lauded in print by two tributes in particular.

First, *Baily's Magazine*:

> Fordham, to whom as many epithets have ben applied as to the heathen gods and goddesses, and whom young jockeys regard with awe, and every sporting writer with a species of religious fanaticism, one hardly knows how to paint for the magnitude of the task oppresses us – especially as he has earnestly asked us not to 'plaster him up so'. However, he must take upon himself the inconvenience of his greatness.

Second, *The Sporting Life*:

> Fordham is a very heavy illustration of a self-made man who has won his way to the top of the tree as much by his faultless character as by his professional skill. He must, during the racing season, very nearly live in the saddle for never before did a jockey so travel, jockey so ride, or jockey so win as this 'devil of a rider' has during the last five years. This 'Pride of the South', this 'Captain Kid', this 'Demon' of a rider are titles earned by great talent, strict integrity, accommodating weight, vast industry, and immense popularity. In 1860 alone his 147 winners came from 471 rides at 51 different meetings, winning £22,414 (*£2.7 million*) in prize-money. He is unquestionably the ablest horse-man that ever held reins.

It was during this purple period that Fordham partnered the fastest horse he ever rode. Certainly he himself was of that opinion. Their association was brief but suitably meteoric. It amounted to seven races. Six were won. The animal was a smallish brown filly called Nutbush.

There was nothing in Nutbush's parentage to suggest she'd have pace to burn. She was by Filbert, who contested the 1853 Derby at odds of 100 to 1, out of a mare called Beauty who failed lamentably to live up to her name. But their daughter demonstrated instant promise as a two-year-old, winning three races at Newmarket (twice) and Liverpool before Fordham sat on her to win Liverpool's Scurry Nursery over three furlongs on 7 November 1860 at odds of 2 to 1 on. At three Nutbush resumed her regular partnership with Harry Grimshaw, which yielded a further five wins numbering the Wokingham at Ascot and the Scurry Stakes at the Curragh. This latter expedition saw her run on three successive days over distances progressively rising from six furlongs to a mile (third) and finally two miles (second). But pure speed was Nutbush's game, and, after an unsuccessful tilt at the Stewards Cup, she was put away until the autumn – when she was united with George Fordham on the first day of October. It's no exaggeration to say that the duo lit up the autumn skies like Halley's Comet.

Fordham's love affair with Captain Hawksley's filly was resurrected in a match race over four furlongs against a decent filly called Little Lady, a match that 'would set the pencils working' in the words of *Baily's Magazine*. Nutbush defied the odds: 'Fordham made very short work of it, as he chopped Her Ladyship in the first 100 yards and all was over to the astonishment of everyone who looked forward to a head-to-head affair, making every yard to win by one and a half lengths.' Two days later Nutbush carried 8st 12lb in a five-furlong handicap. She broke slowly but Fordham got her up to win by a neck. At the second Newmarket October Meeting she scored again despite a similar burden: 'Notwithstanding her crushing impost she won easily by a length and a half,' said *The Times*. Forty-eight hours later Nutbush contested another handicap with no less than 10 stone on her back, and was beaten a head conceding three stone all bar a pound to the winner.

Weight carrying and weight concession of that order were almost unheard of at the time. Indeed, the two qualities are not synonymous or compatible. Physique carries the weight; ability concedes it. Not every horse is capable of both. Nutbush was. And at the Houghton Meeting on the last day of October she demonstrated what a freak she was by winning under a staggering 10st 4lb, conceding 34lb to the runner up. 'Nutbush won in most gallant style by a length amid the shouts of spectators,' reported *The Sporting Life*. 'This achievement stamps Nutbush as the most extraordinary animal we ever had over the TYC. Weight does not appear any object to her and she proved herself to be the greatest flyer we ever saw. She outdid herself and fairly astounded the crowd. People were justified in asking how the filly would be handicapped next time.'

Those 'people' found out on 20 November. She was matched with a colt called Gaberdine over four furlongs at Shrewsbury. She was set to carry 9st 4lb against his 6st 1lb. The concession of 43lb meant sweet nothing to Nutbush. She and Fordham put him firmly in his place. Nutbush never ran again. She threw nothing of note and was shot in 1885 after proving barren for five years. Her jockey went to his own grave convinced he'd never travelled faster on a thoroughbred than he did on Nutbush.

Nutbush was obliged to share Fordham's heart with another 'filly'. Fordham had fallen for Dick Drewitt's niece, two years his junior at the age of 24. Fordham's ardour was reciprocated, and on 21 November 1863 he and Penelope Amelia Hyde were wed in the parish church at Northolt, where her father Isaac was a gamekeeper. The couple set up home - tended by a housekeeper, cook and gardener – in a fine property at Upton-cum-Chalvey, on the outskirts of Slough on the high road to London, that Fordham named Beaufort House in honour of his aristocratic patron. They were not slow in filling it with children. Four followed in quick succession: Penelope Amelia Hyde (1864); George Christopher (1866); Blanche Elizabeth (1867) and Nellie Florence (1869). Here the Fordhams lived until 1876.

Family bliss, however, would be tinged with sadness.

**

Fordham's nine-year reign, that began in 1855 and encompassed new record totals of 147 (1860) and 166 (1862) along the way, came to an end in1864. Even 'The Demon' could not repel the advance of a new young wave of 'feathers'.

At the commencement of the 1864 season Harry Grimshaw bet Fordham £100 (*£12,000*) that his teenage brother Jemmy would take the title away from him. Jemmy Grimshaw, dubbed the 'Pocket Hercules', was the latest 'feather' to graduate to the top echelon. Grimshaw won his brother's bet: he soon stole a march on Fordham, who was on the 'sick list' for much of April and May; indeed, he was fast making a habit of not riding very much until the Craven Meeting in mid April (nor did Fordham care much for Liverpool and Chester, tracks he deemed ripe for accidents). A native of Bolton, the eighteen-year-old Grimshaw racked up winner after winner; and took the title by 164 to 137. At no stage had Fordham led. Nevertheless, the Press was eager to set the record straight. *The Morning Post* stated: 'Grimshaw could not hold a candle to the "Immortal George" as a jockey. He was the originator of what must truthfully be termed the flash school of jockeys that has brought irreparable injury and disgrace.' *Baily's Magazine* spoke in similar vein: 'We cannot quite subscribe to the overwhelming admiration which some of his followers entertain for him as he is careless at times and lost races he ought to have been credited with had he ridden to orders.' Grimshaw squandered his money and after being declared bankrupt in 1869 went off to ride in

Austria and Germany. Trouble followed. He served three months in prison for assault and when he died of cancer in Bohemia at the age of 42 in 1888 he left a widow and six children totally destitute.

'The Demon' smarted – and retaliated as all great champions do by regaining his crown in 1865, trouncing Grimshaw by 20. Then he as quickly lost it again to a second aspiring 'feather' in the form of the illiterate Mancunian teenager Samuel Kenyon, who'd only ridden his first career winner (on his only mount) as recently as 1862. Like Grimshaw, success went to Kenyon's head. He ought to have won the 1869 Two Thousand Guineas on Belladrum but flouted his orders to hold up a horse with known breathing problems by attempting to make all - and got the exhausted animal caught on the line by Pretender. Kenyon was dead of consumption at 23 years of age.

Fordham, it must be added, was unfortunate to lose his title in 1866 for he was hampered by a sprained wrist in the spring: 'Fordham's accident must be very vexatious to him, missing many golden opportunities at the present,' reported *The Sporting Life* from Newmarket on 17 April, 'and we may mention that today he was present on the Heath with his arm in a sling, a mere looker-on at the proceedings.' A month later the paper added: 'The rumour that Fordham's arm is withering and he will be unable to ride again is absurd. He is progressing well and will be back to ride in the Derby.' The prognosis proved false. Fordham missed both the Guineas and Derby meetings. But for this enforced absence it's inconceivable he'd not have exceeded Kenyon's score of 123 as he finished only 11 behind on 112.

Throughout this period, champion or no, Fordham was accomplishing some prodigious feats of riding. Five-timers became routine: on 10 July 1868 he won on all five of his rides at Newmarket, to cite one perfect five-timer; a second conspicuous nap-hand came on Goodwood Cup day in 1866. On the Friday of the 1864 Houghton Meeting he rode six winners: four matches, a handicap and a walk-over, a feat he'd repeat four years later on the card of 8 October. However, 18 June 1867 saw him surpass even those accomplishments. He went one better, winning on all seven of his mounts on an eight-race card at Stockbridge.

Stockbridge racecourse sat some two and a half miles from the town and adjacent to Danebury. The three-day Stockbridge summer festival, dating from 1753, was a picture-perfect example of the provincial race-meetings that provided the centerpiece to a keenly anticipated and furiously celebrated rustic jamboree. It was acclaimed by the Turf historian Charles Richardson as 'one of the pleasantest meetings of the year and one of the prettiest and best in the kingdom'; and following the move of the Cotswolds-based Bibury Club to Stockbridge in 1831, plus a substantial increase in prize-money, the meeting for a time came to rival Goodwood in popularity. The proximity and resultant patronage of Danebury ensured a regular stream of decent mounts for Fordham at the track. Nor did Stockbridge lack Royal patronage: two monarchs-in-waiting, George IV and Edward VII, both had winners here as the Prince of Wales. However, the presence of Turf 'royalty' was exemplified by the June afternoon in 1867 when 'Teddy' witnessed George Fordham show the racing parish how blue-blooded he was.

The opening day's eight-race programme was run under the auspices of the Bibury Club, one of those exclusive bastions of privilege restricted 'by invitation' to nobles and gentlemen that had once been commonplace on the Turf; its origins were linked to Burford races and its members had included the Prince Regent, the Duke of Wellington and Lord Palmerston. Post 1831 the Club was inextricably linked to Danebury and its 'Confederacy' that effectively bank-rolled many of the Club members. To begin with entries were confined to members riding their own horses. In time that ruling was relaxed. Most of the horses still belonged to Club members and many were partnered by them; but in certain races the service of 'professional' jockeys might be enlisted, incurring a 7lb penalty. With the exception of the sixth race on the card, in which he had no ride, Fordham swept the board. *Bell's Life* went into raptures:

> Rich and rare were the gems of the Bibury Club Day; or rather 'Fordham's Day' as it will hereafter be called, the famous jockey's successes having been achieved with the odds so dead against him occasionally that the wonder is he was not knighted on the spot, seeing they were brought off under the very eyes of Royalty. What a day it must have been for his supporters for a little sovereign invested on each race would show a profit of 15 or 16 hundred per cent; and those who commenced with the like amount and doubled stakes every time must have found themselves winners of something like 380 sovereigns.

Baily's Magazine put matters into contemporary context with a colourful turn of phrase: 'By the end of the day the bookmakers were as scarce as Fenians.'

The overture to this virtuoso recital was a routine success in the first on Tumbler, a three-year-old belonging to Lord Vivian. The brown colt won the five-furlong handicap comfortably by a length at odds of 7 to 4.

The following race was a different proposition. It was the most eagerly anticipated contest of the afternoon, the clash in the five-furlong Hamilton Stakes between two juvenile female speedsters. Fordham was up on Athena, a gorgeous chestnut with a blaze-adorned blood-like head, trained by John Day for the free-punting Marquis of Hastings. Her solitary opponent was Leonie, an equally sharp animal owned by the Duke of Hamilton and ridden by Arthur Edwards. Athena opened at odds of 7 to 4 on but, in the words of *The Sportsman*, 'the Danebury party mustered in such strong force and backed their representative with such right-down good will that the long odds of 5 to 2 were laid upon her before the flag fell.' Fordham got the favourite under the flag in a flash and made the best of his way up the hill toward home. But Leonie stuck to Athena like an unwanted house guest and began closing. Many onlookers believed they were witnessing a Fordham 'kid'. They were as soon disabused of that notion. Within a hundred yards of the Judge's chair Fordham began riding Athena in earnest as Leonie inched closer and closer 'amid a perfect storm of excitement which rose almost to a frenzy as the pair passed the post locked together.' The Judge couldn't separate the two fillies. Day's expression suggested Fordham was about to be read the Riot Act for taking things too confidently and upsetting the stable's commission. Thus, rather than divide the stakes, Day pressed for a' run-off' at the end of the day despite Athena showing evidence of being 'dreadfully punished.'

Fordham won the third on Mameluke, another Hastings juvenile, who arrived with a tall reputation. However, the 6 to 4 on favourite was made to work for his victory in the five-furlong Donnington Stakes. Another of the Duke of Hamilton's, Innerdale, was his sole rival. On this occasion it was Edwards who had his mount's head in front inside the final 100 yards and it was Fordham who had to pull out all the stops. This he did 'most vigorously.' And a dozen strides from the post he came with 'a well-timed rush' on his powerfully made bay partner to win a tingle of a race by a head.

He won the fourth, the Bibury Stakes, the main event of the day over one and a half miles, on Mr GJB Morris's three-year-old Ailsbury trained by John Nightingall at Epsom. The colt carried an additional 7lb for his assistance in this welter-weight event. Fordham kept Ailsbury (9 to 2 second best in the field of nine) tucked in behind the leader, Lucifer, who lived up to his name by setting a hot pace down the far side and into the bottom turn. The favourite, Lord Ronald, came to dispute affairs ascending the hill. But 'The Demon' was only biding his time until the moment was right to confront his namesake. When that moment came, it proved no contest. Lucifer was amateur-ridden and conceding a stone. As kind-hearted as ever, Fordham declined to make Mr Bevill look a monkey - and won cheekily by a neck.

Thirty minutes later he took the fifth on the Duke of Beaufort's two-year-old filly Europa 'from a formidable field.' The 6 to 5 favourite beat fellow Danebury juvenile See-Saw for the Biennial Stakes by a neck after a prolonged duel through the last furlong of the five. Languishing in fourth place was Comte de Lagrange's Mortemer on whom Fordham would win the Gold Cup of 1871.

Having sat out the sixth race on the card, Fordham took the seventh on See-Saw – a wonderfully-named son of Margery Daw. None the worse for his exertions an hour earlier, the Hastings colt landed the Champagne Stakes (five furlongs) by three-quarters of a length at remunerative odds of 5 to 1 from the Lagrange representative Rabican.

And, finally, Fordham took the eighth on Merry Monarch (2 to 1) for his old patron Richard Ten Broeck. This Plate over a mile was once again designed with Club members in mind. Mr Bevill rode the 6 to 4 favourite Master Robert, but Ten Broeck knew the value of Fordham more intimately than most. It would require more than 7lb to bring these two jockeys together. Ten Broeck's wager was never in jeopardy. 'That it was one of Fordham's days was pretty evident and he made this assurance doubly sure by securing this victory by a neck.' Having done is job on behalf of Ten Broeck's wagers, the three-year-old was sold for 370 guineas.

Thus did 'The Demon' record a magnificent seven-timer. However, there's a caveat. Athena lost her run-off with Leonie. Many an owner would have divided. But not the punting 'Markis'. The five-furlong course at Stockbridge was too severe for Athena to complete twice in an afternoon and she succumbed to her sturdier adversary. Her defeat reduced Fordham's haul to six. On the second day of the meeting Fordham rode three more winners courtesy of the Duke of Beaufort's Guineas victor Vauban and a pair of bloodless victories from the brightest gem in the Hastings-Danebury coronet, Lady Elizabeth.

Those nine Stockbridge winners helped Fordham finish well clear of his rivals in the list for 1867 with 145 winners. He'd add two more championships before the new decade opened with him finishing 30 adrift of William Gray and Charlie Maidment, who tied on the underwhelming total of 76. Billy Gray was the Sheffield-born son of an Irish groom working in Middleham; his best wins of the season came in two handicaps, the Wokingham and the Liverpool Autumn Cup. He shared Kenyon's unwelcome label of a champion jockey who failed to win a single Classic. The following season of 1871 marked Fordham's fourteenth, and last, title when he finished level with Charlie Maidment on 86 winners.

Charlie 'Lucky' Maidment was a country boy from Dorset who'd cut his teeth riding in Ireland where he became champion jockey in 1866 and 1867 and won the first two runnings of the Irish Derby – a perfect record since he never competed in the race again. Maidment had an attachment to singular feats. He schooled the sisters Emblem and Emblematic before their Grand National victories of 1863 and 1864 and engineered the rare distinction of getting on four winners of the ultra competitive Lincolnshire Handicap in six years. And, of course, his two jockeys championships were ties. The undoubted highlight of the second was a Fillies Triple Crown aboard Hannah; to which he added the Derby on Cremorne (1872) and Kisber (1876) and the St Leger on Wenlock (1872). Maidment's luck didn't last forever. Another incapable of holding on to his money, he went bankrupt in 1895 and was still riding work at Newmarket well into 20th century, dying at the age of 81 in 1926. However, Fordham ought to have won the 1871 title outright. 'He retires for the season with his honours thick upon him,' declared *The Morning Post* on 5 November when Fordham held a lead of two. Unfortunately Maidment didn't call stumps and notched a double at Shrewsbury to draw level.

Of course, no one was left in any doubt as to the identity of the true champion. The evidence was there for all to see at Goodwood when Fordham and Field Marshal fought out a titanic finish with Maidment on the favourite Ripponden. 'If ever a race was won by jockeyship this was one,' said *Baily's*, 'for Fordham never suffered Maidment to come a-nigh until in the straight George flattered the latter a little and the favourite got his head in front. Both horses were done to a turn at this point, and white with lather, struggled on to the Chair – but Field Marshal had got the most in him thanks to a bit of nursing from Fordham and won by one and a half lengths.'

Only Gordon Richards has headed the list more times (26) than Fordham. Fordham's totals declined markedly in the 1870s; his failing health and growing disenchantment was reflected in his failure to reach the century mark again until the 1880 season.

***

If quantity diminished quality did not. If anything the quantity of 'quality' races won increased. Fordham was now the jockey every owner and trainer wanted on their animals in the Classics, Cups and principal Stakes. Indeed, Fordham expected to be put up. He knew he was the best. And if his confidence in that knowledge was regarded as sacrosanct by any detractor, so be it.

One trainer who never settled for anything other than the 'best' when he brought his horses south was Malton's John Scott, the greatest Northern trainer of the age, or any age for that matter - the man revered as the 'Wizard of Whitewall'.

In the 1871 Goodwood Stakes Scott engaged Fordham for Taraban. The seven-year-old belonged to John Bowes for whom Fordham had ridden on and off for 30 years – yet he'd only met Bowes twice in all that time; Bowes stopped attending the races in 1855. Bowes was the illegitimate son of the Earl of Strathmore and a shy unemotional fellow – the two in all probability not being entirely unconnected. He resided mainly in Paris where his French wife was an actress. However, his choice of principal habitation failed to prevent Bowes from becoming an MP as a young man or winning the Derby on four occasions. His fortune, already increased by shrewd investments in coal mining and shipping, was augmented by equally shrewd betting. Bowes cleared £20,000 (*£3.4 million*) in bets on his first Derby winner, Mundig; £23,000 (*£3.9 million*) on the second, Cotherstone; and £30,000 (*£5.1 million*) when West Australian won the 1853 Derby en route to the Triple Crown. Bowes won eight Classics, all with the assistance of Scott - who trained a record 40 in all, including a record 16 St Legers. Neither mark is likely to be beaten. In an era of inadequate long-distance transport Scott disliked sending horses all the way from his Malton stables to the likes of Epsom, Ascot and Goodwood, and when so obliged he'd base them at Leatherhead where the young Fordham worked for Drewitt. Thus was the connection set in motion.

This renewal of the Goodwood Stakes seemed an exceedingly open one. Cherie had won a Cesarewitch; Indian Ocean had been the runner-up in the Stakes 12 months ago; but it was a 'talking horse' from William Day's yard named Cedric the Saxon that was backed down to favourite. Taraban was a 10 to 1 shot in the betting rooms – with the proviso that Fordham was in the saddle. The old gelding (who'd run in Hermit's Derby four years back) had won this season's Northumberland Plate, but he was a bit of a rogue. 'Once tried as a two-year-old to be a very good horse indeed, but since afflicted with a temper which would have broken the Bank of England,' opined *The Times*, 'he recovered a little of his reputation by winning the Northumberland Plate the other day under the seductive influence of a bottle of port.'

Booking Fordham to ride a horse reliant on a pre race tincture of port might be viewed as courting trouble - and both horse and rider were said to have enjoyed 'a sponge of port' in a Goodwood paddock bathed in warm sunshine. In Fordham's comforting hands the rogue behaved like a gentleman. Fordham nudged the old reprobate into an early lead, but once he'd got Taraban into a relaxing rhythm he took a pull and allowed the favourite to go on. Coming down the hill and into the straight the leader was joined by Cherie. But the 'dreaded' Fordham was seen to be in close attendance next to the rails, sitting as still as a cat at a mouse-hole. It was evident Taraban could go past whenever his jockey so desired; 'Fordham then brought up the old horse with a rush and was a clever winner by half a length from the favourite.' Or as *Baily's Magazine* described it: 'Taraban and old port had been triumphant under Fordham's skilful riding.' A few days later Taraban contested the Lewes Handicap minus Fordham and, in Press opinion, 'chucked it.'

Taraban proved to be Fordham's last big winner for Scott. One foggy morning the following month the trainer went out on to Stockton racecourse to watch some of his horses work, and caught a chill from which he failed to recover. He was 77. Bowes died in 1885. The last time Bowes saw Fordham sporting his silks was at Newmarket when two horses, own brother and sister, won two succeeding races – the winning distance being a head on both occasions. And the toping Taraban continued mixing alcohol and racing until 1874 when he was retired to an honourable postion between the shafts of Bowes's brougham.

Three months after Taraban's Goodwood success, Fordham rode what was generally acknowledged to be second of the four great defining races of his career when he got William Graham's Sabinus home by a short head from the dead-heaters Sterling and Allbrook in the 1871 Cambridgeshire.

Sabinus was a four-year-old by Newminster and something of a late developer. The bay had two unsuccessful races in the April of his juvenile year before Henry Woolcott had him gelded. Afterwards he was regarded as the best youngster at Beckhampton; his galloping companion was no less than Formosa, with whom he lost no cast. Beckhampton backed him throughout the winter for the Epsom 'Spring Double' of the City and Sub and Great Met. Carrying just 5st 9lb in the former, Sabinus duly landed the competitive 28-runner handicap over 10 furlongs before doubling up under a stone more in the equally difficult Great Met over almost twice the distance. Fordham wasn't in the pigskin for those two wins, or the 1870 Gold Cup that followed (geldings were still eligible at this point). But he was sorely needed in the Cambridgeshire.

Their Cambridgeshire task under 8st 7lb was a stiff one. It's hard to overstate how difficult winning this nine furlong handicap was in the 19th century. The entries invariably included several classy individuals with Classic form – often Classic-winning form. The 1871 renewal was no exception because the field of 29 contained not only the previous year's Derby winner Kingcraft (8st 4lb) but also the latest in Favonius (8st 11lb), besides the Guineas runner-up Sterling who'd won at Ascot and had just added the Free Handicap to fully justify his 8st 11lb. Lurking down the handicap on 6st 9lb was Sir Frederick Johnstone's Allbrook, a five-year-old with a win in a division of Ascot's Wokingham to his name before latterly disgracing himself with a lacklustre display when favourite for the Great Eastern Handicap. In addition, the unbeaten three-year-old colt Henry (7st 9lb) had recently come over from France to win the Ascot and Newmarket Derbies with consummate ease in the colours of 'Mr T Lombard' – alias M C-J Lefevre, a French financier with offices in London's Lombard Street; the following summer this handsome son of Monarque would win the Gold Cup.

News of sensational trials against other animals with decent English form had ensured Henry 'paralyzed' the Cambridgeshire betting. Even the two Derby winners were not expected to cause him trouble at these weights. Accordingly, he was backed down to favouritism, at the unusual odds of 17 to 4. Sabinus went off at 33 to1. *Bell's Life* uttered the damning comment: 'Sabinus is not to be trusted.' The previous season's form of the 'despised outsider,' in the words of *The Times*, 'was unaccountably overlooked.'

Sabinus would need every ounce of Fordham's strength plus the acumen of his every brain cell if he was to upset the favourites. The omens were not propitious. The previous day found Fordham under the weather, a condition the evening did nothing to improve. Deep in his cups in Newmarket's White Hart he took a bet of £1,000 to £30 about Sabinus with one of his drinking companions. Next morning, however, he'd no clear recollection of what had happened the night before and couldn't remember the name of the bookmaker who had laid him the wager.

The Cambridgeshire was his only mount on the card, due off at 3pm; plenty of time for him to shake the drink out of his system. Sir George Chetwynd rode part way to the starting post with him, whether from cordiality or to ensure Fordham did not fall off is not recorded. At any rate, during the course of this journey, Fordham swore the gelding was so well he thought he just might win. Chetwynd needed no further prompting. He galloped back to the Ring and took £1,000 to £30 four times about Sabinus.

How glad the Prince of Wales must've been to have journeyed up by special train from St Pancras to see the Turf's master magician pull another rabbit out of the hat. On an unusually warm and calm late October afternoon Fordham enjoyed further minutes to gather his strength at the start: 30 of them, to be accurate, owing to repeated breaks-away. Henry was 'chopped' at the start, and lost all chance, as Allbrook, greatly fancied owing to his low weight, made the running to such good purpose that he'd soon established a four-length advantage over Sterling. At this stage Sabinus was lagging, his fate seemed terminal. Fordham was sitting 'crouched like a monkey' in the words of Chetwynd, trapped on the inside behind a wall of horses. 'My horse wins!' screamed Lord Alington, the owner of Allbrook, galloping madly along the rails by the side of the leader, his covert coat open and flying in the air. 'I stand to win £20,000 on that horse, and I wouldn't take £19,999 for it!'

His Lordship spoke too soon. Allbrook began to tread water, his exertions finally catching up with him. He'd been galloped to a virtual standstill. Sterling was responding to everything Tom Chaloner was hurling at him. But hardly were the words 'Sterling wins!' out of the mouths of his backers, when a yell went up from the Ring as Fordham, scarcely noticed in the hubbub so close was he to the near-side rail, suddenly began to ride with satanic determination. A chink of light had finally pierced the wall. That's all the incentive 'The Demon' required. This was one of the rare occasions when Fordham's whip cut through the air like cheese-wire. Sabinus responded to the wizard on his back and got up on the post to 'snatch the race out of the fire and win this most astonishing race by a short head'. Sabinus only prevailed, according to Chetwynd, 'by dint of the superb skill and judgement on the part of Fordham.'

Fordham had been 'kidding' – both jockeys and spectators. The Cambridgeshire was invariably a close-run affair. He'd long reached the conclusion that in any desperate finish on the Rowley Mile the Judge always favoured the near side, directly beneath his box. That's where he wanted to be. No matter how crowded and frantic the circumstances might become, experience told him he'd get a run eventually so long as he held his nerve. He brought Sabinus back to the Birdcage smiling the smile of a genius who wonders what all the fuss is about. Chetwynd was as much awed by the jockey's unflappable performance as the effortlessness of it. 'It is a curious fact with regard to Fordham that although he never wasted and took little exercise, he never seemed to blow, even after such a finish as this.'

Fordham returned to a Roman triumph. 'Fordham's riding,' said *The Morning Post,* 'was the perfection of jockeyship and determination.' *The Sporting Life* agreed: 'Fordham never rode a finer race and it was altogether owing to the splendid horsemanship of this celebrated jockey that the race has gone back to Beckhampton.' Wise after the event, the paper added: 'The stable must have fancied Sabinus greatly, for although he started at an outside price, Mr Graham came to Newmarket expressly to see him run and he must have been gratified at the success of Fordham.' *The Illustrated Sporting and Dramatic News* sang from the same hymn sheet:

> The most extraordinary instance of patience and judgement and jockeyship within living recollection, and therefore that the Turf has ever known. Fordham sat, keeping Sabinus going without pressing him, ready to take instant advantage of the 100 to 1 chance that might arise. Sterling, tiring under his heavy weight, was, he saw, no longer dangerous, and under the vigorous but clumsy administration of the whip Allbrook was gradually stopping. So 'The Demon' made ready for one tremendous last effort, got his horse ready for one run home, waited till that tick of a second when it was a case of now or never, and concentrating all his energies, made his final rush and beat Allbrook to the post.

There was an amusing post script to this latest Fordham masterclass. Fordham was staying in Newmarket with Tom Cannon who, years later, related to a reporter what ensued. Cannon had been sweet on Allbrook's chances in the Cambridgeshire and when Fordham retorted he was 'only half a horse' promptly suggested a bet of £500 on the outcome. Cannon watched the race from his hack a furlong or so from the finish. On noting Fordham's apparently hopeless position as Sabinus passed, he turned his mount for home confident the 'monkey' was already in his bank account.

That evening, suitably refreshed and changed for dinner, Cannon greeted Fordham with an exultant 'Well, what do you think of Allbrook now? If he's only half a horse he's better than the rest of the whole ones!'

Fordham was perplexed.

'He'd settled you some distance from home, I noticed!' continued Cannon. 'I saw that and then I came back!'

The penny dropped. Fordham realized his friend had no idea of the result. And he decided to milk the situation for all it was worth.

'Well, you know,' he said in customary faltering style, 'I didn't think your horse was good enough to win, you know, but we all make mistakes.'

'Yes,' said Cannon in a concerted effort to rub it in, 'but there wasn't much mistake made about Allbrook! The boy did all he could to throw away the race with his whip, too, but we could give that in and chance it!'

'Well, it's no good chafing about it now, you know,' said Fordham, with a shrug of the shoulders and a deadpan expression. 'It's all over now!'

Fordham maintained the pretence over dinner. After the table had been cleared, a visitor arrived – and immediately strode toward Fordham, hand outstretched. 'The most wonderful bit of riding I ever saw in my life!' he said. 'It looked 100 to 1 against you so close to home!'

'Well, you see, the other didn't quite stay home, you know,' said Fordham modestly while casting a sly glance in the direction of Cannon.

Now it was Cannon's turn to be momentarily baffled – until the truth dawned on him. 'You won?'

'Oh, I won, you know. Allbrook nearly did it, but he wasn't quite good enough.' Fordham permitted himself a chuckle before adding: 'I told you I didn't think he would win!'

Not for the first time – or the last - Fordham had confirmed he was in a class of one, measured only by the extent of his own talent. *The Illustrated Sporting and Theatrical News* paid him this compliment:

It has been imagined that he delays his finishing almost too long, and draws it a little too fine in that respect; but, doubtless, he is the best judge of his animal's capabilities and is aware to an ounce what is left in him. But be that as it may, nothing can equal the vigour and the determination of his 'rushes' and many a faint-hearted backer has been overjoyed to see him just level on the post when to all appearances the race was lost.

He has nothing to fear from the rivalry of his peers. There were few, if any, of the great giants in the pigskin who are dead and gone that could have equalled, much more, surpassed George Fordham.

Comte Frederic de Lagrange

SIX

THE FRENCH CONNECTION

When Henry won his Gold Cup in 1872 it was with the assistance of Fordham. Twelve months earlier the jockey had won the race on Mortemer. These two victories in the nation's highest profile race outside of the Classics celebrated a new and exciting association – the 'French Connection'. Comte Frederic de Lagrange and Christopher-Joachim Lefevre may have been French but they were chalk and camembert. Like many stupendously rich men they were not interested in second best. Only the best jockey would do. They'd seen enough of Fordham in France to know he was the man they wanted whenever possible – even if this might not be as often as they'd like owing to Fordham's allegiance to Danebury, Manton and Beckhampton.

The Frenchmen waved money under Fordham's nose at every opportunity. He rejected four-figure retainers. But he welcomed their flattery and accepted the hefty 'presents' rewarding each big win. At a time when the fortunes of French horses on England's historic prizes were rising, Fordham's frequent alignment with French owners did not always sit favourably with the inhabitants of the racing parish. 'Argus' of *The Morning Post*, for one, took grave exception;

> I am no great admirer of Fordham because I conceive him to be completely spoilt by the flattery that has been administered to him, and also because he has shown an inclination to kick down the ladder by which he mounted to his present position. Let me express the hope that Fordham will properly recognize the obligation he is under to the Press for the kind and generous treatment he has received at its hands and not to be led astray by designing individuals to doubt its power and influence on society.

Had Fordham's status gone to his head? 'Fordham is dreadfully irate at "Argus" for having the audacity to subject him to the same rules of criticism to which every public man is liable,' said *Baily's Magazine* with tongue firmly in cheek. 'No doubt the wholesome advice given him has been of service.' Though conceit can be an involuntary reflex to sporting fame and adulation, it's unlikely from all testimony to Fordham's character that his hat size would've increased. But the Turf Establishment was rattled. Richard Ten Broeck's arrival in the 1850s marked the first outright challenge to the English Turf from overseas. Ten Broeck's foibles and frailties were, in the main, accepted with a smile and a knowing wink. And nobody castigated Fordham for hanging on to the American's coat tails. Turf grandees proved less charitable, however, when Frederic de Lagrange came calling during the 1860s.

Lagrange was born the year after Waterloo. He was the eldest son of Joseph de Lagrange, veteran of the Revolutionary and Napoleonic Wars, promoted to General by Napoleon in 1805 and ultimately elevated to the peerage in 1831. As a result Frederic de Lagrange inherited a considerable fortune of £16,000 (*£2.7 million*) a year which his practical mind multiplied by investing in mines, canals, railways and glass factories – and marrying the daughter of a prince. As a Senator in the Second Empire he held a leading position in Parisian society and was a close friend of the Emperor, Napoleon III. His reputation was that, in the words of Thormanby, 'of a model French gentleman, an intellectual companion, a genuine sportsman, and a perfect host.'

Lagrange also liked a 'flutter'. However, his betting diminished once he decided to invest in thoroughbreds. In 1856 he spent £11,200 (*£1.9 million*) on purchasing 23 animals from M. Alexandre Aumont, plus the right to buy all the foals from his broodmares for the next two years. In partnership with Baron Niviere, he soon became responsible for what the French termed the 'Big Stable'. The animals acquired from Aumont provided the bloodlines for the winners of three French Derbies and six successive renewals of the French Oaks between 1857 and 1862. In 1861 the 'Big Stable' won no fewer than 111 races on the continent worth £50,000 (*£6 million*). Stated the *Pall Mall Gazette*: 'To record all the races won by the Count on the French Turf and the English would require a small volume for the lord of the racecourse in his own country and as the doughty champion who undertook the supremacy of the horse-taming islanders even on their own ground.'

Survival of the fittest was the Lagrange principle. At Haras de Dangu, his private stud and stable near Chantilly, all the yearlings were tried on the rides cut through the forest of Compiegne. As these grassy tracks could only take four or five horses abreast, the trials were arranged in the form of a knock-out competition leading to a final. Thus were Dangu's representatives imbued with courage, toughness and bottomless stamina. Lagrange capitalized on these qualities by racing on a major scale, both in France, where it was estimated his racing expenses were £120 a day - or almost £44,000 (*£5.3 million*) per annum - and in England. In total Lagrange won the Prix du Jockey Club eight times; the Prix de Diane five times in his own name and on three occasions in Niviere's; and the Grand Prix de Paris twice.

Lagrange's hopes in the 1861 Prix du Jockey Club rested with the filly Gabrielle d'Estrees, trained by Tom Jennings – and ridden by Fordham. The 7 to 2 second favourite was only sixth rounding the last turn, but Fordham quickly pushed her past Éclair to win by a length. There was no respite for the filly. Lagrange was not content with merely plundering French prizes. The following day she was packed off to England to try her luck in the Oaks at the end of the week. Not unsurprisingly she finished out of the money.

From the outset Lagrange determined to win the great prizes on the English side of La Manche. Among the racing stock acquired from Aumont was Monarque – the 'French Eclipse' according to the Press - who'd already won the French Guineas, Derby and St Leger of 1855, and it was he who became Lagrange's maiden winner in England when taking the 1857 Goodwood Cup. Monarque would become Dangu's resident stallion, alongside 23 broodmares - and a pack of staghounds. The following year Madamoiselle de Chantilly won the City and Sub; a rich vein of success ensued. His English string was trained at Phantom Cottage in Newmarket by Tom Jennings and, owing to Fordham's other commitments, most were partnered by Harry Grimshaw. Lagrange's best finish in an English Classic was Dangu's fourth place in Thormanby's Derby of 1860 until Fille de l'Air– or 'Filly de Layer' as the bookmakers called her - won the 1864 Oaks. This maiden victory was not well received.

The filly's form seemed strangely in-and-out. Following a bad loss in the Two Thousand Guineas she'd landed the Prix de Diane. Tempers flaired after the Oaks and the filly had to be escorted to the winner's enclosure by a phalanx of hired prizefighters headed by the redoubtable champion Jem Mace and her trainer had to be locked in a room at the back of the Grand Stand for 45 minutes for his own safety. 'The French Jockey Club is most interested in the question of the conduct of one of its members,' suggested *Baily's*. Lagrange never did quite blow away lingering doubts surrounding the running of his horses. As late as 1879 the public, it seemed, had not forgotten or forgiven. When Phenix won the Rous Memorial over a stiff mile at Ascot after being declared a non-stayer in the wake of running unplaced as a hot favourite at Epsom, the hissing and booing rang out all over again. Even Lagrange's finest horse, the mighty Gladiateur, did not escape brickbats. This son of Monarque won the Clearwell Stakes on his juvenile debut in 1864, before retiring into winter quarters incurably lame according to some touts. This supposed 'cripple' then added a Triple Crown under Grimshaw – surviving insinuations of being over age from certain Francophobes – besides the Grand Prix de Paris in his spiritual home. Sheep and oxen were roasted and cider casks emptied back at Dangu in celebration of his Derby victory and Lagrange was appointed Oficer of the Legion of Honour. Thanks in the main to his Triple Crown winner, Lagrange topped the list of owners in England for 1865 with a total of £24,655. The so-dubbed 'Avenger of Waterloo' - guarded at all times by former bare-knuckle champion Harry Broome - went on to add the Gold Cup of 1866 by 40 lengths. His eight wins made a rich man richer by £26,000 (*£3.1 million*).

When the Franco-Prussian war broke out in 1870, Prussian troops overran Dangu and Lagrange broke up his racing establishments on both sides of La Manche. Forty of his animals, including Gladiateur, were sold at Tattersalls; mares and yearlings were retained, as was Monarque with whom Lagrange couldn't bear to part. Some of his best horses in training were acquired by M. Christopher-Joachim Lefevre, the face behind the *nom de course* of 'Mr T Lombard'. He also leased the Dangu yearlings for three years to acquire a powerful Turf presence for himself. The change was seamless – albeit the French newcomer had to melt a degree or two of frostiness. Lefevre was cold-shouldered on his initial appearance at Newmarket after detrimental tales of shady Stock Exchange transactions in connection with the 'Honduras Railway Loans' had entered circulation. Time would see this skeleton come rattling out of the cupboard to haunt the mysterious M Lefevre.

Had Fordham kept Lefevre at arm's length few would've judged him foolish for so doing. Born the son of a lawyer in Senlis, near Chantilly, in 1835, Lefevre led what *The Times* came to describe as 'a checkered existence'. Acres of wild oats were sewn during his youth which soon exhausted his slender financial resources; after borrowing money from some friends and embezzling money from others he received a two-year prison sentence for 'breach of trust'. Lefevre quietly disappeared before the sentence could be imposed. He re-surfaced in America, earning a precarious livelihood and enduring 'vicissitudes which would illustrate the adage as to truth being stranger than fiction.' Eventually he began working on the construction of a railway in Honduras, that led to him making a number of useful contacts when the 'Honduras Railway Loans' were being negotiated.

Some Turf stalwarts extended a welcoming hand straight away. 'I shall certainly be introduced to a man who runs his horses so straightforwardly, enters them in every available race, and whose friends say he is in all respects a worthy associate for a gentleman,' said George Payne. Sir George Chetwynd also found Lefevre to be 'a straightforward gentleman, always good-tempered and pleasant in spite of being a martyr to gout – which I believe is saying a great deal.' Sir John Astley echoed their sentiments: 'I don't believe there was ever a straighter owner of racehorses than Lefevre. He was a princely supporter of racing, was generous to a fault and, unlike Count Lagrange, there was no mystery to his horses.'

Sailing close to the wind was no bar to acceptance into the raffish fellowship of the English Turf – quite probably the reverse if truth be told. Chetwynd, Payne and Astley epitomized those habitues of the Victorian Turf whose finances were inextricably linked to their fortunes on the racecourse. They owned racehorses; more importantly, they kept themselves in port and cigars by betting on them. Inside information might - but only might - be shared with like-minded individuals. That was the *lingua franca* of the Turf. Keep oneself in the highest company and one's horses in the lowest. By such means was it possible to avoid another Turf maxim: the only way to make a small fortune on the Turf is to start with a bigger one. Money talks; the Chetwynds, Paynes and Astleys weren't overly concerned by any 'mystery' pertaining to the funding of Lefevre's new-found interest in the Turf.

The Frenchman soon got his feet under the table. In October 1871 the *Sporting Gazette* reported him to have inherited £½ million under the Will of a cousin whom he'd never met: the benefactor had gone to America and made his fortune thanks to a £500 loan from Lefevre's father when all his other relatives had turned their back on him. Conversely, the entire story could just as easily have been a fiction to cover Lefevre's embarrassment of riches following the Honduras scam. Lefevre also accessed money through more conventional means by marrying into a well-heeled French family. At any rate, he was not slow to boost this accumulated wealth through shrewd financial operations in the City of London. As far as the English Turf was concerned Lefevre was copper-bottomed: his credit was good.

Lefevre's business acumen was mirrored in his equine operation. He aimed to save an estimated £10,000 (*£1.2 million*) per annum by trying his yearlings over three furlongs in order to weed out any slow coaches lurking at his Haras de Chamant base near Senlis. The estate was rented from Prince Lucien Bonaparte and Lefevre ensured it was fit for equine blue-bloods: a staff of 200 men cared for 100 horses. Among the broodmares were no less than two heroines of the English Turf in Lady Elizabeth and Formosa. The yearlings were pampered. They were 'lodged two-by-two,' Lefevre maintained, 'to prevent them finding it dull, to enable them to chat, play and live like chums. They are all anxious to come and lick you or thrust their muzzles in your pocket.' Or, on one occasion, to bite Lefevre's arm down to the bone.

Employing such a focused philosophy ensured it was not long before Lefevre made his mark in the calendar's elite events. 'He is the only French owner who turns his attention almost exclusively to racing in England,' stated the *Gazette*, 'and the success which attends his colours cannot fail to arrest the attention of anyone taking but the most casual interest in sporting matters.' His chosen ally in the pigskin was Fordham. So keen was Lefevre to retain Fordham's services that he offered him £1,500 (*£180,000*) per season for the privilege. Fordham said no. He preferred a 'good cheque' after each big win. Nevertheless, every autumn he'd demonstrate his commitment by crossing the Channel to test the Chamant yearlings. And he was much amused to find the 'races' were started on a loud bark from a black retriever.

M Lefevre shows how it's done.

The opening Lefevre-Fordham onslaught on English prizes came via Lagrange-bred animals. The first event of note to fall to them was the Ascot Gold Cup of 1871 with Mortemer, one of the principal runners Lagrange sold to Lefevre, as he put it, 'to frustrate the design the Prussians entertained of making him a part of the spoils of war'. This six year old proven racer by Compeigne was a multiple winner in France and Germany for trainer Edouard Fould and had won the Stockbridge Cup on one trip to England in 1870. Jennings immediately placed him to win at Newmarket before sending him to Chester for the Cup in which he ran second under 9st 3lb in heavy ground, conceding 43lb to the winner. Although his six opponents at Ascot included winners of a Guineas (Bothwell) and a Derby (Kingcraft), Mortemer gained his reward for persistence. On a cold and blustery afternoon he was turned out looking a picture, 'as grand a specimen of the racehorse as ever came out on the Royal Heath', and went off at even money. The result was never in doubt. Fordham collared Bothwell late in the straight and 'amid load cheering came on hard held' to win by two lengths from a second French animal in the form of Verdure. *The Times* lamented: 'And so in one of our chief Cup races, and over the severest course in England, we have to stand by and see French-bred horses first and second. No one grudges the honour to our neighbours, who deserve all they have gained, but we trust the lesson it inculcates may not be thrown away upon our breeders. Fields are small, Cup races are unfashionable, and today our Derby favourites and our Cup winners are beaten by the foreigner.' *Baily's Magazine* felt a new champion was unveiled: 'M Lefevre may whip or challenge creation with Mortemer if he is so disposed.' Mortemer won from Admiral Rous the plaudit of being the best horse in the world between six furlongs and two and a half miles.

Twelve months later it was the turn of a second ex Lagrange animal in Henry, winner of the previous year's Ascot Derby, to bring home the patriotic Lefevre colours of 'red, white and blue hoops'. The Derby winner Favonius was as hot in the market at 5 to 2 on as the Prince and Princess of Wales were in warm sunshine; the Fillies Triple Crown winner Hannah was demoted insultingly to the role of his pacemaker. Tom Jennings, for his part, bemoaned the fact he'd nothing to make the pace for Henry, who, reported in some quarters to be 'amiss', could thus be backed at a generous 6 to 1. If Henry had been 'wrong', Fordham soon put him 'right'. Hannah's gallop was hardly testing and when the Derby winner passed her in the straight it was only on sufferance because Fordham had Henry poised on his tail. Henry just cantered away in his own time to win by a length and a half.

The next Lefevre target had to be a Classic. In duly arrived in 1872 when Fordham won the Oaks on Reine. The filly was bred in the purple by Lagrange, being a daughter of Monarque and Fille de l'Air, and bought by Lefevre for 400 guineas. Not that Rcinc was as appealing on the eye as her imposing mother. She was a rusty looking bay whose good shoulders were let down by rather droopy quarters; 'Wiry and by no means a good looking specimen,' stated the 'Special Commissioner' of *The Sporting Life*, 'but she looked remarkably well.' His colleague 'Augur' declared Reine 'about the pick of a moderate lot.' He continued: 'It does not speak highly of the quality of the field when it is considered the French mare, in addition to to being beaten twice in France, has had so much travelling by sea and land since her victory in the One Thousand Guineas.'

Reine had finished placed in a pair of maidens at the Houghton meeting as a two-year-old prior to registering a shock neck victory under Henry Parry in the One Thousand Guineas (she started 20 to 1 in a field of 11); Fordham had partnered Graham's Germania who finished last. The two abortive trips to France referenced by 'Augur' saw her finish second at Longchamp and in the Prix de Diane. With her nearest pursuer in the Guineas, Derelict, having died from influenza, there was less reason to believe Reine would be troubled to add a second Classic and she started a 5 to 2 favourite. The pundits looked elsewhere for the likely winner. They latched on to the debutant Louisa Victoria, a full sister to the Derby and Leger runner up Albert Victor.

Fordham left nothing to chance. He had Reine in front well before the descent to Tattenham Corner closely followed by Custance on Louise Victoria and Fred Webb on Landlady. Custance chased Fordham all the way to the line but he could never quite get close enough to look Fordham in the eye. The master 'Kidder' had kept a little up his sleeve, always looked comfortable and won by half a length.

The Field and *Bell's Life* were united in their despond: 'If the Derby horses were moderate, some thought the Oaks fillies worse,' said the former. The latter added: 'Reine's victory speaks volumes as to the poverty of her opponents, and once more the foreign-bred horses threaten to teach us some sharp lessons. It is sufficient to say that the stake fell to the lot of a most popular and deserving sportsman' – who, it was noted by his increasing number of creditors, declined to put in an appearance at Epsom. *The Times* sought positives: 'This is good vindication of public form, and right and proper that a daughter of the great mare Fille de l'Air should repeat her dam's performance of eight years ago. French winners were rather scarce in those days but we had our eyes opened by Gladiateur and are pretty well accustomed to them by now. But still the victory of the tricolor was hailed with a good deal of cheering.' Almost all of that cheering was dedicated to Fordham who, 'Augur' said, 'must consider himself considerably recompensed for his disappointments in the Derby.'

Reine returned to France for the Grand Prix de Paris with Fordham in the saddle, and finished a respectable third to the Derby winner Cremorne. As she wasn't engaged in the St Leger she went for the French equivalent, the Prix Royal Oak, and again occupied third spot. For all the disparaging comments she received following her Oaks victory, Reine was good enough to supplement her Classic laurels with further successes as a four-year-old. After being thwarted in the final three strides of the Royal Hunt Cup by Fordham and the Drewitt-trained Winslow, she was reunited with her Oaks pilot the following afternoon to win the Ascot Plate with consummate ease.

One of the most durable performers on whom Fordham wore the Lefevre jacket was Dutch Skater who ran and won consistently over three seasons. A brown horse by The Flying Dutchman, he was bought as a five-year-old in 1871 to act as lead horse to Mortemer. Despite wins at Baden-Baden, in the Cup at Deauville and a Queen's Plate at Warwick, he was regarded as a slow, staying horse a good 21lb inferior to Mortemer. However, Dutch Skater quickly outgrew his intended role, albeit falling between the two dreaded stools of handicapper and genuine Cup horse. He was never quite good enough for the latter class of staying race; in 1872 he beat only two horses, one of whom was his pacemaker, to capture 'such a miserable entry for the Doncaster Cup never seen before.' In lesser company Dutch Skater came into his own whenever the handicapper gave him half a chance. He and Fordham defied top weight of 8st 13lb to settle the 1872 Great Met with a devastating 'rush' in the final six strides. But what Dutch Skater really loved were the Queen's Plates which might be run over anything from two miles to four miles. He won a dozen of them, on the smaller stages of Chelmsford, Hampton, Egham and Northampton to the grandest at Epsom, York, Newmarket and Goodwood. He and Fordham even travelled back to France in 1872 to pilfer the Prix Gladiateur over three miles and seven furlongs at Longchamp. The pair won their final Queen's Plate at the Epsom Derby meeting of 1873 to fully merit a Press tribute as 'one of the gamest of the game.'

Another Lefevre animal in training at the same time as Dutch Skater was a genuine Cup horse. This was Flageolet, a sweet-tempered and handsome chestnut, who came to defy his, by Chamant standards, somewhat plebeian pedigree. He was by the moderate Lagrange handicapper Plutus out of a Monarque mare from whom he inherited a set of large flat feet. Flageolet soon showed he was more like his maternal grandsire than his sire by winning five races as a two-year-old under Fordham including the Hopeful and the Criterion. The winter saw him trading freely as second favourite for the Two Thousand Guineas. In consequence his 'never prominent' fifth place in the Classic was a blow. Further disappointment ensued when sent back to France for the Prix du Jockey Club. Boiard beat him a short neck – setting in motion a frustrating trend. Flageolet just could not get the better of Boiard whenever they met. A short neck again divided them in the Grand Prix de Paris; the following season Boiard franked the form with further victories over Flageolet in the Prix du Cadran, Ascot Gold Cup and Prix Rainbow. That 1874 Gold Cup was truly a vintage renewal. The other four runners were Marie Stuart, Doncaster, Gang Forward and Kaiser – which meant the race featured the first and second in the Two Thousand Guineas; the first three in the Derby; the Oaks winner; the first three in the St Leger; and the three placed horses in the Grand Prix de Paris. Flageolet humbled them all bar his Gallic nemesis. His best English successes came in the 1873 Goodwood Cup (for which Fordham couldn't make the weight), the Grand Duke Michael Stakes and the inaugural Jockey Club Cup at Newmarket. Flageolet eventually joined the stallion ranks at Haras de Chamant alongside Mortemer.

Lefevre had begun to make Midas appear cack-handed. Everything the French owner touched seemed instantly to turn gold. He was leading owner in 1872 with winnings of £23,634 (*£2.8 million*); and again in 1873 when he won no fewer 105 races, which stood as an English record for over 100 years. Some meetings were farmed. At the 1872 Craven, for instance, he collected nine races; Fordham rode all bar one. Twelve months later Lefevre won seven at the Craven, all partnered by Fordham; at Goodwood his horses won no fewer than 10 of the 16 races - Fordham rode seven of them. In 1874 the partnership scored another seven. But by then the wind was changing direction and blowing Lefevre toward the rocks.

It was only a matter of time before the scandal connected with the 'Honduras Railway Loans' was exposed – and Lefevre's shabby role in it. In the spring of 1875 Lefevre's part in the scam was highlighted in the findings of the Commons Select Committee on Foreign Loans. Three loans exceeding £5.7 million (*£684 million*) in total were raised between 1867 and 1870 to stimulate economic growth in the central American country through the construction of a railway from the Gulf of Mexico to the Pacific by which timber might be exploited and exported to Europe. The loan of 1870 was for £2.7 million to cover unsold paper from the earlier two. The bankers handling the deal were Bischoffscheim and Goldschmidt and the agent selling both old and new bonds to the public from an office in Lombard Street in order to fund it was Lefevre. He'd capitalized on his Honduras contacts to line the President's pockets with a sweetener of £10,000 and the country's London ambassador with the gift of £4,000-worth of diamonds for his wife. Lefevre then hired 100 agents to create an artificial market in which to sell off the bonds at relatively high prices. The value of the bonds soon plummeted from £50 to £6; only £562,000 of the £2.7 million wound up funding a mere 53 miles of railroad; and not a single splinter of mahogany reached Europe. The bulk of the net proceeds from the three bond issues went missing. It was estimated Lefevre pocketed almost £¾ million. The financial world was disgusted. 'If honesty were among the qualifications for these loans, it is obvious that Messrs Bischoffscheim and Goldschmidt and M Christopher-Joachim Lefevre would not be eligible,' opined the *New York Times*. The British authorities agreed, and a warrant for Lefevre's arrest was issued. But the bird had long flown the coop. It was to Lefevre's good fortune that his French prison sentence from the 1850s had been lifted. In the autumn of 1872 he'd pre-empted English justice by returning to native soil.

The slippery speculator lived a charmed life. The writer Anthony Trollope was so fascinated by the Frenchman's blend of venality laced with mendacity that he allegedly based the swindler Melmotte in his 1873 novel *The Way We Live Now* on Lefevre. It's not known whether Fordham was one of those fleeced. An affluent yet unsophicticated sportsman would seem to be the perfect 'mark' for a con-man. Gossip of the day suggested he'd been taken for £60,000 (*£7.2 million*). Fordham denied the rumours. And the fact that he never stopped riding for Lefevre suggests he wasn't a victim – either that or he was extraordinarily forgiving.

With Lefevre obliged to lie low in Senlis, Lagrange regained centre-stage with the resurrection in 1874 of the 'Big Stable'. The details of how this new Lagrange-Lefevre operation was organized are imprecise; but whatever the small print, all prize-money was pooled. The Lagrange colours instantly picked up the thread. Where it had once been Lefevre exploiting Lagrange's Dangu bloodlines it was now Lagrange profiting from mares Lefevre had gathered together at Chamant – most of which were English-bred. Normal service was resumed in the Classics. In 1876 the alliance finished the English season as leading owner with over £17,000 in stakes; and thanks largely to eight wins from the St Leger winner Rayon d'Or, the 'Big Stable' again topped the owners list in 1879 with an even mightier haul of £26,376 (*£3.2 million*).

The Lagrange-Lefevre partnership was terminated at the end of 1879. Lagrange's string went with Tom Jennings Senior (who moved to a new yard named in honour of his principal patron) while Lefevre's horses stayed at Phantom House, now under the auspices of Tom Jennings Junior. The pinnacle of Lagrange's fortunes on the English Turf had passed. Always on the portly side and blessed with a complexion 'ruddier than a cherry', he began suffering severely from gout and heart problems. He'd no children to comfort him; married twice, both wives had died during confinement. Dangu and its stock were sold off in September 1883. Two months later Lagrange died in his Paris apartments on the Rue de Cirque that were decorated throughout in his racing colours of blue and red.

***

The Fille de l'Air contretemps of 1864 brought into the open a festering resentment toward French horses in England. This ill-feeling stemmed from the contrasting treatment accorded English and French horses in the other's country. French-bred horses were free to harvest English races. But English-bred horses were barred from the elite French races promoted by the Societe d'Encouragement, the governing body of French racing. National pride was wounded. *The Times* thundered as only 'The Thunderer' could:

Foreign horses can hold their own on even terms with those in this country, and should induce the authorities of the French Jockey Club to throw open their chief races to English horses. There is not a single race in France open to English thoroughbreds with the sole exception of the Grand Prix de Paris. The time seems to have arrived when a treaty of reciprocity should be entered into between the Turf Senates of the two countries. French owners understand the principle of breeding and training quite as well as ourselves. They spared no pains and no expense to buy our best bloodstock, and they have turned our own weapons against us with a considerable measure of success.

Sir John Astley embarked on a personal offensive, suggesting to the Jockey Club that 'no horse be allowed to enter any handicap in Britain unless it has been trained for at least three months before the date of entry in Great Britain.' Lord Falmouth, one of the country's foremost owner-breeders, went further. He proposed all English races should be closed to 'foreigners' He bemoaned the fact French owners were pocketing prize-money derived from the entry fees and forfeits paid in the main by English owners – conveniently forgetting the amount contributed by French owners for horses that did not fulfill their English engagements.

Such rampant xenophobia provoked the *Pall Mall Gazette* into presenting the opposite view:

We should surely be moved to make every effort for the recovery of our old prestige than to exclude foreigners from participating in our sports and our prizes because they refuse to reciprocate our apparent generosity. If we exclude the foreigners from our racecourses we should lost the best, if not the only, test to prove the superiority or inferiority of our thoroughbreds and might go on deteriorating in self-complacent unconsciousness till we lost our commanding position among the horse-breeding world.

The anomoly eventually drove Admiral Rous to lobby the Societe for a change of heart: 'Non' came the reply.

The ban on English-bred horses in the French Classics did not extend to English jockeys – even if their participation was greeted by their Gallic counterparts with something less than cordiality. All bar three of the 17 jockeys in Fordham's first victory in the Prix du Jockey Club were English. And the ban certainly didn't apply to the English aristocracy who were drawn to Chantilly, home to the Prix du Jockey Club and Prix de Diane, like iron filings to a magnet. So many of England's nobility regularly crossed *La Manche* for these two summer Classics that English reporters were requested not to name names on the off chance the holder was meant to be elsewhere. Instead the many English reporters (interest in racing across the Channel having spawned the emergence of the 'French Correspondent' in the trade papers) gushed about their surroundings. They sang hymns of praise to Chantilly's nightingale-populated trees and manicured lawns that provided a serene and beautiful atmosphere completely at odds with the raucous hubbub associated with a major race day at home. One gushed: 'Frith might on such a day have conceived a grand comparison picture of "The Derby in France". The contrast would be great: the low-life of Epsom would be absent. Another marked distinction is the practice of Stewards filling the positions of Starter and Judge; our neighbours think there is a greater probability of satisfaction following the exertions of gentlemen of high character and position.'

By the time Fordham won the Prix du Jockey Club for a second time the event had lost some of its gloss in the eyes of the English *cognoscenti*: 'The French Derby has got so popular that it is no longer as pleasant as it was won't to be.' His mount in 1868 was Suzerain, sporting the colours of Baron Schickler, a Prussian by birth but French by marriage and sympathies. The latter ensured his Chantilly mansion received particularly destructive attention from occupying Prussian troops in 1871; and conscious of his Germanic name he chose for a time to race as 'M Davis'. Threatening weather failed to dissuade Chantilly's largest ever crowd from thronging the track; and one spectator, through ignorance or idiocacy, elected to wander onto the track during the opening race and was fatally injured.

Although only ten went to post, the contest was judged likely to be close; four colts headed the market at odds below 4 to 1. Suzerain had been well backed throughout the morning of the race and started a warm 3 to 1 second favourite to the Duke of Hamilton's French Guineas winner Gouvernail, partnered by Tom Chaloner. The two English jockeys kept their mounts close to the lead off a woefully slow gallop. When the sprint came it was Suzerain who possessed the superior turn of foot. Said *The Sportsman*: 'Bringing up the winner with his consummate skill, Fordham won on the post only, by a neck.'

There was one notable exception to the ban on English-bred horses competing in France: the Grand Prix de Paris, the country's greatest race. Founded in 1863 at the instigation of the Duc de Morny as a means of testing Gallic bloodstock against the best Europe could offer, it outranked even the Prix du Jockey Club. It was confined to three-year-olds and run at Longchamp over one mile and seven furlongs in June – a tough assignment for horses of that age. It boasted a prize of 100,000 francs raised equally by the Municipality of Paris and the nation's five leading railway companies. The fears of French owners and breeders that the race would be a gift to the English were proved correct when The Ranger defeated the winners of the Prix du Jockey Club and the Prix de Diane to win the inaugural race. In 1866 the Duke of Beaufort won with Ceylon. And the first four runnings had all been won by English jockeys.

But for illness Fordham would've partnered Ceylon. However, his initial success was not long delayed. In 1867 he put on a tour de force to win on M de Montgomery's Fervacques. The visiting Press was once more entranced by Gallic ambiance: 'The drive through the Bois de Boulogne was delightful, the air quite refreshing and the dust well laid by a constant system of watering. Grand Prix day may be compared to the Ascot Gold Cup day with regard to the attendance of the ladies and the splendour of the toilettes.' Or at least most of them were. *Baily's* man in Paris spluttered: 'I would rather run a mile on a hot Sunday afternoon rather than face the crowd of another Grand Prix. I have a holy horror of the weight of more than one heavy man on each instep at a time.' Nor had he much time for the race itself: 'What a pity that such a splendid prize should be run for at such a season! How can you expect Englishmen to come over to Paris, for, say, 48 hours, between Epsom and Ascot? At any other season it would attract half England! At present we have a great stake disputed by four or five horses - and usually have to bet five to one on the winner!'

One person at Longchamp forced to work up a sweat was Fordham. Fervacques was a forlorn 60 to 1 no-hoper in the morning exchanges and started at a forlorn 33 to 1. No one could see beyond the favourite, Patricien, victor in the Prix des Longchamps and the Prix du Jockey Club. Fervaques was a well-beaten fourth behind Patricien in the latter after running second in the French Guineas. On both occasions he was ridden by Tom Chaloner, who once again had the mount when winning the Prix de la Neva 24 hours before the Grand Prix. What might Fordham do on Fervaques to reverse the Jockey Club form?

Patricien led the field into the straight closely pursued by Fervacques. The two colts were soon locked together in a hammer-and-tongs battle to the post. The Judge couldn't separate them. A run-off was ordered for after the last race, obliging Emperor Napoleon to wait until six o'clock to discover who would carry off the piece of plate he'd donated. Patricien was again made favourite, this time at shades of odds on. But this was now a match race. And Fordham had no peer in this form of combat. Fordham allowed his opponent to lead at a crawl for the first mile. When Patricien began to increase the pace he drew Fervacques alongside ready for the inevitable sprint down the straight. A second ding-dong struggle ensued. All of a sudden the French crowd began behaving like an English one. The duellists were roared on. Fervaques lasted the longest. Fifty yards from the post Fordham forced his nose in front. And only by a nose he prevailed.

This race may not have forced its way into Fordham's 'Top Four' according to contemporary chroniclers but it must've been damn close. When the two colts met again later in the season in the Prix du Prince Imperial Patricien beat Fervaques pointless. On this occasion, however, he lacked the priceless assistance of 'The Demon'.

De Montgomery did nothing to placate green-eyed xenophobes in the English Press. The Frenchman sent Fordham back across La Manche with a parting gift of £400 (*£48,000*) tucked safely away in his luggage.

The Fordham seat.

SEVEN

JUST MANAGING TO WIN

'It is the gift of brains which makes the jockey. Jockeys are born and seldom made. They have been given the brains which enable them to do the right thing at the right time. They have no time in a race for hesitation. Their brains must act quickly.'

When expressing that view in his autobiography trainer Richard Marsh might've had George Fordham in mind. Fordham was not an educated man and in consequence could easily be accused of lacking 'brains' in the general sense of the word. But this is not to say Fordham lacked 'brains' in a specific sense of the word. He was rich in horse sense. And he had a 'double first' in jockeyship and horsemanship from the 'University of the Turf' to prove it.

Unfortunately, Fordham could never advertise the fact in any *viva voce*. He wasn't the most articulate of men; a Fordham conversation with winning connections might get no further than vague meandering along the lines of: 'Well, don't you see, I just went up and, er, don't you know, I, er, just managed to win.' He gave another memorable tongue-tied demonstration to George Hodgman after the gambler's Victorious had landed some huge bets in the Goodwood Nursery by a neck: 'Well, you know, I got a nice place, you know, and I was always going easy, always easy, very easy indeed, you know, you know...'

However, although Fordham displayed an unerring talent for tying himself in verbal knots, it was his good fortune to be articulate in a language granted to few human beings. He could communicate with the equine. The reins were his voice. The silken touch of his hands on them, accompanied by a nudge, or a whisper, or a 'cluck', his vocabulary. His genius was totally instinctive. And sublime genius is incapable of explanation. 'Than George Fordham,' declared the Turf writer Alfred Watson, 'it is probable that no one else lived who understood horses and the delicate art of racing them more thoroughly.'

Fordham was both jockey and horseman. The two are frequent bedfellows but they are not one and the same. The *Pall Mall Gazette* put it neatly: 'It was the head, and not the muscle, that made Fordham a great horseman.' Fordham would get horses running that no other jockey could. After he'd ridden Westwick to beat the favourite Strathconan for the Great Northern St Leger of 1866 *The Morning Post* declared: 'Fordham had Westwick going as quiet as a sheep while with Jemmy Adams he was all over the track at Goodwood.' That was a typical endorsement of Fordham's rapport with the unruly equine that one comes across time and again throughout his career. The beau ideal is a blend of jockeyship and horsemanship. Such alchemy produces someone above the norm. A paragon. A champion like George Fordham.

Fordham the jockey is easily defined by his career statistics - the number of winners, the Classic winners, the jockeys' championships, the countless races he pulled out of the fire where others would have gone up in flames. They all speak for his powers as a jockey; his supreme jockeyship. Such success only comes to a rider who is a master of jockeyship. He must be one who understands pace, one who can implement a variety of race tactics, who knows when to seize a gap and when to wait for a better one. An exceptional jockey must have ice in his veins and rely on brain rather than brawn.

Was George Fordham a master jockey: yes. A master horseman: yes. But he was not a master stylist. On that contemporary observers were of one mind: his was rather an ungainly seat.

Baily's Magazine found Fordham's seat and success difficult to reconcile:

> For a jockey of such eminence, it is extraordinary that Fordham should have such an ugly seat, and he makes it the more conspicuous by the careless manner in which he sits when going down to post, and the habit he has of shrugging up his shoulders, which is contrary to all ideals of the old school. Indeed, Mr Parr, who, as a judge of horses and riding is second to none, has two lads in his stable whom he will not bring out for some time for fear they will copy our hero's style of seat.

Alexander Scott watched Fordham ride at nearly every racecourse in England between 1868 and 1883:

> I shall never forget his peculiar seat, unlike that of any other jockey of his time. Fordham rode with fairly short leathers, got well down on his mount's back, and slewed his head and body almost sideways during a race, with his shoulders hunched up high. This last mannerism was very effective in keeping his mount balanced throughout a

race, very seldom taking up his whip, but riding his mount home with his hands. In fact, Fordham got more out of a horse with his hands than any other jockey I remember.

His judgement of the winning post was of the first order, and to see him get up and win, body and head cocked on one side, with only his hands asking the horse a question, was an education in the art of timing a finish. It was by no means uncommon to hear the cry 'Fordham's beat!' in races which he eventually won, and no jockey could wish for a greater compliment than that.

Sir George Chetwynd was another devotee:

> How many times and with what enthusiasm have I watched the marvellous riding of Fordham, with his little short legs looking almost pinned at the knee to the saddle, on which he appeared propped up rather than sitting down, his left arm rather high in the air, flourishing his whip, and riding more with his body and shoulders than his legs, yet getting every ounce out of his horse to the very last stride to the post. And a perfect exponent of race-riding. I feel the inadequacy of this description of a horseman whose fame will be kept alive in the annals of the Turf, judging, that is to say, by results and not by appearance, for though unsurpassed as a horseman not his greatest friend could say that his style was graceful or elegant.

Prior to embarking on his own training career, John Porter had worked for John Bahram Day and William Goater which enabled him to observe Fordham at close quarters. However unattractive Fordham's version of the 20th century 'crouch' may have appeared, John Porter was adamant:

> His is the style of riding that should be taught and encouraged - the happy medium. He rode with a medium stirrup just short enough to clear the pommel of the saddle with little to spare. Taking tight hold of his horse's head, he leaned slightly

forward, with his hands resting on the horse's withers, thus throwing the weight on to the shoulders. The position enabled him to drop into the saddle and control a horse when in difficulties and drive him straight home at the finish of a race. He had beautiful hands and horses that stronger men could do nothing with went kindly enough for him.

A third fan among the training fraternity was Charles Morton:

> His style of riding, if not precisely the forerunner of the modern crouch, was as near perfection as anything I have known. He was the best judge of pace I have ever seen and the brilliant finishes he rode were masterpieces. He would never hit a horse except in the last two or three strides, just sufficient to make the animal win. Only now and again have I come across men who could save a horse for one last effort and land him on the post a winner by a short head. George Fordham had the art.

Renowned scribe 'Thormanby' put it thus:

> He was not a graceful rider, he was awkward in his seat, and the high manner in which he carried his shoulders gave him an ungainly appearance. See him on his way to post, how careless, almost slovenly was his gait! But as soon as he was in the pigskin, how splendid were his hands, how marvellous was his judgement of pace, how perfect his knowledge of every inch of course. Then what stubborn John Bull courage he had; he never believed a race was lost till the numbers went up against him! George was very fond of "kidding", especially when opposed to some youngster. A few hundred yards before reaching the winning post, he would apparently show signs of distress and then, just as the greenhorns were chuckling over anticipated victory, 'The Demon' would fly past them like a whirlwind.

John Radcliffe was a third contemporary chronicler awarding laurels:

Fordham's ugly seat was always made worse in appearance by the careless manner he adopted in going to post, and an incurable habit he had of shrugging his shoulders. His eminence and almost phenomenal success as a jockey were as much due to his talents as to his good fortune. When he had established a reputation, he naturally had a choice of good mounts. He had good hands, which were only surpassed by his expertness in 'kidding.' Another element of his success was that he never gave up riding a horse until he was past the post, so as to be there in the count for any mishap taking place to the leader, and never was this policy better exemplified than in his riding of Starke in the Goodwood Cup.

In judging the subtleties of jockeyship one is almost inclined to believe in the transmigration of souls, for it is often evidenced that a horse runs more generously in the hands of a certain jockey than he does in any other. Fordham was a striking example of this truism, for often enough a horse would run a stone better under him than when piloted by a less sympathetic man. Fordham, by subtle influence, had the power of conveying his will to stimulate the speed, the courage, and the heart, even the soul, of the horse he bestrode. Nor was this end achieved by the ruthless use of whip and spur, which only too often marked Archer's efforts in a desperate finish. It was attained by the velvet touch of the hands on the reins, which acted as a conductor of the human current to the equine, inspiring confidence and energy in the horse. Only on rare occasions did Fordham apply whip and spur, and these happened mostly when he was on a slow, muddling rogue, who would never do his best under the milder method of riding with the hands.

Never was there a fairer or more generous rider. In riding, he never even availed himself of the advantages he was entitled to, nor could he ever be induced to make an objection unless the case was most outrageous. So much could not be said of Archer.

Fellow jockey John Osborne described a man he counted 'a good fellow':

> Perhaps he had an ungainly seat. He used to get all out of a horse. He and Archer had two different styles altogether – as different as possible. Fordham rode short and Archer long. Fordham rode more with his hands than Archer. Fordham didn't punish his horse so much, though I have seen him give 'one, two, three' on the post. You never knew you were done with Fordham until you got past the post.

Another weighing room colleague equally awed was Tommy Heartfield:

> No jockey had a lighter hand than Fordham. He had a marvellous knack with horses that no jockey except himself ever had. Old Fordham was a man to sit and nurse 'em. Yet he was a powerful jockey at the same time – no jockey more so when it came to real riding a race out. But he had a knack of 'kidding' to horses somehow which was most astonishing. I rode a horse at Newmarket once and was beaten to blazes. Fordham got up on the same horse in the same sort of race, and he won in a hand trot. I never knew how he could make horses win races that nobody else could.

Finally, Fordham's close friend, and fellow jockey, Henry Custance:

> Fordham was very short and rode short; whilst Archer was very tall, and rode extra long. Neither of them had the graceful seat of Tom Cannon, who was the happy medium, but, still, they were fine horsemen. I always say that Archer was the best man at starting that I ever saw. I must now say where I think my friend Fordham excelled him. That was at the finish of the race. Here again their style was totally different. Fordham sat back in the saddle, and, as it were, drove his horse from him, never having loosed his head, both acting together. One great peculiarity about horses which Fordham rode was

they always finished straight and seldom changed their legs. Now, with Archer riding long, he invariably got up the horse's neck, very often finishing with a loose rein, consequently his mounts frequently changed their legs a time or two. Anyone who knows anything about riding at all must agree that every time a horses changes his leg he shortens his stride, and loses at least a neck. It is, of course, a matter of opinion, but I myself give Fordham the palm, as I think the finish is certainly the most important part of the race.

Although Henry Custance was Fordham's friend and contemporary it was Tom Cannon who bore his legacy and exposed his exquisite skills to the next generation, winning Classics and a jockeys championship. The young Cannon rode for Danebury and was Fordham's protégé. In return Cannon served as Boswell to Fordham's Dr Johnson. Cannon became a renowned trainer – of jockeys as wells as horses. And in contrast to his mentor, he'd no problem explaining his methods and took pains to educate his apprentices (who included his sons Morny, Tom and Kempton) in a manner that Fordham would've approved. Cannon's doctrine was set down for his aspiring jockeys to read. It's impossible not to hear the voice of George Fordham running through Cannon's discourse. This is Cannon on the art of riding the finish so admired by Custance. There's little doubt it's straight from the gospel according to Fordham:

> Before sitting down to finish, it is generally advisable, especially if the race has been run at a strong pace, to take a 'pull' at one's horse for a few strides, so as to enable him to catch his wind and to collect himself before he makes his effort.
>
> When a jockey wants to finish, he should sit down in the centre of his saddle with his seat as much under him as possible. He should catch a good hold of the horse's head so as to collect him at each stride; he should lean slightly

back; should grip the flaps of the saddle tightly with his knees...should draw his feet well back...the hands and arms should yield to the extension of the horse's neck at each stride...the hands should be within five or six inches of each other and kept low. The seat and thighs should appear as if glued to the saddle. As the rider's legs are the only other parts which connect him to the horse, the 'lift' if there be one, must proceed from them, and may be be the result of weight being taken off the horse's back at each instant his hind feet make their stroke.

A large number of horses are annually ruined for life by needless punishment. A horse, at the end of a race, cannot go farther than 100 yards at his very utmost speed without beginning to shorten his stride and go slower; hence we may conclude that our last resource, the whip, should not be used until we are within 100 yards of the winning post. When the moment comes, it should be quickly 'picked up' while the reins are grasped firmly in the other hand; the rider should sit well back in the saddle, should keep his shoulders square, should lean back, draw his feet back, and keep his body as steady as possible so that it may not get any sway from the arm which may interfere with the motion of the horse.

Practically speaking, the whip should be very rarely indeed 'picked up' until before the last 30 or 40 yards, nor should more than two or three cuts be given.

And any assessment of Fordham's prowess in the saddle cannot be concluded without consulting Fred Archer. 'The Tinman' was as astute a judge of jockeys as he was of horses. What did he think of Fordham the horseman and jockey? Archer's appreciation of his arch adversary's wiles knew no bounds – along with his frustration at constantly being played for a fool.

I could always make out what every other jockey was doing, but I never could understand what old Fordham was up to.

In one race George comes and taps me in the last stride on the post. I am determined not to have this happen again, and then in the next race he just gets home and I beat him a stride past the post. With his clucking and fiddling you never know what the old chap is up to.

One time he was cluck-clucking at his mount for the whole of the race. I thought I had him beaten two or three times in the two miles. But with his infernal cluck-clucking he was always coming again. Still 200 yards from home I supposed I had him dead settled. 'I'll cluck-cluck you,' I thought – and at that moment he swoops down on me and beats me easily!

Baily's Magazine had its own theory for Fordham's success:

Partly to good fortune, without which the finest abilities in the world are good for nothing; partly to good mounts that are given him; partly to his good hands and knowledge of pace; but beyond everything, to his consummate skill in 'gammoning' boys that he is done with, and catching them on the post when they have let their horses heads loose. In this art, which in slang language is termed 'kidding', he has no equal. And another secret of his many successes is that he never gives up riding his horse until past the post in case of any mistake occurring to the leader.

'The Demon' took immense delight in 'kidding' whether he was riding against an arch rival like Archer or a young greenhorn. Races, even some over short sprint distances, still tended to be run in snatches with the pace only quickening toward the finish. This was a scenario ripe for subterfuge and 'kid-ology'; Fordham would feign distress, perhaps 'cluck' at his mount, thereby encouraging the imprudent to make their efforts prematurely. Then, just as the victim sensed triumph, Fordham would pounce – to the amusement and financial gain of his countless disciples who worshipped 'The Kidder'. Fordham's wiliness drove Archer to distraction. And Fordham knew it – which is why he took immense delight in making his younger rival look stupid at every conceivable opportunity.

The *Pall Mall Gazette* indulged its readers with a lyrical account of the technique at work:

> Fordham throws a keen glance to right and left, then, perhaps actuated by a charitable desire to kindle once more a ray of hope in the breasts of the now silent bookmakers, or, which is more probable, thinking that the two boys have got more left in them than the horse quite fancies, he sets his shoulders higher than ever, and a convulsive movement agitates his elbows. Fordham will pretend to be 'riding,' that is 'squeezing' his horse; he will seem to flog his horse while all the time he is holding him well together, not hustling him, and timing his own 'rush' to come when the others shall have shot their bolt. For the hundredth time the old ruse has succeeded, the two lads, thinking they had the great horseman in difficulties, plunge simultaneously into the fantastic ecstasies of a flogging finish which settles the winning horse in the next dozen strides; with the semblance of a shake Fordham shoots out, and canters home the easiest of winners by two lengths.

From a vantage point on the sidelines, however, only the truly perceptive might discern whether or not 'The Demon' was 'kidding'. George Lambton recounted watching a seller at Newmarket in Archer's company in which Fordham rode a certainty called Nimble for Leopold de Rothschild.

> Fordham was riding one of his 'kidding' races, and for once was caught. Mr de Rothschild declared his intention of buying the winner. Fordham begged him not to, but having seen nothing apparently wrong in the race he did so. The horse turned out to be no good. When I saw

Fordham's whip go up 200 yards from home, I thought he was beaten, but Archer, who had studied his methods so closely, assured me that he was only 'kidding'. He lost the race by a head, and I turned to Archer, saying, 'Well, you made a mistake then.' 'No,' he replied, 'I made no mistake, but the old man did and threw his race away.' It took an expert like Archer to know whether Fordham was all out or had a stone up his sleeve.

As Archer knew to his cost, reading Fordham from the saddle was near impossible. And reading Fordham from the sidelines was not as easy as it appeared. There was an oft-recounted tale of a man at Newmarket who said he could always tell just how well Fordham was going on a horse. He maintained he'd not once been deceived. One day the man has backed Fordham and sees him look over his shoulder toward the finish. It's a 'kid', thinks the man. He's got plenty left; and will go on to win. But Fordham's horse is soundly beaten. The man approaches Fordham after the race and asks why the 'kid' had failed. Fordham eyed him up and down. Then said softly: 'I was looking at a dog. I was four lengths beat at the time.'

Fordham had soon cottoned on to the fact that the majority of racehorses preferred the carrot to the stick. In his youth he'd been unsparing, drawing the colourful quote from *The Morning Post* that 'he wore out a whip' when urging Knight of the Kars to victory in Doncaster's Fitzwilliam Handicap. But although horses were still habitually subjected to severe punishment from whip and spur, Fordham grew to eschew either; on Formosa and Petronel in the Guineas for two significant examples. One day he explained himself:

> I never do knock them about, you know. If I hit a horse once, and he does not answer, I stop. There's a chance of the others stopping and coming back to you, perhaps, but it's no good flogging away at him. They whip a horse

a mile from home. Sometimes, as we've been going in a race, I've seen them begin, and I've said to them, 'How the deuce do you expect to get home if you're whipping him now?'

The elder statesman was often at pains to pass on the 'knowledge'. To the apprentice Edwin Martin, mounting Don Juan prior to the 1883 Cesarewitch, he said: 'Dear me, that's a pretty whip that is, my boy, but what a pity it is that these pretty things lose so many races. Don't you think that you had better leave it behind?' Whereupon he thrust it in his pocket and walked away. Don Juan proceeded to justify public support, winning at odds of 11 to 2. Commented the *Post*:

> It will be something for little Martin to boast of hereafter that riding the winner of the Cesarewitch without a whip, mainly by the advice of Fordham who forcibly impressed upon him beforehand the important advantage of having two hands to ride his horse with instead of one if it came to anything like a finish. That many a race has been thrown away by the too free use of the whip, more especially by the disciples of the 'windmill school'. It is to be regretted that Fordham's laudable example is not more frequently followed by some of the senior jockeys.

One occasion that saw Fordham uncharacteristically employ both aids came at Newmarket in 1871. The race was a humble seller. Only two started. Fordham rode the aptly-named Badsworth, a notorious jade. Fordham jumped him off and never ceased riding with whip and spur from start to finish. Badsworth tried to swerve one way and then the other. Fordham deftly switched his whip from one hand to the other in response. Badsworth had no option but to gallop on. Fordham never gave him a moment's rest. Badsworth won by a short head. For Fordham to ride this severely was the rarest of occurrences. But he knew the horse he was on – and the only way to deal with him.

Few horses got the better of him. One who did was General Peel in the Gold Cup of 1865. Lord Glasgow's Guineas winner and Derby runner-up was a soft-hearted brute. After dead-heating with Ely he was sent out for the run-off looking as clean as a new pin and as fresh as a daisy. But he decided enough was enough for the day. He sulked so abominably in the decider that Fordham threw the reins on his neck in disgust and made no effort to complete the race. The jockey was taking a risk. Lord Glasgow possessed a temper that made typhoons appear puffs of wind. As a young sailor he'd fallen from a mast top and fractured a neck vertebra which, it was supposed, caused him to suffer excruciating agony whenever he turned his head to address people and thus left him in an almost constant state of irascibility. True to form Glasgow's stormy temper erupted in a towering rage – which, on this occasion, was directed more toward his cowardly horse than Fordham.

Although accorded god-like status by his fellow jockeys Fordham occasionally showed he was human after all by making a mistake. When riding Warlock in the Cumberland Plate of 1856 he misjudged the finishing post and almost stopped the horse, thinking he'd won. Realizing his error as the field rushed past, he took up the chase but failed by a head to catch Fisherman. On another occasion at Goodwood an animal called Serge II bolted with him to post. The horse began walking around on his hind legs, thoroughly enjoying himself. Fordham grew so disgusted with the beast's antics he dismounted and turned him loose. George Hodgman recalled another rare instance of Fordham losing his rag: 'Only once, in a friendship extending over a great number of years, do I remember being thoroughly "at elbows" with him. This was over a mare called Heiress. I sent her for the Bibury Stakes. She was not in high racing trim, and I told Fordham not to knock her about. He came to win the race to find, when he had clapped on full steam, that his opponent had a bit up his sleeve. He lost his head, and freely plied whip and spur. "Well, Mr Butcher," I said to him as I looked at the bloodstained sides of the mare, "you've done a nice thing." Well, Fordham, with me, was "Mr Butcher" for some time.'

Fordham's 'butchery' of Heiress was a hen's tooth. His hands were invariably used to coax rather than coerce the unwilling. He was the master of finesse. The Druid opined: 'Fordham can communicate his fine confidence to a nervous horse beyond almost any jockey of the day.' Allied to his judgement of pace, this lightness of touch made him the ideal partner for a two-year-old – however skittish they might be. At Goodwood in 1871 a juvenile filly belonging to William Graham tried to bolt on the way to the start and threw him clean up in the air before galloping away up Trundle Hill. There was much laughter and ribaldry at the sight of Fordham picking himself up and dusting himself off. His dodgy knee was intact but his pride was not. This state of affairs would not do; not do at all. Once reunited with the filly the wooing began in earnest. Tamed and reassured, the filly went on to win.

Aboard the young thoroughbred kindness was king as far as Fordham was concerned. 'When I get down to the post on these two-year-olds,' he told his patron Baron Leopold de Rothschild, 'and I feel their little hearts beating under my legs, I think "Why not let them have an easy race, win if they can but don't frighten them."'

In a rare interview from 1884 Fordham spoke further about his approach to riding juveniles:

> It's no use knocking the young ones about. I never did it, you know. You see, they understand what they've got to do, and if they have not been taught, it's very certain you can't teach them on a racecourse, where there's often guns and shouting and bustle all around to take off their attention, you know. Poor little brutes. They look at you

sometimes, if they can't go the pace, to see if you are going to hit them, turn their heads and look at you, they do, expecting the whip. They are outpaced, they can't go any faster, and they dread they are going to catch it.

It comes as no surprise, therefore, to find the list of Fordham successes in the calendar's principal juvenile events is long and comprehensive, encompassing the principal juvenile events at all the major tracks. In some instances the haul was impressive. Fordham won Ascot's New Stakes seven times; Newmarket's July Stakes on five occasions; the Lavant at Goodwood four times; Doncaster's Champagne Stakes five times; and he enjoyed a fruitful harvest of the important events at Newmarket's three autumnal meetings viz the Hopeful (four), Clearwell (six), Criterion (seven) and the Prendergast (five). Despite the Middle Park and Dewhurst only being inaugurated in the twilight of his career, Fordham still won the former with Beaudesert and St Louis and the latter with Ladislas. Such was his reputation on two-year-olds that he frequently picked up 'spare' rides on horses not usually associated with him. He won the Champagne Stakes on Derby winner Thormanby and Guineas winner The Marquis; the Clearwell on the Fillies Triple Crown victrix Hannah. Besides these elite stakes races there were several valuable nurseries. The nursery, even more than the ordinary handicap, was rife with sleight-of-hand. 'A premium of vice,' declared *Baily's*, 'generally won by a horse which has probably made its first effort to win and for the first time in its life has been brought to the post fit to run.' Fordham was the first name on an owner's lips when, for instance, Goodwood's valuable Nursery came around. It certainly was in 1859 when Ten Broeck's Umpire advertised his Classic potential by bolting up in Fordham's hands.

The identity of the best juvenile he rode regularly is a question open to heated debate. Lord Clifden (Woodcote and Champagne),

Thebais (Criterion) and Hauteur (Champagne and Clearwell) franked their promise with Classics. But there's an argument for saying that as two-year-olds they were inferior to Lady Elizabeth and Ecossais (alias 'The Flying Scotchman'), who each landed the prestigious New Stakes-July Stakes double.

Certain individual performances demand detail. Marksman's success in Goodwood's Molecomb Stakes of 1866 illustrated why Fordham's powers of conveying human will to the equine youngster became the envy of all. Mr James Merry's colt was generally regarded a bit of a rogue. In the previous afternoon's Findon Stakes the colt, ridden by the journeyman jockey Harvey Covey, ran unplaced behind Friponnier and Bismarck. His trainer, James Waugh, refused to concede the colt was unreliable. He believed the youngster was too resolute and took too much out of himself if his jockey rode him too hard too soon. Fordham watched the race and was so convinced Marksman had not shown anything like his best form that he urged Merry to run the colt in the Molecomb and to put him up. Merry was not keen on the idea. Marksman would meet Bismarck at exactly the same weights and risked a second drubbing. Fordham persisted and at length was allowed to have his way. Odds of 5 to 4 were laid on Bismarck, while 5s were obtainable about Marksman. 'Fordham's Marksman,' crowed *Baily's Magazine*, 'did more execution than the needle gun, and, using him tenderly, he turned the tables on "The Prussian". Without the slightest wish to disparage the merits of other jockeys, Fordham alone seems to understand Marksman and his kind riding mainly contributed to his victory.' Marksman won in a canter – one of a Fordham five-timer on the day that included the Cup. 'There, that'll give him confidence,' said 'The Demon', patting the colt on the neck afterwards. Marksman won twice more that season and in 1867 was only denied the Derby by a neck despite the handicap of a 'dicky' leg.

Lord Clifden: one of the best two-year-olds Fordham partnered; and, ultimately, possibly the best horse he ever rode.

It is perhaps fitting that the oldest race in the calendar confined to two-year-olds, the July Stakes, should exhibit, by comment consent, Fordham's finest display on a juvenile. In 1875 it yielded a mesmerizing demonstration of his unique brand of horsemanship and jockeyship reliant on silken hands, quick wits and no-nonsense; one endorsing the view of Messrs Heartfield and Radcliffe that some horses ran more generously in his hands than in any other. This victory on Levant was spoken of as the third in Fordham's quartet of greatest triumphs.

Levant seemed to have everything going for her. Her dam was the One Thousand Guineas winner Repulse; and although her sire Adventurer had cast his net in calmer waters on the track, the City & Sub and the Gold Vase yielding his principal laurels, he'd proved himself in the stallion shed by getting a Derby winner in Pretender and two exceptional fillies in Wheel of Fortune and Apology who each won a Fillies Triple Crown. She also looked the part, a rich bay or brown of beautiful conformation. And was a splendid mover in the walk and at the gallop. But she'd proved something of a disappointment. She belonged to Lord Rosebery and was trained by James Dover at East Ilsley in Berkshire – and, thus, was not in a yard for which Fordham would normally be expected to ride. Reputed to be far and away the best of Dover's juveniles, she was developing a nasty habit of saving her best for the gallops and not the track. And it wasn't as if she was being ridden by an incompetent. Her regular jockey was Harry Constable, champion in 1873 with 109 winners. Levant had run five times prior to the July Stakes and had one win to show for it: a moderate race at Epsom. Any hopes entertained by Rosebery and Dover that she'd finally turned the corner were cruelly exposed by her subsequent abysmal effort in the Hurstbourne Stakes at Stockbridge in which she was beaten a dozen lengths. So unreliable had she become that the Press began labelling her a 'jade'. Her owner concurred; and was on the verge of taking her out of training. As a last resort Constable suggested to Rosebery and Dover they turn to the matchless hands of George Fordham in an effort to work the oracle on their impeccably bred but decidedly wayward filly. Once the engagement was announced there was a rush to back Levant.

The new partnership was faced by nine opponents, five of them debutants. The best of these was thought to be the colt Gilestone who started favourite at 100 to 30. Rosebery could back Levant at 9 to 2 – if he dare. Levant took virtually no part in the race for all bar the last 100 yards of its six furlongs. Fordham had convinced the filly she was back home on the Berkshire gallops she preferred by keeping her wide of the remainder. Up ahead Gilestone was disputing the lead with a much fancied filly called Camelia and a slashing unnamed chestnut colt out of Lady Coventry, latter named Farnesse, who was partnered by Fred Archer. Running up the hill out of the Dip the three of them were upsides. Only then did Fordham wake Levant up; and one of the great Fordham 'rushes' unfolded. At first it appeared as if Levant wanted to answer him in the negative. But 'The Demon' was in no mood to let the recalcitrant filly behave like a spoilt child. In a furious four-horse finish he forced Levant up to collar Farnesse right on the post by a short head with Camelia and Gilestone dead-heating the same distance in arrears.

The Sportsman was unequivocal: 'A better race has seldom been witnessed at Newmarket or elsewhere, and Fordham's effort on Levant was so admirably timed that the filly just got home.' And *Baily's Magazine* went into raptures: 'Fordham caught hold of Levant and squeezed her in the last few yards to win narrowly. We make no reflection on the riders of the others – Archer, Wood and Parry, but every community has its king, and as the king of jockeys is

George Fordham, it is not too much to say that he could have won on any of the others. There is no doubt Levant is a jade and that she tried to cut it, but she found her master this time.' *The Times* agreed: 'That jockeyship had much to do with the issue of the race it is impossible to doubt. Levant put up her head towards the finish, as if half inclined to cut it, but Fordham administered punishment, and kept her straight, and it is not too much to say that in so close a finish any one of the four, if it had been ridden by that accomplished horseman, would have won.' That Fred Archer was up on Farnesse doubtless made the victory and that final sentiment all the sweeter in Fordham's eyes.

Levant was awarded a walk-over on her next start, but thereafter failed to win again in six outings that saw her beaten by Camelia and Gilestone at Brighton and involved progressively poorer opposition. Crucially, she wasn't ridden by Fordham. Her last race of the season was a match at Newmarket. Given that her rival was partnered by Fordham the result was a foregone conclusion.

EIGHT

A WONDER IN A MATCH

Nowhere was Fordham's tactical acumen and wizardry more evident than during the match-races that were such a staple ingredient of the Victorian racing scene. Fordham had no equal in these jousts. Not even Fred Archer managed to usurp his status in such tilts without lances. In the 1860 season, for example, Fordham won no fewer than 13. He'd benefited from a thorough grounding in this form of combat from having cut his teeth in an era when some races were still run in heats between two horses: he took his first in a Tunbridge Seller back in 1853. 'His luck in deciding heats is a wonder,' declared *The Sporting Life* somewhat disingenuously because there was no 'luck' about it – only skill.

Match-races were one of the oldest, quite possibly the original, form of horse racing. Owners simply challenged each other and staked money on the outcome. Wagering soon came to assume monumental proportions: when the Northern champion Hambletonian beat

Diamond, for example, in a 3,000-guineas match over four and a quarter miles at Newmarket in 1799 the cost to losing punters was estimated at £500,000 (a staggering *£187 million* in today's money). Mindful of such figures, it's no surprise to find match races being celebrated in verse and prose. Two instances quickly entered folklore.

The first, on 24 August 1805, was between Louisa and Allegro over two miles at York. Louisa won by a short neck. And so she should've considering she was receiving four stone from the colt. What made the result sensational, however, were the identities of the jockeys. Allegro enjoyed the priceless assistance of Frank Buckle, 'a rider of the first celebrity' in the words of *The Times*, prolific winner of Classics, the man who'd steered Hambletonian to victory, and the first truly great jockey of the English Turf. Louisa, by contrast, was aided by 22-year-old Mrs Alicia Thornton (nee Meynell), the daughter of a Norwich watchmaker. She rode side-saddle and dressed for the contest in a purple cap and waistcoat, buff-coloured cotton skirts, purple satin shoes and embroidered stockings. Mrs Thornton kicked her mare into the lead and came again after Buckle had stolen a narrow lead near the finish. 'Her close seat and perfect management of her horse, and her bold and steady jockeyship, amazed one of the most crowded courses we have for a long time witnessed.'

The second was the most celebrated match framed by Admiral Rous at York in the spring of 1851 between the two Derby winners, The Flying Dutchman and Voltigeur. The year older 'Dutchman' conceded 8½ lb and won by a length to avenge his half-length defeat in the previous year's Doncaster Cup in concession of 19lb.

Although match races were contested on any racecourse the greatest number were fought at Newmarket where they helped swell many a dull card. The process invariably commenced in the Jockey Club Rooms once the snuff had been taken, from the box fashioned from Eclipse's gold-mounted foot, and the port and brandy was circulating after a splendid dinner. Those owners cajoled (or lured) into pitting their horses against each others for a named stake wrote on slips of paper the relevant names and at what distance the 'match' was to be made. These slips were handed to Admiral Rous. Then the acknowledged 'Dictator of the Turf' would set the weights. The match was duly made if each party then handed Rous a half-crown. Then the wagering commenced. As Rous professed on more than one occasion: 'Racing has always been a gambling speculation.'

As implied by his oft-quoted pseudonym, the Hon Henry John Rous bestrode the Victorian Turf like no other. And, like every other jockey, owner and trainer, it was in Fordham's interest to keep on the Admiral's good side. Rous held as low view of jockeys as he did heavy bettors and bookmakers. He believed they should be kept in their place. They were the 'servant' not the 'master'. He disliked the trend of rewarding victorious jockeys with excessive presents, which had gradually come to exceed more than 'a hard-working professional man' might earn in a year. He preferred treating them with a patrician courtesy. They were not his dining companions of choice. In truth, Rous probably undervalued fine jockeyship. Bearing that in mind, it was perfectly possible for a crack jockey to be worth a pound or two that Rous hadn't bargained for when drawing up the weights. Nat Flatman he liked; Fordham mustn't have put a foot wrong because later on 'The Demon' was the Admiral's blue-eyed boy whom he'd put up whenever he had a horse of his own in a match.

And Rous would've taken some winning over. He'd been a mettlesome youth born to an Earl and raised near the marshes of Suffolk with the salt of the North Sea in his blood. It was the time of the Napoleonic Wars and life in the Royal Navy beckoned. Rous served 27 years in the Navy; sailed, among others, in HMS Victory; nearly drowned when clinging to an unpturned boat for five hours in darkness; and was awarded the rank by which he's come to be so instantly recognizable in 1852. His seamanship was unquestionable. On one occasion he brought his rudderless vessel 1,500 miles from the rocks of Labrador to Spithead while shipping water at the rate of two feet per hour. He might have gone further in the senior service had it not been for a love of the Turf engendered as a boy by the sight and sound of his father's young racehorses galloping in the paddocks at home. But after leaving the Navy in 1836 he commenced serious study of the Rules of Racing. From that date his life was given to the Turf, body and soul. In April 1838 he was nominated for the position of Senior Steward; no one guessed that for the next 40 years he was to be the 'Perpetual Steward.'

Rous had been a member of the Jockey Club since 1821. During this period his unusual knowledge and understanding of the Rules of Racing had constantly found flaws that he invariably conveyed to fellow members who much preferred being left to their newspapers and armchairs. The reformed poacher, one may presume, was thought to make the best gamekeeper. And so it proved. Rous became the most famous of all Turf administrators and reformers. He was vigorous, determined and unafraid of shouldering responsibility. He was friendly and straight-talking albeit prone to impetuosity – 'if not so violent and precipitate as Lord George Bentinck,' averred *Baily's Magazine*. The magazine went on to extol his virtues: 'He is slow and sure, considerate, perhaps wisely, that a conciliatory position with those whose co-operation it is necessary to secure is the best for him to adopt. His manner may be said to favour the quarter-deck but it should not be forgotten he was brought up in a school where to hear was to obey. His unsullied honour, kind-hearted disposition and matchless abilities will go far to atone for any shortcomings.' In 1850 Rous published *The Laws and Practice of Horse-Racing*; five years later he accepted the role of public handicapper despite having said that for 30 years he'd searched, and failed, to find someone to fill the role with those priceless qualities of Caesar's wife: 'above suspicion, of independent means, a perfect knowledge of the form and actual condition of every public horse, without having the slightest interest in any stable.'

Fordham grew accustomed to the sight of the Admiral sat on his old bay horse at his usual vantage point near the Bushes from which he might scrutinize every race at Newmarket for signs of any horse being 'pulled'. A splendid pen picture of this image came from William Day: 'He became like an equestrian statue, silent and motionless, with the reins resting on the neck of his horse, and the long loop at the end of the handle of his whip round his arm left him the free use of his hands for the more steady support of the glasses. His eyes, once fixed on the runners, were seldom removed till he had discovered all he wanted to see in the running of the different starters.'

Very little - if anything - escaped Rous. He'd frequently be abroad early in the morning to study each trainer's string to check if there was any shirking at work with a view to tempting him into bestowing a lenient weight. Truly it might be said that one had to get up very early in the morning to put one over on Admiral Henry Rous.

Rous was fascinated by match races since the key to them was the delicate issue of how much weight each participant was asked to carry: in other words, applying the principles of handicapping that, theoretically, gave each horse an equal chance of victory. The age of the animal had to be considered; a mature horse should carry a heavier weight than a younger one. A filly – the 'weaker' sex – warranted an additional allowance. Previous form had to be considered, especially over the distance chosen for the match. In time this recurring puzzle led to Rous evolving his enduring legacy to the Turf: a weight-for-age scale applicable for different distances and for different months of the year. Although minor adjustments have been made down the years, the Rous template remained.

Admiral Rous

However, no handicapper, not even Rous, could be expected to get things right every time. Many a time he was heard to mutter 'I'll eat my hat if that wins' which served to make a fortune for his hatter while ruining his digestion. 'Every great handicap,' he averred, 'offers a premium to fraud, for horses are constantly started without any intention of winning, merely to hoodwink the handicapper.' Not for nothing does the phrase 'staying one step ahead of the handicapper' feature in every trainer's lexicon. Money, a lot of it, might change hands if Rous was proved to have miscalculated or blundered. And if there was one thing Rous loathed more than man's taste for 'that vile and pernicious weed' tobacco it was the racing man's predilection for heavy betting.

Betting had long moved on from owners just wagering with each other over match-races. Any race became fair game. Arising from the gaming houses of London, such as Crockford's, emerged a new breed of Turf personality: the bookmaker. The bookmaker might bet an individual £20,000 to £10,000 against a horse in a race – and lose. But if he'd betted also against every horse in the race, what he drew from the losers was, in theory, enough to pay the winners and leave him some profit. Thus developed the simple process of 'betting round' that became the foundation of all bookmaking.

During the decades when George Fordham was the 'banker' jockey - and nowhere more so than in match races - the men whose living depended on correctly judging if Fordham was on 'their side' were individuals such as John Gully, Harry Hill, George Hodgman, William 'The Leviathan' Davies and his Yorkshire counterpart John Jackson 'The Leviathan of the North'. *Baily's Magazine* took the time to define their qualities:

> A bookmaker, like a poet, has been said to be born not made. A successful competitor, a broad chest in a black silk

waistcoat, plenty of brass, a voluble tongue and a ready-calculator are the stock in trade. Their very profession is haunted with suspicion and every successful practice makes dishonesty almost indispensible. Their associations have opened to them a vein of information upon which they are induced to trade. There is scarcely one of these men who would not have made a very superior artisan, be it shoemaker, stockinger or carpenter, but they make very indifferent purveyors of sport.

The bookie who uttered the defining remark for a one of his calling was Frederick Swindell, a personal friend of Fordham's, and a Liverpudlian who rose from a cleaner of railway engines to be regaled as 'Lord Freddy' or 'The Napoleon of the Turf'. When asked what he should do were he paid twice over by a debtor in error Swindell shrugged and replied: 'Do? Look hard at him and the next time thee meets him perhaps he'll pay thee a third time!' Swindell's proud boast was that he refused to bet on 'anything that talks.' Little wonder 'Lord Freddy' left £146,000 (*£11.7 million*) in his Will.

***

Fordham's inexhaustible box of tricks ensured his was the first name on an owner's lips after a match had been announced – particularly if it were taking place at Newmarket. Although he'd participated in numerous run-offs following dead-heats, his very first 'match' in the proper sense of the term came on 31 October 1857. The location was Newmarket. The distance was just short of six furlongs. He rode The Happy Land, on whom he'd recently won the Criterion for Lord Ribblesdale. Lining up against the juvenile colt was the filly Heroine to whom Rous insisted he concede 8lb instead of the 3lb sex allowance. The money went on the colt who was 7 to 4 on by the off. Fordham stalked Heroine and while her jockey, Ben Bray, was looking one side he brought The Happy Land up the other to win by a length.

Thus was the precedent set. As time passed it was not uncommon for 'The Demon' to win three matches of an afternoon - and occasionally more. During a protracted Newmarket card on a cold and raw 26 October 1864, that commenced at 11 in the morning and finished close to five in the evening, he rode six matches and won four, claiming the scalps of Henry Custance, Sam Rogers and 'Brusher' Wells twice. Two days later he rode in four more and won them all: two on behalf of Ten Broeck, one for the Marquis of Hastings and one for the Duke of Beaufort. This time the vanquished jockeys were Tom Ashmall, Tom Chaloner, Henry Parry and Custance.

Fordham frequently did his pals a good turn in match races. One such instance took place on the Friday of the Guineas Meeting in 1867. Fordham rode the five-year-old Ostregor for Sir John Astley against Captain Machell's Two Thousand Guineas runner up Knight of the Garter (on whom Fordham would eventually win the Chester Cup) for 200 sovereigns a side. Ostregor conceded two stone weight-for-age to the three-year-old, who was a firm odds-on favourite. But the younger horse didn't have Fordham. 'The best looking, best tempered, and gamest horse of his day,' according to his owner, Ostregor was a grand mover with a tremendous stride on ground he liked. Harvey Covey valiantly tried to win from the front but he could never shake off Ostregor who pounced close home and, 'won by half a length thanks to Fordham's inimitable nursing', in the opinion of The Life.

'The Kid was a wonder in a match, and no mistake,' stated Astley. 'The Mate' had good reason to be so unequivocal. His funds rose and fell with the regularity of a barometer. In May 1875, during another of his frequent financial shortages, Fordham won him two matches on the same Newmarket afternoon. In one of them Fordham jumped out and made every yard of the running to win in a canter. In the other he had to beat Fred Archer on the raging favourite Tripaway to put drink on Astley's table. This time 'The Demon' took a pull. After stalking Archer all the way, he produced May Day in the shadow of the post to frustrate his arch rival by a head.

Any two-horse race demanded Fordham be put up. The clamour for his services in any run-off was as keen as it was after the triple dead-heat in the 1857 Cesarewitch – often to a colleague's disadvantage. For a Newmarket run-off in the 1879 Cheveley Stakes, for example, anxious supporters of Cannie Chiel begged his owner Prince Batthyany to replace Jack 'Deafie' Morris with Fordham for the decider after the well-backed favourite had been caught on the line by Tom Cannon aboard Mirth. Morris was so vexed at being displaced he sent in his cap and jacket (and in due course, penniless and forgotten, was found dead in a Newmarket cellar from cirrhosis of the liver). Fordham won the decider readily.

Some races cut up into two-horse contests. The 1874 renewal of the Grand Duke Michael Stakes between Novateur and Leolinus enabled Fordham to shine. The prize appeared to be on a plate for Leolinus who had just run second in the St Leger. But this was now a 'match' and Fordham was on Novatuer. Tom Jennings, the trainer of Novateur, assured Sir George Chetwynd when they bumped into each other before the race that in these circumstances his horse would win. Chetwynd promptly took a bet to win a 'monkey' with the first bookmaker he saw. Fordham secured Chetwynd's 'monkey' by a short head.

One jockey to whom Fordham always enjoyed issuing a dunce's cap in matches was Tom Chaloner who narrowly deprived him of victories in a Derby and two St Legers. There were just two runners for the Brighton's Champagne Stakes of 1871, Vulcan and Fordham versus Sterling and Chaloner. The Brighton track exhibited many similarities to Epsom; its descent, turns and cambers were, if anything, even more dangerous. The distance was a mile and the seven-year-old Vulcan had to give Sterling, the Guineas runner-up, four years and 18lb. Vulcan was as tough as old boots, a prolific winner who seemed to be in action every other week. Since being acquired by M Lefevre following two wins in the spring that included the Lincolnshire Handicap, he and Fordham had notched eight victories. Nevertheless, the form experts believed the old horse's task to be impossible; Sterling went off at 11 to 4 on. Fordham recognized he'd no chance unless he stole a march on his rival. He knew Vulcan would not be inconvenienced by the steep descent: the old horse possessed beautiful shoulders and would take it in his stride. Fordham dashed Vulcan down the Brighton hill at an alarming pace that must've convinced the naysayers that his dislike of Tattenham Hill was a myth. By the time Vulcan reached the bottom of the hill Sterling was lagging well behind and although Chaloner set him alight thereafter there was still a neck between the pair at the post. 'Fordham on the old horse never gave Chaloner a chance,' reported *Baily's*, 'for he made play at such a pace that the latter could never get on terms and when it came to the final struggle Vulcan won very cleverly. Vulcan is such a wonder that he puts racing calculations all on one side. He is quite out of the pale of handicapping and stands alone, such an extraordinary species of a horse as these later days have seen.'

The crowd went berserk. Fordham had stolen the race. Nothing pleased him more than to best Tom Chaloner by a head or a neck. 'Winners and losers alike, according to Sir George Chetwynd, 'were impressed with this magnificent piece of horsemanship, the result of careful forethought, thorough knowledge of the animal and the course, and ability to carry out the scheme so cleverly devised.' *The Sportsman* spared a thought for his partner: 'Poor Vulcan, never was a horse so maligned. No one ever knew how to ride him until Fordham got into the saddle. At Brighton he drove him along from start to finish to beat Sterling, and he did the same thing on the following day when he made mincemeat of his field in the Sussex Cup conceding up to 45lb. It's to be regretted that Vulcan was not timed for these races, for never has a horse carrying 10 stone gone at so grand a pace.' Vulcan and 'The Demon' were not finished; the partnership raised their total to 11 by the end of the season.

Other Fordham match races owed more to their novelty value. In October 1859 Fordham beat Tom Aldcroft in match at Newmarket between ponies, winning by 12 'pony lengths.' Three years later he fought an equine duel for £100 a side with bookmaker John Jackson, 'The Northern Leviathan'. The match arose out of a dispute as to the relative merits of Fordham and Ralph Bullock as jockeys. Jackson favoured the latter and fully intended to put him up on his colt Neptunus when the match against Fordham, on his pony Levity, was to be decided - and brought him to scale for that purpose. But Fordham pointed out that the match had been made for *owners* to ride. Jackson reluctantly donned silks. There was only going to be one winner of that match. Poor Neptunus, good enough to have run fourth in the Derby, was unable to carry his owner for more than a furlong or two before breaking down, leaving a smiling Fordham to canter in alone. 'Jackson went well to hounds, but not much racing, you know. I beat him easy,' reminisced Fordham years later. 'I also rode my pony Babylon in a 100 yards race on the July Course against a wonderful pony of Jackson's. It had beaten all the running men at

Sheffield. But mine was a bit better. Started by pistol, we were. The starter stood up in the July Stand. I think I only won about a head.'

The last of Fordham's novelty matches might have gone either way. At the end of the 1867 season Fordham and Tom Cannon fought out a pony duel over two miles of Warwick's steeplechase track for £50 a side. Fordham's mount, Nelly, had to be cajoled at a few fences but eventually bested Cannon's Wasp by three lengths. 'Both jockeys were in rare form and throughout set a good pace,' said *The Sportsman*, 'but Nelly was the better fencer, although Wasp made up a lot of ground on the flat. Fordham was loudly cheered on passing the post and appeared highly pleased with his success.'

The artistry Fordham displayed in match races stayed with him to the end. In his final season of 1883 he rode in 12 and won eight; five of those successes came at the expense of Fred Archer. If one adds races that season reduced to two-horse contests a further six may be included, of which Fordham won five. Altogether he thus won 13 out of 18 – seven at the expense of the regularly bewitched and bemused Archer. Other jockeys to suffer humiliation were Fred Webb (twice), Tom Cannon, Jem Goater, Charlie Wood and Charles Loates. All bar four of these duels took place at Newmarket, the canvas on which Fordham painted eternal pictures with the race-horse as his brush.

The last such picture was painted at his local track, Brighton, on 30 October. Needless to add the jockey who felt the dab of his brush was Archer. And the torture was strung out over two miles, a rare distance for matches by 1883. Fordham rode his own horse, the three-year-old colt Oliver; Archer rode Mr Reynolds' aged gelding Beddington, a recent winner at Croydon. Oliver had run three times at the last Lewes meeting partnered by inexperienced young riders and could barely finish in front of another animal. Now Oliver had the master on top. Despite Beddington's superior form and the presence of 'The Tinman' in the plate, the market was only going to bet one way. Oliver left the starting post the 11 to 10 on favourite and passed the finishing post ten lengths to the good. Subsequently reunited with lesser mortals, Oliver ran twice more down his field.

Some horses only respond to genius.

***

Despite the many renowned match races in the annals of the Turf, it is to the 1860s that one must turn for three examples that stand head and shoulders above the rest. Fordham rode in all three. And he won all three. Each one is etched into Turf history; each one for an entirely different reason.

The notoriety of the first transcended the sport. Its ramifications spilled over into the law reports and letters pages of the newspapers. It raised points of honour and threatened to tarnish reputations. It questioned the leeway an 'officer and a gentleman' should be permitted in furtherance of landing a bet, for the weight of money wagered on match races always invoked the spectre of skulduggery. And greed was at the core of the Tarragona-Michel Grove match of 3 October 1862. Run over the last half of the Abingdon Mile at Newmarket, it resulted in Fordham being a key figure in a four-day enquiry that kept the racing parish in a fever of anticipation and gossip for weeks.

Michel Grove had won easily in the hands of Fordham – as he ought at 3 to 1 on; yet Tarragona and her jockey (and trainer) John Nightingall were 'loudly hooted' by the crowd as they passed the post. Admiral Rous believed he knew why: he suspected the result was fixed by the two owners involved, a 'Mr Wyon' and a 'Mr Trowson'. One of them, the owner of Tarragona, was loathed by

Rous because he was one of the sly Army officers who'd engineered the 'Reindeer' bubble bet that duped Richard Ten Broeck: 'Mr Trowson' was the *nom de course* of Colonel Edwyn Burnaby. His alleged accomplice in this latest wheeze, 'Mr Wyon', was a fellow officer in the Grenadier Guards, the Hon Captain Arthur Annesley, who owned Michel Grove. The Stewards, at Rous's instigation, posted a notice at Tattersalls calling for Burnaby to explain 'several incidents connected with the running of the match...recommending no settlement of bets until after the investigation.' The issue at stake was a matter of honour.

Fordham's knowledge and expertise in match races, not to mention his status as a champion jockey beyond reproach, ensured he'd assume a key role in the enquiry convened by the Jockey Club. Rous presided over the committee duly assembled on 14 October, which included the Duke of Beaufort among its six members.

Burnaby huffed and puffed. He maintained the match was properly contested; and he and Annesley had wagered accordingly. 'We had not backed Michel Grove in concert. I declare this upon my honour.' He stood to win £435 or lose £397 on Tarragona; Annesley £400 and £685 on Michel Grove. Harry Steel, the Sheffield bookmaker, stated that he was present when the bet of 'an even £100' was struck – a fact corroborated by the Duke of Beaufort who was standing within earshot. The betting books of the two officers were produced and examined by an expert from the Bank of England, and by Rous (with the aid of a microscope) for any sign of irregularity or alteration. None were found. Nightingall said he thought the match was a 'bad one and would not have stood money on it...I called upon the mare with the spur but she could not keep up'; and he was promised £25 should he get Tarragona home a winner. The starter, Tom McGeorge, reported watching the horses run together for a hundred yards or so before Nightingall pulled Tarragona six lengths behind Michel Grove: 'I assumed he was riding a waiting race but had 'misjudged the pull.'" His assistant, William Norton, concurred: 'Nightingall had got the "strings" on,' declared the man who rejoiced in the nickname of 'Squirt'. However, had Nightingall been trying to 'pull' Tarragona to lose he'd hardly have done so in the first 100 yards. At the other end, the Judge, John Clark, saw nothing wrong: 'If either of the jockeys had "dogged" their horse 10 or 15 lengths from home I must have seen it.'

Burnaby maintained McGeorge was a biased because he'd only recently reported him for allowing 'a flying start' to stand uncorrected at Hungerford races. And so, he added, was Beaufort because he'd openly admitted having had a bet on the match. Burnaby then went for broke. He protested Rous's presence in the chair, asserting Rous was also prejudiced against him; Annesley had overheard Rous say he 'utterly abhorred' Burnaby owing to the 'Reindeer' bet. The investigation into the match was just a ruse to bring the 'Reindeer' bet into the public domain so that the Turf Establishment, and Rous in particular, might exact revenge by humiliating Burnaby and ruining his reputation. This was a case of Rous throwing his weight around; trying to portray him, an officer and a gentleman, as an utter cad. 'He treated me with the utmost hostility and a serious prejudice to poison the minds of the other members of the committee against me,' swore Burnaby. 'We were as much at enmity as two men could be.'

As far as the running of the race was concerned Fordham's evidence would be crucial. Rous began by bowling him a succession of long hops relating to a deposition Burnaby claimed he'd freely submitted. Fordham agreed he'd been told to make the running on Michel Grove. But he refuted any suggestion he'd said that, having ridden Tarragona, she couldn't win under any circumstances; or that

Nightingall had done everything he could to win; and that 'possibly he punished her too severely, more so than I should have liked to do for any of my employers.' He concluded by saying: 'I never authorized Colonel Burnaby to give this paper as my deposition, and saw it yesterday morning for the first time.'

Burnaby was allowed to cross-examine. He maintained Fordham was being economical with the truth. He produced a letter he insisted was handed to Fordham the previous week at Lewes races: 'I am anxious to know if you consider Nightingall rode Tarragona up to her form in the match with Michel Grove. I only saw the last few strides of the race, but I am told by some that he had pulled her. Your opinion will tend to satisfy me the more, from your knowing my mare so well from having ridden yourself, and the fact of your having ridden her only the very day before will enable you to form a better opinion than anyone else as to the merits or demerits of my jockey's riding.' Furthermore, continued Burnaby, when this letter had been read to Fordham the previous morning he'd agreed 'the substance of it was correct' - and would be happy to state the same before the Stewards.

Burnaby's attempt to shake the champion jockey's testimony fell flat. When Fordham had won his match on Tarragona, the jockey explained, she didn't seem 'to be in such good form as she'd shown him previously'. He agreed the owner had told him 'to come hard through, as hard as you can.' And that's what he did. By contrast, in the disputed match, Fordham added, 'Nightingall was never nearer than the first three strides. I heard his whip, flogging at the finish.' Fordham would not be moved; Burnaby ran up the white flag as far as enlisting the champion's support was concerned.

Burnaby did score one minor victory: Rous withdrew from the committee in the face of his accusation of bias – but only after all the evidence had been taken. The committee's judgement was that both charges viz (i) Tarragona being 'pulled' and (ii) a fictitious bet being made, were 'Not Proven'; the bet may have been *bona fide*. Burnaby and Annesley, however, were not absolved. The committee clearly believed the charges were true but were annoyingly unable to prove them. Rous's best hope was that much of the mud slung at the pair would stick. Burnaby aspired to have the last word: 'It would be impossible for me to convey in adequate language the pain which we have experienced from the mode in which this enquiry has been conducted.'

If Burnaby thought he'd had the last word he was mistaken. He was about to be publicly smeared for his role in the 'Reindeer' affair which was revived in the letters page of the newspapers. Rous was not a man to hold his tongue when he felt strongly about something. Via the columns of *The Morning Post* he raked over the coals of 'The Reindeer Bet' in the context of the 'Tarragona Affair' and poked its embers into life - 'his duty, as a Steward of the Jockey Club' - by referring to the un-gentlemanly and unsportsmanlike trait that was 'cheating.' Burnaby had form: he 'cheated' at Mamhead; and he 'cheated' at Newmarket. His words were instantly reproduced in *The Times* which felt obliged to print 'the full details of one of those scandals which from time to time crop up into light and give us specimens of transactions which we fear are but too common in the soils from which they rise.' The 'Reindeer Bet' was underhand; without honour. 'It is not lawful for two men to ascertain some fact beyond the possibility of mistake, and then to introduce the topic while in conversation with a third person, to pretend to get up a bet between themselves upon it, and then craftily to induce the third person to join in their betting with the certainty that he must lose.'

Annesley was quick to point out to the paper he'd had nothing to do with the 'Reindeer Bet' and connecting him with it in order to blacken his role in the 'Tarragona Affair' was unjust. Letters from Burnaby and Stewart followed swiftly. Burnaby's stated: 'I assert that the bet with Mr Stewart was *bona fide*...the subject was not introduced by either Mr Stewart or myself...I did not name Dr Johnson as an authority.' Stewart's letter said: 'I never referred to Johnson...my impression was Mr Ten Broeck claimed Johnson as his reference, but owing to the loud discussion going one, I am not quite positive on this point.'

Rous joined in on the 8th, wondering why the gentleman in whose presence Stewart had admitted the bet was fictitious had subsequently recanted. On the same day Burnaby forwarded letters from witnesses supporting the accounts provided by himself and Stewart, principally to the effect that no *specific* dictionary was mentioned until *after* the bet between Ten Broeck and Stewart was made. Stewart stressed that no fewer than 21 dictionaries spelt 'raindeer' with an 'a' and not just Johnson's. Other correspondents questioned why Burnaby should be penalized for exploiting his knowledge of etymology. Is it wrong, they postulated, for Turf men of an evening in their clubs to argue over, for example, the colour of some named thoroughbred and back their knowledge of the Stud Book with cash? What neither man could shake was the fact that their initial bet of £5 on the spelling had been recorded on paper and passed round the dinner table at Mamhead. Culpability rested with them for escalating the betting.

That there was no love lost between the Jockey Club and the Press was evident: the latter was firmly on the side of Burnaby and Annesley. 'The "Reindeer" question was the hinge on which the enquiry turned,' stated *Baily's Magazine*. 'The Jockey Club was hasty and inconsiderate in prejudging; it has exhibited an over-zeal. If two or three gentlemen at a house cannot now lose bets of £5 or £10 each without all Europe being agitated about it then there is an end to society. Mixing it up with the Tarragona enquiry is very bad taste and altogether uncalled for.' Scorn also poured forth from *The Field*: 'We have to regret that the spirit evinced in the investigation savours more of a prosecution in a court of law than of a tribunal whose course of action should only have been guided by the code of honour recognized among English gentlemen.' The *Sporting Life* buried the knife to the hilt: 'We will say that Admiral Rous is at times impatient and despotic. The authorities arrogated to themselves a power to treat gentlemen as pickpockets by declining to hear them or believe them upon their oaths or solemn words of honour. The power of the Jockey Club possessed they have stretched to a degree scandalous and utterly overbearing.' *The Morning Post* was the most vociferous: one of its writers, Irwin Willes, aka 'Argus', had already been 'warned off' by the Jockey Club for what he'd written: 'Since the Running Rein affair we believe no case has created a greater sensation in the racing world. It has been customary to believe that, whatever might be the delinquencies of some members of it, there was at the head an association of gentleman of rank and fortune incapable of being influenced by passion, prejudice or self-interest. That a man of the Admiral's reputed ability and judgement should make such strange havoc of all our notions of fair play is astonishing. His want of discretion is deplorable.'

The one man who walked away from the tawdry 'Tarragona Affair' with reputation intact was George Fordham.

***

After cutting his teeth in two-horse contests against jockeys the calibre of Nat Flatman and 'Brusher' Wells, Fordham appreciated better than most that 'kidology' was paramount and that the first jockey to 'blink' was apt to make the mistake that cost him the duel. His eye was invariably beady; his trigger finger rock steady.

It was in 1869 that he claimed his biggest scalp when Vespasian was pitted against the Derby winner Blue Gown. The match was made for £500 a side, to be run over ten furlongs at Newmarket on 26 April.

The six-year-old Vespasian was the elder brother of Sabinus. He was a powerful 16.1 hands son of Newminster whose good looks were marred only by his forelegs: he turned both his toes outwards so much that he always ran in black leather boots to keep from hitting himself. He was owned by Sir Charles Legard and trained by George Bloss at Bedford Lodge, the Newmarket yard controlled by the arch schemer Captain Machell. Instead of running at the regulation level weights, Vespasian received 4lb from his two years younger adversary. He was a game and extremely tough handicapper, who'd run no fewer than 21 times the previous season and won a dozen of them; later in 1869 he'd win the Chesterfield Cup under 10st 4lb. But Vespasian was not from the same drawer as a Derby winner. Blue Gown had already defeated him twice at Doncaster and Epsom, and the 7 to 4 on odds offered about the Derby winner seemed no more than realistic. Blue Gown was ridden by his usual partner, John Wells. Machell engaged Fordham for Vespasian.

The sense of anticipation was immense on the Heath that afternoon. The opening race on the card was a two-horse stakes which Fordham won for Lionel de Rothschild aboard Mahonia; the owner was in such a high state of excitement about his win and things to come that he steadfastly refused to believe Fordham had ridden his horse until he saw him dismounting from it. Enormous sums were bet on Blue Gown who, in the words of *The Sportsman*, 'appeared to be as fit as any horse in the world.' Vespasian, too, appeared as if 'he'd received a very careful preparation.' Machell knew Epsom was not a course that played to the strengths of a long-striding animal with suspect forelegs like Vespasian; and his fellow had been giving Blue Gown weight – he was now 11lb better off. The paper's preview ended: 'Captain Machell summed up the match so nicely that he thought Vespasian had just a neck in hand.'

The match evoked widespread astonishment. It was apparent from flag fall which horse was going to prevail. Newmarket's broad expanses might've been made to measure for a big powerful galloper like Vespasian; the writing was soon writ large. 'Vespasian looked as if he could carry the Derby winner, who appeared a little stale and hardly moved with his usual freedom,' reported *The Times*. 'He was never in it, for Vespasian pulled over him all the way and when Fordham let his head go it was all over by a couple of lengths.' Up to that point Fordham's arms were growing longer by the second. He'd even resorted to hauling Vespasian right behind Blue Gown passing the Bushes in an effort to contain him, so hard was he pulling. *The Sporting Life* likewise shook its head in wonderment: 'Vespasian never appeared brighter or better. It was palpable from the start that he could gallop over his rival at any moment. Vespasian cut him down in a common canter. Fordham actually turned in the saddle as he was passing the post and gave a glance of exultation at Blue Gown and Wells in their difficulty.'

This victory was a triumph for all involved: Vespasian, Machell and, of course, Fordham who'd upset the apple cart yet again.

Sandwiched between these victories on Michel Grove and Vespasian was the third of Fordham's trio of great matches in the 1860s: that between the two-year-old filly Lady Elizabeth and the three-year-old colt Julius at Newmarket on 11 October 1867. The events that preceded and followed this epic duel belong to the story of the 'Queen of Danebury'.

Lady Elizabeth going down to post for the New Stakes.

NINE

THE QUEEN OF DANEBURY

The velvet subtleties transmitted by Fordham's hands, his empathy with fillies and his feeling for two-year-olds found its finest expression during the summer of 1867 aboard Lady Elizabeth.

Even so, the story of Lady Elizabeth is one of the saddest in Turf history. Thirty years after Lady Elizabeth retired some judges still considered her the best two-year-old to set foot on the English Turf. Writing in 1901 Sydenham Dixon, for so long 'Vigilant' of *The Sportsman*, dared suggest she was absolutely the best two-year-old that ever lived'; and Turf historian Edward Moorhouse referred to her as 'probably the most brilliant two-year-old that ever trod the Turf'

Lady Elizabeth was bought privately (along with her dam) from ex jockey Sam Rogers. She was a bay by Trumpeter who'd won a pair of Biennials at Newmarket and Bath before finishing third in the 1859 Derby where a leg gave way, causing his retirement. As a stallion his appearance was highlighted by a small Arab-like head and ears of remarkable beauty – characteristics he passed on to his sublime daughter. She stood a trifle under 16 hands; possessed magnificent shoulders, great depth and big wide hips. Only her straight thighs and hocks offended the eye although her high-spirited, fiery demeanour constituted more than enough shortcomings on the score of temperament. She had to be led to post where she'd often grow fractious and tend to give away three or four lengths. But Lady Elizabeth proved so fast she could afford to be generous. And with George Fordham on her back she couldn't have found a better mate. After all, he'd also won on her mother, Miss Bowzer.

The 'marriage' between the flighty but beautiful Lady Elizabeth and the sympathetic George Fordham seemed one made in heaven. However, the purity of this partnership was obliged to withstand the shadiest possible influences because Lady Elizabeth was trained by the artful John Day junior for Henry, 4th Marquis of Hastings whose reckless penchant for gambling had also seen him fall under the dangerous spell of Henry Padwick.

Some say a picture paints a thousand words. Whether or not that is a universal truth, a glance at Hastings' portrait suggests occasional accuracy. It reveals a weak baby face seemingly on the verge of tears or the expression of some other extreme emotion; but a slim figure, small sensitive mouth and brown spaniel eyes were the kind of looks that set female hearts a-tremble. Yes, he was both self-centred and selfish. But this little-boy-lost persona stirred maternal instincts and could charm vultures off a carcass. One so smitten was Lady Florence Paget, the 'Pocket Venus', younger daughter of the Marquis of Anglesey, as high-spirited and spoilt as she was beautiful. That she was betrothed to Hastings's equally rich friend Henry Chaplin made not an iota of difference when Hastings turned on the charm. The morning after this privileged threesome had attended a performance of *Faust* at Covent Garden, Florence took a cab to Marshall and Snelgrove's store in Oxford Street. She went in one door and walked straight through the shop to exit by another - on the arm of Hastings. The lovesick pair went direct to St George's Church in Hanover Square to be married. Chaplin was left a note assuring him she would be the wife of Lord Hastings when he received it.

There was an underlying vulnerability about Hastings, both physical and mental. He did not enjoy the best of health. Yet he caroused endlessly; and not just in the refined atmosphere of polite society. Hastings was the epitome of the rich and feckless young aristocrat with more money than sense who surrounded himself with a coterie of venal characters eager and capable of exploiting the latter to extract the former. If it's true that people exist sad or stupid enough to bet on which of two raindrops would first reach the bottom of a window pane then Hastings would be among their number. His parents set a poor example. His father cared for nothing but hunting; his mother was a born gambler who sought her pleasures at the roulette table. Donington Castle, the Hastings seat in Leicestershire, had been in the family since the 15th century. The Scottish estates of the Earls of Loudoun, the Irish estates of the Earls of Moira and the English estates of the Earls of Rawdon and the Earls of Huntingdon augmented Hastings's wealth. 'The Marquis quickly threw himself into the pursuits which were congenial to his rank, youth and his purse,' observed *Baily's Magazine*. He loved nothing more than leading an expedition of like-minded toffs into the lowest, most notorious dives of London in search of a night's entertainment filled by smoking, cursing and swilling strong drinks while wagering cock-fights or rat-catching – followed by a restorative breakfast of mackerel fried in gin and caviar on devilled toast washed down with claret. It might be said of him that he represented the last of the Regency bucks and the first of the Edwardian swells; or, as one of his obituary notices opined, he was 'The perfect cocker.' However, burning the candle in the middle as well as both ends sealed his fate. His plans became too grandiose. His love of gambling and thirst for popular acclaim had inevitably drawn him to the raffish world of the Turf. His ambition, no less, was to break the 'Ring'. What better accomplices in this design than the Days of Danebury.

John Day junior was already an experienced trainer when introduced to the young Oxford undergraduate Henry Weysford Charles Plantagenet Rawdon Hastings in 1862. Despite his own privileged education at Winchester and Oxford, he'd been moulded in his father's image. He'd ridden a Classic winner and trained half a dozen within ten years of assuming control of Danebury. In consequence the training side of the Confederacy was secure. But by 1862 John Gully was a dying man and, in the manner of Gully replacing Bentinck, 'The Nestor of the Turf' was now in need of a replacement - preferably by someone with more money than sense. Hastings apparently suited the role to a tee. 'One of the most important acquisitions to the English Turf that has been made in decades,' declared *Baily's*. Day would be a good mentor for the young student. The servant would be the master. 'Open-hearted and confiding, he placed himself in hands he knows full well will protect his interests and his property.' The magazine had misjudged the situation entirely.

Henry, 4th Marquis of Hastings

Hastings was a pupil for a short time only. He was a quick learner. Young as he was, a good many soon came to regard him as having few superiors as a judge of racing. He'd need to be, because, betting on the colossal scale he did, very little could be left to chance. And Hastings lived at a rate that could only be maintained by unlimited wealth. Rich as he was, that equation might prove as untenable for him as Mr Micawber: much coin flowed in, but just a tad too much streamed out – resulting in misery.

Hasting's obsession with the Turf lasted six years. In 1862 he could ride through Newmarket unrecognized. In 1868 the very sight of him brought forth the cry 'The Markis - Gawd bless 'im!' Seldom having less than 50 horses in training with John Day, he might easily have made racing pay were it not for his compulsive gambling. In 1864 he won £10,000 in stakes; in 1866 it was £12,837; and a year later the enormous sum of £30,353 (*£3.6 million*). But moderation was not in the Hastings lexicon. 'Whether he wins or loses, he evinces no undue hilarity or despondency.' He blazed through the Turf firmament like a comet. Hanging to the comet's tail were, inevitably, unsavoury individuals who let go when things got too hot. And then there were innocent passengers like George Fordham whose lot it was to be Danebury's principal jockey during this infamous period.

The pattern was quickly set. In July 1862 Hastings bought, on Day's advice, a filly named Consternation. Running her in the name of 'Mr Weysford', she ran a dozen times and won twice for him, once with Fordham aboard. Hastings made plans for expansion. He came of age the following year and began exploiting a seemingly endless supply of funds. He was elected to the Jockey Club as a matter of Turf etiquette, abandoned his *nom de course*, and instantly his 'scarlet and white hoop, white cap' became a familiar sight on the racecourse. The Days had never spared their charges and for Hastings to punt with 'inside' knowledge his horses had to run frequently, irrespective of their age. A juvenile colt called Garotter, won at Northampton in March and ran a further 17 times that season. Other youngsters, Tippler and Recap, were subjected to two races on one card; the unfortunate Lady Barbara endured three races in one afternoon at Salisbury. These ordeals were necessary to Hastings's way of thinking because travelling horses was still bedevilled by poor transport networks and opportunities had to be seized where they could be found. At the smaller, 'backwoods', meetings – the Northamptons and Shrewsburys long since vanished from the *Racing Calendar* – several sweet little fish might be netted to equal any one large tastier fish landed at Newmarket, Epsom, Ascot or Goodwood.

In 1864 Hastings landed his first major coup when Ackworth netted him £70,000 with victory in the Cambridgeshire. The following year he'd hoped to win the Derby with The Duke, a 500-guineas purchase whom Day rated the best horse he ever trained. Even though it was impossible to try The Duke very often as he took so much out of himself, he made a winning debut at Stockbridge and enjoyed a very useful two-year-old campaign. Unfortunately, the colt missed the Derby with influenza and in the St Leger he overpowered Fordham when finishing fourth behind Gladiateur. Lost money, however, was soon recouped in a pair of match races at Newmarket. The following season saw The Duke win 12 of his 16 races, eight of them shared with Fordham, that icluded the Goodwood and Brighton Cups. In essence, The Duke was a miler who was able to use his burst of speed at the conclusion of stop-start staying races because in 'The Kidder' he found the perfect partner to capitalize on this attribute.

Hastings still fielded a candidate for the 1865 Derby. Incensed that his love rival Henry Chaplin had prospective runners he had to have one. Consequently, he bought a colt called Kangaroo from Henry Padwick. It had recent winning form at Newmarket and, importantly, a Derby entry. He paid the astonishing sum of £12,000 (*£1.4 million*), the highest amount ever outlaid on an English thoroughbred. 'Mr Padwick's bargains and sales have never been equalled,' observed *Baily's*, 'and would furnish a most interesting paper for the sporting writer.' Whether the animal found Day's regimen too harsh or whether it was a 'dud', Kangaroo proved a useless acquisition, and wound up breaking a fetlock joint in a steeplechase at Hambledon. Hastings, most probably, had been swindled.

Hastings was finally rewarded with a Classic in 1866, the One Thousand Guineas with Repulse – partnered by Tom Cannon owing to Fordham being sidelined with a sprained wrist. When Lecturer added the Cesarewitch at odds of 9 to 1 Hastings pocketed over £60,000. Rous had given the pony-sized Lecturer what he considered a 'stopping weight' of 7st 3lb - too low for Fordham to scale. But Rous had been duped. Lecturer was entered for the race under a false owner and he was ignorant of a significant trial at Danebury. Desperate to conceal Lecturer's true ability, Day replicated the Duke of Beaufort by rounding up all the touts and carting them off to Stockbridge's Grosvenor Arms where they were royally entertained at what has come to be known as the 'Tout's Luncheon.' Lecturer had repaid his purchase price of £600 many times over.

Hastings felt he could do no wrong. He was betting on every race he watched, often in units of £10,000. But, more dangerous even than risking such enormous sums, was his prediction to take under the odds if he really fancied a horse. And yet he still bought into the Ring's flattery: 'Heaven's been very kind to you,' one bookmaker fawned, 'for you look a fool and you ain't one.' A depressing pattern had been established. Vaulting ambition; reckless gambling; exploitative counsel; naive spending. Up one minute, down the next.

By the spring of 1867 Hastings was in freefall. His health and fortune, ravaged in equal measure by the dissolute lifestyle that left him looking older than his 24 years, had begun to nosedive. What might be interpreted as the pivotal moment in Hastings's life occurred that summer when Chaplin won the Derby with Hermit. Hastings had only the rank outsider Uncas to represent him in the race (in which Danebury fielded the favourite in Vauban with Fordham up), and had bet against Hermit as though Chaplin's horse was already on the knacker's cart. He'd debts of £120,000 (*£14.4 million*) – which included upwards of £10,000 to Chaplin. Hastings had been well and truly repaid for his betrayal. Hastings settled with all his creditors at once and in full.

Hastings's saviour was Lady Elizabeth. He owed this temporary liquidity largely to her dozen victories and associated punts. She was the brightest gem in a coronet of Danebury juveniles that sparkled throughout 1867 for Day possessed five other crackerjacks by any normal standard. Athena, an attractive chestnut filly by Stockwell, won 10 of her 14 races and featured in Fordham's Stockbridge septet; in any other yard Athena would've been the star but Danebury knew she was 11 to 18lb behind Lady Elizabeth. Europa was a chestnut filly by Lady Elizabeth's sire Trumpeter; she won six from seven in a brief career extending from Ascot to Goodwood yet was regarded two stone inferior to Lady Elizabeth. Of Danebury's colts, See-Saw won five times; another called Mameluke won Stockbridge's valuable Donnington Post Stakes; lastly, there was a backward colt called The Earl – who was fated to play a more sinister role the following season. This son of Young Melbourne was a half brother to The Duke and cost Hastings 450 guineas. He was a rather large and plain bay (possessing one white stocking on his hind leg like his elder sibling) with a common head and lop ears. Being so overgrown the few trials he was subjected to as a yearling made him out to be worthless. It needed half the season for the backward colt to get the hang of things – whereupon he won four times, including a two-length success in the Gimcrack. Each of these precocious talents was aided and abetted by the equine conjurer in chief, George Fordham.

Lady Elizabeth had run, and won, four races before Hastings' disastrous plunge on the Derby. Her career commenced in typical Danebury fashion, with two wins in as many days at Northampton in early April, quickly followed by third in the Salisbury Stakes. Bath's Weston Stakes a week later would prove a sterner test since, in the words of *Bell's Life*, the opposition included 'some good-looking, clever-shaped animals' such as John Porter's colt Blue Gown, recently victorious at the (subsequently discontinued) Ascot spring meeting, and Formosa, a filly destined to relegate Lady Elizabeth to minor status in the annals of the Turf. Lady Elizabeth had to give Blue Gown 2lb. He went off favourite at 2 to 1 with the filly at 5s.

The bitterly cold east wind buffeting the Downs contributed to an unsatisfactory start. Blue Gown got away particularly badly and Fordham, just ahead of him, saw to it that he remained trapped on the rails. In so doing, the initiative was handed to Grimston, and this game little colt made the most of it until Fordham, realizing the seriousness of the situation, got to work on his filly and snatched the decision by a short head. Commented *Baily's Magazine*: 'The fine stride and gameness of Lady Elizabeth were put into competition with the same qualities of Grimston and at the last precedence was given to the softer sex.'

Grimston faced Lady Elizabeth again at Epsom, the day after Hermit's Derby. The colt had already won once at the meeting and at the weights held a splendid chance of reversing the Bath result. After several false starts, Fordham let Lady Elizabeth stride along in front; she'd become fractious owing to the false starts and he didn't wish to restrain her. Grimston came alongside as they met the rising ground near the finish and forced a dead-heat. Lady Elizabeth looked desperately tired before the re-run, but Fordham was peerless in such circumstances. He led all the way to win the run-off by a head. Lady Elizabeth had salvaged some of Hastings' losses.

Ahead lay Ascot, the best week's racing in the year. Said one fastidious socialite: 'The Ascot is to the Derby what genteel comedy is to broad farce. All London goes to the Derby, only the West End goes to Ascot.' This snobbery flourished in spite of Queen Victoria's absence. Once a regular visitor, she'd gradually surrendered to Prince Albert's disinterest in the sport; the incident in 1854 when, becoming over-excited by the finish of a race, she'd put her head through the glass window of her box, had done little to alter Albert's opinion of Ascot's attractions. One regular visitor needing to avoid calamity was Hastings. He had to be sure Lady Elizabeth could be counted upon to play her part in the meeting's premier juvenile event, Thursday's New Stakes. To this end a secret trial was arranged at Danebury for the Tuesday beforehand. To maintain the subterfuge Day left for Ascot as usual, leaving the arrangements to his head man Joseph Enoch.

Trials were an essential ingredient of the Victorian training regimen – and, quite probably, significantly more influential than at any time since. The trial book of a Victorian trainer was more valuable than a Shakespeare first folio; deemed so vulnerable to misuse that they were frequently destroyed every few months to prevent any chance of their contents being glimpsed by the wrong people. Secreted within were the weights carried in these trials, the lead in the weight cloth equating to gold for profitable investment; information only relayed on a strictly need-to-know basis. If jockeys or touts – and ultimately even Admiral Rous if he got wind of the trial - had no knowledge of the weights carried they might be fooled. Being conversant with the weights of the lads or jockeys involved meant nothing if the weights in the saddle cloth spoke adversely; the horse with a heavier jockey who trounces the horse with a lighter jockey may not be one pound superior if the beaten horse was burdened by two stone of lead in its saddle cloth. Lads who rode in trials were never privy to the weights actually carried and were frequently locked in their dormitory in order to prevent loose lips sharing any trial information whatsoever until such time as their master (plus his owners and cronies) had secured the best price via the stable's commission agent. Of course no trial was foolproof: public form tends to be infinitely more trustworthy than private trials. Some horses try at home and refuse to do their best on the track – the 'morning glories' forever reported to be 'catching pigeons'. By contrast, the lazy worker is often invigorated by the shouting and excitement of the crowded racecourse. Nevertheless, Danebury swore by them.

This make-or-break trial took place over six furlongs on Stockbridge racecourse at the ungodly hour of 3am. Enoch still decided to take no chances; once again the touts were rounded up and driven into Stockbridge for a champagne breakfast. Lady Elizabeth received just 2lb from the three-year-old Challenge and 10lb from the five-year-old Lord Ronald; that is 27 and 32lb less than weight-for-age. Another older horse was put in to make the pace – but he could never get to the front. The filly, partnered by her usual work rider, Bob Salter (generally known as the 'stable jockey'), waited on her elders and then cruised past to win by a couple of lengths. The magnitude of this performance was not lost on Danebury. Lord Ronald had recently won the Salisbury Cup under top weight; Challenge would win five on the bounce including the Liverpool Summer Cup. There'd not be a trial by a two-year-old of this magnificence, and significance, until The Tetrarch annihilated his trial 'tackle' on these same Hampshire Downs nearly half a century later. Once the news was relayed to Hastings he lost no time in placing bets totalling £16,000 on Lady Elizabeth to win the New Stakes.

The scene was set: that Thursday, 6 June 1867, would be the happiest day of Hastings's life. The threatening weather held off; his old Oxford chum the Prince of Wales was in attendance; he felt he held a strong hand. 'The great assemblage was at its fullest and most animated,' in the words of *The Times*, when the ten runners for the Gold Cup came out onto the track. The barely 15 hands Lecturer, who made even Fordham look a giant in the saddle, had to overcome a vintage field. The strongest opposition was likely to come from the unique presence of three Oaks winners: the five-year-old Regalia, the four-year-old Tormentor and Hippia, who had defeated Achievement in the latest renewal. Hastings's cash ensured Lecturer was sent off the slight favourite at 11 to 4. Danebury ran John Davis (a winner himself of six races that season) to make a strong pace for him.

For much of the journey Fordham restrained Lecturer in the middle of the pack, keeping the three Oaks heroines under close scrutiny. Lecturer was easily picked out. He carried his head so low that it was almost clipping the grass, his extraordinary round action demanding he be shod with 'half tips' to prevent him from cutting his elbows. Then, approaching the final bend into the short straight, John Davis's role came to an end, and Tom Cannon pulled him off the rail to allow Lecturer free passage. Before Fordham could act Tommy Heartfield on Regalia snatched the gap instead. It seemed certain Regalia would prevail. Fordham had no alternative other than steady Lecturer and come round on the outside. The manoeuvre cost him a length and momentum.

'The Demon' began to justify his soubriquet. Fordham sat down into his horse and rode one of his most powerful finishes to land his gallant and willing little partner in front at the post by one and a half lengths. 'Fordham seemed literally to lift his horse in,' declared the awestruck reporter from *The Sporting Life*. It took an awful lot to upset Fordham's equanimity but he told Heartfield he'd have objected had the result not gone his way. In the words of Sydenham Dixon 'a less consummate artist than Fordham might easily have got into trouble at the finish, but the great jockey grasped the situation in an instant, and, instead of running the risk of bumping and fouling, or of getting pinned on to the rails, pulled Lecturer right back and came up on the outside. It seemed a bold thing to do when they were so close home, but his knowledge of the wonderful little bit of stuff that he had between his knees fully justified it.'

Hastings immediately invested £16,000 of the £50,000 won with Lecturer on Lady Elizabeth. Starting at evens in a field of 12, the filly broke smartly as, for once, McGeorge's flag fell at the first attempt. Fordham saw no need for restraint. Despite her 5lb penalty, he let Lady Elizabeth stride out, down the centre of the track. The further they went the more pointed the arrowhead became. She won in a canter by six lengths 'like another Blink Bonny' opined *Bell's Life* in deference to the Derby and Oaks-winning filly of 1857. 'Lady Elizabeth made such an exhibition of one or two candidates for Derby honours next year that their backers must have been disconcerted.' It was Lady Elizabeth's coronation. And her acclamation rebounded onto Hastings. Lecturer took an encore in Friday's Alexandra Plate. Hastings went back to London to celebrate. His Derby losses had been recovered. Tranquillity had returned to his gilded world, thanks in no small measure to Fordham and the 'Queen of Danebury'.

Betting opportunities there would be a-plenty before Lady Elizabeth attempted to emulate Eleanor and Blink Bonny as a Derby-winning filly. She won twice at Stockbridge in June (beating The Earl in the first) before travelling to Newmarket for the July Stakes, the oldest juvenile event in the calendar and run over a distance just short of six furlongs. The contest threw up a serious challenger in the Duke of Hamilton's filly Leonie, who'd defeated Athena for the Hamilton (Post) Stakes at Stockbridge in the run-off that spoilt Fordham's 'perfect' seven. The Duke's support for Leonie enabled Hastings to obtain odds of 5 to 4 about Lady Elizabeth, and knowing her to be at least a stone superior to Athena, he invested heavily. Fordham allowed Leonie to lead until the dip before unleashing Lady Elizabeth. 'She never suffered Leonie to touch her,' reported *The Times*, 'and won with 10lb in hand'; 'she won as if she had been doing regular work at Danebury,' added *Baily's*.

Lady Elizabeth was rested until the Middle Park Plate at Newmarket in October, the season's richest contest for youngsters. Her winning streak now stood at 11. Few people, least of all, Fordham, Day and Hastings, thought she could be beaten. While it was true her behaviour at the start often cost her several lengths, it was of no consequence because nothing could live with her once she found her stride. Fifteen opposed, 'altogether a finer lot of two-year-olds has not been seen for some years.' These included Formosa (winner of three races since Bath, including a victory over Leonie and Athena in the Chesterfield Stakes), Mat Dawson's leggy filly Lady Coventry, and three from the up-and-coming yard of another graduate of the Danebury 'academy' in John Porter – Blue Gown (an Ascot winner), Rosicrucian and Green Sleeve. 'The amount of money that went on

Lady Elizabeth was large even for these gambling days,' said *The Times*. 'Lord Hastings put down the money as if the race was over.' He'd backed his filly to win £50,000.

All was not well, however, with the filly's partner. Fordham was struggling with depression. He should have been a happy man. He was about to become a father for the third time. But a family tragedy had struck. Shortly before the birth of Blanche Elizabeth, the Fordhams were devastated by the sudden loss of three-year-old Penelope, who died on 9 September from sepsis following gastric fever. One cannot imagine the ordeal endured by Fordham and his heavily preganant wife as they watched their little girl suffer a painful and prolonged death. The mite was in agony for four days as the poison seeped through her system. Fordham was grief-stricken. This most sensitive of human beings was brought to his knees. He quit the saddle for a month, missing the St Leger meeting and not returning until the first Newmarket autumn meeting on 24 September. When he felt able to resume his judgement and his confidence were in tatters. Prior to the Middle Park he suffered a run-off defeat aboard The Earl in the Bedford Stakes; quickly followed by a losing match against his perennial bête noir, Tom Chaloner.

A day of teeming rain did nothing to dampen the even-money favourite's antics at the start. Lady Elizabeth repeatedly broke away and when the flag finally dropped she was almost sitting on her haunches. Fordham was seemingly unperturbed and with less than two furlongs to run he still had the filly's head pulled round to his knee. But this was a race as rare as a dodo. He'd miscalculated. 'The Kidder' had got things wrong. She was left with too much ground to recover. Lady Elizabeth trailed in fifth behind Green Sleeve. *Baily's Magazine* stated what everyone was thinking: 'It is years since Danebury sustained so decisive a blow. John Day was flabbergasted.'

Fordham shouldered the blame for the filly's defeat. The derision of those speaking through their pockets had given a voice to his paternal grief. It was as if he was determined to atone for his daughter's death through an act of contrition. 'I ought to have won many a length,' he muttered. *The Sporting Life*, however, was quick to share out the blame for the filly's reverse by stating 'We never saw an animal run more like a non-stayer, as Lady Elizabeth was "all out" at the foot of the hill. Fordham is too sound a judge to have eased her for such a stake and such heavy "plunging" behind the horse had she not been fairly and squarely exhausted.'

Hastings was crestfallen; not so much at the blow to his pocket as that to his heart. He was seen to turn ashen and to stagger as if about to fall. 'Still, when we consider how often Lady Elizabeth has been called upon during the season,' wrote one chronicler, 'her having to lower her colours cannot create much wonderment.' Her owner was determined she be given the opportunity of redeeming herself as quickly as possible. He couldn't bank on Lecturer bailing him out this time. After adding the Hurstbourne and Stamford Cups to his tally, the little horse's endeavours caught up with him and a string of defeats demonstrated he was not within a stone of his proper form. Only Lady Elizabeth might replenish the Hastings coffers. Consequently, a match was arranged between her and the Duke of Newcastle's colt Julius for £1,000 a side, to be run over the last six furlongs of the Rowley Mile two days after the Middle Park. The naysayers shook their heads. Not in awe but in disbelief bordering on despair. This would be the filly's thirteenth race of the season.

Julius was a three-year-old who'd finished behind Lecturer in the Gold Cup. Since then he'd run third in the St Leger and won the Cesarewitch carrying eight stone, a record for that age. Admiral Rous set his weight at 8st 11lb; John Daley had the mount. The filly, one year younger, was allotted 8st 2lb, which amounted to a stone more than weight-for-age. At those weights Julius had to start favourite (11 to 10 on), enabling Hastings to wager with abandon. Fordham, too, was on a recovery mission. What with riding a rare stinker in the Middle Park and tasting defeat on The Earl he owed Hastings a victory.

The match was a classic of its kind with no quarter asked or given. Nose to nose and tail to tail they galloped toward the stands. 'They ran locked together to within three or four strides of home,' observed *The Times*, 'whereupon Fordham "put on the screw" and landed Lady Elizabeth the winner by the shortest of heads.' The exhausted filly trudged through a melee of admirers cheering and calling out "Urrah for Lady Elizabeth!' *Baily's* correspondent was so overcome his hyperbole extended beyond even its own habitually florid standards: 'The most sensational match since Voltigeur and The Dutchman! Fordham rode as desperately as if he had felt a garroter's claw on the point of clasping his neck! Amidst shouting so loud the Clerk of Ely Cathedral was compelled to stuff his ears with cotton, Lady Elizabeth's number was hoisted and Danebury went its way rejoicing!'

To the greatest private performance put up by a two-year-old Lady Elizabeth could now add the finest public performance accomplished by a two-year-old – thanks to the priceless assistance of 'The Demon'. Honour was restored. Both owner and jockey were convinced Lady Elizabeth would win the Derby of 1868.

Others were less sure. One dissenting voice belonged to the 'Special Commissioner' of *The Sportsman*:

> I do not believe that Lady Elizabeth will train on into the extraordinary three-year-old some people imagine, for she appears to be of a fretful disposition, and though her greyhound like symmetry is about perfection for speed itself, she looks just like one of those early and precocious animals that we see the best of as two-year-olds.

Hastings ended the 1867 season as leading owner with winnings of £30,451 – of which Lady Elizabeth had contributed £9,165. However, despite his filly's efforts, Hastings was in deep financial trouble. He'd lost an estimated £90,000 over the various Newmarket meetings that autumn; and fuelled by alcohol he was also losing on the throw of the dice or the turn of a card at Crockford's of an evening. He was more heavily in debt than ever. He'd already sold his Scottish estates for £300,000 (*£36 million*). Next it was his racehorses. They were auctioned at Stockbridge racecourse on 23 November. He could not bear to part with Lady Elizabeth or The Earl, and they were bought-in for 6,500 and 6,100 guineas respectively. Even this additional 37,495 guineas could not save him. In just five years on the Turf, and despite numerous good days in his battle with the Ring, not least on the recent Gold Cup day, Hastings had somehow managed to lose £½ million (*£60 million*). That a member of the Jockey Club was one of the Turf's biggest defaulters had not gone unnoticed. He was left with no alternative but apply to Padwick for a loan. He was instantly accommodated, of course. But in addition to the normal securities, the Shylock demanded a bill of sale on various other assets – including The Earl.

For Danebury 1867 was an *annus mirabilis*. The stable had won 146 races, a record that stood until 1987. At Goodwood alone it won 14 races with just 16 horses – causing the prices of Danebury horses to be shorter than they might have been and left some sections of the Press suggesting that 'whether John Day likes it or not, unless the handicapping of his horses is altered, the members of the stable will have to race by themselves.' For Hastings it had not quite been an *annus horribilis*. However his ultimate salvation quite possibly lay with the apple of his eye and a blind faith in George Fordham's wizardry continuing to get the best out of her.

But his immediate rescue depended on Henry Padwick.

The Ring at Ascot.

TEN

THE SPIDER AND THE FLY

Any gauche spendthrift who fell into Padwick's clutches might expect to be ruined. Earlier in the decade John Bayton Starkey had been fleeced of £300,000 (*£36 million*) and his Wiltshire estate of Spye Park within six years of becoming involved with Padwick. Harry Hastings would be no different – particulary if Lady Elizabeth failed to deliver.

The filly wintered badly – and there's little doubt the tremendous battle with Julius had broken her. She grew nervous and irritable. She'd turned sour. The grand 'doer' became a delicate feeder. Day was afraid to try her and confirm his worst fears that the strenuous juvenile campaign had sapped her spirit and that she'd not trained-on from two to three – a tendency common among hard-raced juvenile fillies. Whenever Hastings came down to watch her gallop, excuses were made for her not to appear. In the early spring she was rumoured to have gone poorly in a rough spin with Athena – which later events suggested may not have been a total disgrace for the latter proved she'd trained on by achieving places in the One Thousand Guineas and Oaks before winning the Coronation at Ascot, the Park Hill at Doncaster and the Grand Duke Michael at Newmarket. We do not know whether Lady Elizabeth was partnered by Fordham in this work; this was usually Salter's job. Hindsight would suggest not. But it's impossible to think he was ignorant of these lacklustre displays. He knew too many people at Danebury to be kept in the dark.

The first harbinger of things to come arrived in April: Lady Elizabeth missed the Guineas. Yet still money poured on her for the Derby, her odds contracting from 6 to 1 to 3s and 7 to 4 by Derby Day thanks to the stream of fictitious reports emanating from Danebury concerning her well-being and continued prowess: 'Lady Elizabeth has wonderfully improved, having thickened a good deal and laid on muscle in abundance,' telegraphed the 'Special Commissioner' of *The Sporting Life*. 'She stands about 16 hands and I am pleased to report that instead of the vicious and bad-tempered animal some would make her out to be, she is as quiet as a lamb. In her work she takes no notice of anything except her companion, Athena, and the two are almost inseparable while they are at exercise. She is pleasing her trainer in every way.' One or two scribes adopted a more cynical stance: 'I take off my hat to that darling,' said *Mr Punch*, 'and if wishes were horses and beggars could ride, I'm the beggar that would ride her into glory and win the battle of Hastings.' And an anonymous poet in *Bell's Life* predicted:

> *For Lady Elizabeth in spite of her wins*
> *Will have to cave in when the fighting begins*
> *And all you gay gallants of old London town*
> *Must put your spare cash on old bonny Blue Gown.*

On a warm May afternoon Day had gained permission from the Stewards for Lady Elizabeth to be saddled in Sherwood's stables near the start – ostensibly to spare unnecessary strain on her temperament but most likely to keep her condition a secret for as long as possible. There she waited with stablemate Cock of the Walk for company. Hastings, now off the defaulter's list and temporarily solvent, strolled across the Downs arm-in-arm with Day (Padwick, naturally, in tow) to see his sweetheart. He was greeted by the sight of a fretful filly in a muck sweat. To any horseman the signs were ominous. Fordham, certainly, would've known there and then that the game was up. He cooed to her. But the 'sweet nuthins' had no effect. He abandoned any thought of a preliminary canter and did not mount till she reached the start. She bucked him off the instant he dropped into the saddle. 'Immediately Fordham got her to post,' reported *The Morning Post*, 'she put her head between her legs and kept sawing away at the reins to the great dislike of her jockey.'

The word soon spread through the enclosures. The bookmakers were prepared. Their bush telegraph was seldom wrong. They were not stupid. They'd guessed for weeks that something must be amiss with the favourite. The evidence was now plain. The Ring reacted swiftly. Lady Elizabeth's odds lengthened from 5 to 4 to 7 to 4 while those of Blue Gown shortened from 6 to 1 to 7 to 2.

The skies were clear and the silks stood out brightly as McGeorge sent them on their way. But the scarlet and white aboard Lady Elizabeth were never seen with a chance in the race. She got away all right in spite of a recalcitrance that encompassed further attempts to send Fordham airborne. She was done for by the mile post and finished one of the last three (of 30) behind Blue Gown. The lovely rhythmic action of her two-year-old days had gone. 'The Derby showed us that an animal which had won 11 of her 12 engagements is not worth a £50 note,' the *Post* noted caustically. Another newspaper described her as looking like 'a dried-up bag of bones'.

The public was told that Day and everyone connected with Danebury could not believe their eyes. She had reportedly 'galloped fine' on the Monday and had not been out of Enoch's sight ever since – scotching any tittle-tattle about her having been nobbled. But one face which betrayed acute chagrin and vexation was that of George Fordham. 'Fordham will look on the Epsom Derby as proverbially unlucky for him,' lamented the *Post*, 'for while called upon to ride in the French Derby and win, he invariably has the mortification of a disappointing mount at Epsom.' On this occasion not even the worst grouch could blame him for the abject failure of this Derby favourite - as Hastings was quick to inform reporters: 'Not the slightest blame should be attached to Fordham.' Lady Elizabeth was sent out on the Friday to fulfil her Oaks engagement. Fordham had seen enough. He'd another iron in the fire, his Guineas partner Formosa. He begged off Lady Elizabeth; she finished tailed off with Tom Cannon aboard as Fordham and Formosa won in a canter.

It seemed matters couldn't get any worse. But they did. The fact that Lady Elizabeth could scarcely raise a gallop in the Derby smelt fishy. The fact that The Earl (who'd beaten Blue Gown at Newmarket in April) arrived at Epsom only to be scratched from the Derby at the eleventh hour and was then sent over to France to win the Grand Prix de Paris ponged like the hold of a Grimsby trawler.

Fordham was winning France's greatest race for the second year in a row. In fact, he enjoyed a day to remember. In the race preceding the Grand Prix he was engaged to ride the Duke of Hamilton's Cristal in the Prix de la Ville de Paris, a handicap over two miles. He won 'cleverly by a length'. For the day's showpiece he'd been obliged to forego the mount on his Prix du Jockey-Club winner

Suzerain who, at 3 to 1, was regarded the main threat to The Earl, a hot favourite at 5 to 4 on. The colt looked the part, fully living up to his name. He circled the paddock area, observed *The Sportsman*, 'with a regular peacocky strut and looked every inch a gentleman.' The Earl looked like a Derby winner and won the Grand Prix like one. The seven runners got away at the first attempt; Fordham kept the favourite tucked in the shadows as Sedan led at a slow pace past the windmill. Entering the straight Suzerain took it up amid a Gallic roar of 'Suzerain wins!' But his position was only on sufferance. Fordham 'clucked' and The Earl swept into the lead. Though Suzerain chased all the way to the line he never got closer than a length. This was a third victory for England in six renewals of the Grand Prix for the vast influx of English visitors to crow about; and, in the presence of the Imperial family, in the words of *The Times*, 'it was not altogether satisfactory to the French.' *The Sportsman* chose to applaud the jockey: 'Fordham has now become as much a hero in France as he is in England. The fates are against his winning the greatest of our three-year-old races but this is fully made up to him by his victories on French soil – two winners of the French Derby and now two winners of the Grand Prix.'

The Earl had trounced the French Derby winner with the authority and panache of a Derby winner. It appeared Hastings would've had his desperately needed Derby win after all if only he'd not heeded, averred *The Times*, 'friends and advisors who assisted him to forfeit all claim to the character of a sportsman while preventing him from retrieving his fortune.'

Fordham returned home to read newspaper reports like the above that bordered on the libellous. Day must've known Lady Elizabeth had lost all semblance of form, yet he allowed Padwick to persuade Hastings that withdrawing the colt from the Derby was in his best interests because 'Lady Elizabeth was nearly a stone better than The Earl.' That The Earl was withdrawn from the Derby was attributed to Day, Padwick and Hill, having laid so much money against the colt the previous year, when they were confident of victory with Lady Elizabeth, they'd have wound up losing on the race. The Ring was not bothered one iota: it lost over Blue Gown but its liabilities were much worse over Lady Elizabeth; and the public wept no tears because it had plunged on Blue Gown.

'Vigilant', lead writer in *The Sportsman*, was beside himself:

> Amidst the almost unprecedented features of a week which will ever be memorable in the history of the Turf, and which no true sportsman will ever regard without deep dissatisfaction, not the least noticeable was the proceedings in reference to The Earl, which, it is not too much to say, have aroused deeper disgust and called forth more general condemnation than anything that has for a long time occurred in connection with the sport. Was it necessary for his Grand Prix preparation that he should be conveyed with lady Elizabeth to Epsom and there flashed in the eyes of the whole sporting world? Those who have stated she looked 'a fine powerful mare' must surely have been describing The Earl by mistake!
>
> I ask anyone who heard the significant hissing with which the Marquis of Hastings and Lady Elizabeth were greeted if his subsequent conduct does not justify the severest condemnation. I admit with the utmost candour that this language is severe, but it may perhaps be remembered that a great moralist expressed his belief that one may be angry without sinning. I have no doubt that I shall again be accused by his lordship's toadies of 'meanness', 'cowardice', 'scurrility', 'insolence', 'intimidation' and 'pusillanimity' because I once more venture to protest, in the name of the sport, against a course of conduct which I cannot help believing is scandalous.

When The Earl won no fewer than three races at Ascot within three days of returning from France (the Ascot Derby, the St James's Palace Stakes and a Biennial) while Lady Elizabeth finished last of eight in the Prince of Wales's Stakes, the storm broke with the ferocity of a hurricane. Admiral Rous was overheard to say that if he'd taken as much laudanum as Lady Elizabeth had been given he'd have been 'a dead man'. The remark was reproduced in *The Sporting Life* and then quoted in the *Pall Mall Gazette* – and gave rise on 15 June to the Admiral writing his infamous 'Spider and the Fly' letter to *The Times*.

Rous had not digested the lessons of the 'Tarragona Affair' six years earlier. His tongue was as loose as ever. He denied the laudanum comment, but otherwise pilloried Danebury. He maintained the Days knew in March that Lady Elizabeth had lost her form and that they reversed a commission to back her for the One Thousand Guineas. Moreover, Hastings was repeatedly denied the opportunity to watch her gallop because 'had he seen her move, the bubble would have been burst.'

He continued:

> Lord Hastings has been shamefully deceived. She has never been able to gallop the whole year. But the 'touters' reported she was 'going like a bird'. £10 will make a horse fly if a trainer wishes to make it rise in the market. With respect to scratching The Earl, Lord Westmoreland came up to town early to beseech Lord Hastings not to commit such an act. On his arrival in Grosvenor Square, he met Mr Hill going to Weatherbys with the order in his pocket to scratch The Earl; and Padwick closeted with Lord Hastings. In justice to the Marquis of Hastings, I state that he stood to win £35,000 by The Earl and did not hedge his stake money. Then you will ask 'Why did he

scratch him?' What can a poor fly demand from the spider in whose web he is enveloped?

The Sporting Life continued to back the Admiral: 'The Earl must have been a "corpse" all winter. It will never be forgotten how the "spiders" having got the owner into their web and foisting a gaunt skeleton called Lady Elizabeth on the public sent The Earl to Epsom only for the iniquitous purpose of extorting every shilling out of backers and then to scratch him on the eve of the race.'

Hastings strongly rebutted any suggestion he'd been duped. For his part, Padwick, 'The Spider', tried every dodge he knew to escape any culpability. He responded in *The Times*:

> I had no control over, or interest in the horse, and I was no party to his being scratched. Lord Hastings, in the presence of the gentleman I have mentioned (Lord Westmoreland and others), accepted exclusive responsibility for the act. I beg most unhesitatingly to state that I had not betted one shilling either on or against The Earl for his Derby engagement.

Hastings dispatched his own riposte to the 'greatest astonishment' engendered by Rous:

> I can only characterise that letter as a tissue of misrepresentation from first to last. There is no single circumstance mentioned as regards my two horses, Lady Elizabeth and The Earl, correctly stated. I wish also to add that so far from being shamefully deceived, The Earl was scratched by my express authority and that no one either prompted me, or suggested to me, to adopt that course.

Events hurried to a close. Day consulted his solicitors. Padwick badgered the Jockey Club to instigate 'a strict investigation' into matters surrounding The Earl owing to the 'abuse and imputations' cast on him. Hastings owed the Ring £40,000; his wife had fallen out of love with him; he backed The Earl for the St Leger with as much as he could raise but the colt broke down on his near-fore in a stripped gallop six days beforehand and missed the race – a misfortune regarded as retributive justice by Danebury's enemies and critics. The colt had cut such a wretched figure following his four races in five days with a journey to France thrown in that on seeing him arrive back at Danebury the normally hard-hearted Enoch was rendered close to tears. The Earl never ran again.

On 19 October Hastings paid a last visit to Newmarket. He was wheeled around in a basket chair and watched Fordham bring Athena home the winner of the Grand Duke Michael Stakes. But, thankfully, he didn't return to see Lady Elizabeth and Fordham finish third of five in a lowly £100 plate. Three weeks later he was dead, his body wasted by drink (officially he died of kidney disease) and his soul destroyed by gambling. He was 26 years- old. His will was proved at £90,000, but there were liabilities outstanding. His last words epitomized his tragic tale: 'Hermit's Derby broke my heart. But I didn't show it, did I?'

His obituary in the *Daily News* was compiled by Henry Hall Dixon and began : 'That poor coroneted youth who had crowded into six years more Corinthian excitement and weightier Turf cares than many "fast men" know in a lifetime, has laid down his weary load. A craving for the odds had really become a disease. He worshipped chance with all the ardour of a fanatic. His public coups were often so brilliant...but the Ring had marked him for their own and never left him.'

Baily's Magazine professed to have seen it all coming: 'We had hoped that the first burst of recklessness might have succumbed to the entreaties and warnings of reason and that the season of reflection might have cooled the hot spring-like tide of youth. He was only his own enemy and surely bore the responsibilities of the chicanery of others upon his shoulders. He, no doubt, at the end of his career, saw his folly, but there was no time given to him to carry a Reform Bill.'

Day's suit against Rous was never heard: his evidence, and that of Padwick, under oath, would've been fascinating to say the least. The combatants settled out of court. In January of 1869 Rous wrote a half-baked apology to Day, which Day insisted was published in *The Times*. Rous and Day later made up; Rous never apologized to Padwick. 'Now we trust Admiral Rous will write no more letters to the newspapers,' chided *Baily's*, 'and John Day bring no more such favourites to the post as Lady Elizabeth for the Derby.' Within a few years the trainer was himself in financial bother that demanded Padwick's intervention. Before his death in 1879, plagued with gout and ill-temper, Padwick was himself skewered by the ruin of the Duke of Newcastle which cost him £60-70,000. His passing was largely unacknowledged by most Turf writers of the day; the less said about him the better. The odour from his dealings with Hastings lingered. One writer who did stick his head above the parapet was *Baily's* 'Van Driver': 'The death of Mr Padwick removes from the scene a name for the last 30 years or more intimately associated, for good or evil, with Turf history. Those who knew him well esteemed him for warmth of heart and general kindness of disposition for which the outside world hardly gave him credit.'

Hastings' widow sold The Earl but kept Lady Elizabeth. The filly ran once more, in May 1869, at Northampton, ridden by Cannon. She came nowhere. Sent to the paddocks her first foal was born dead, and she was sold to Hungary's Imperial Stud for £3,000. She had two foals of no worth. But her story did end on a sunny note.

Christopher-Joachim Lefevre paid £300 to install her at Chamant with his other broodmares. The change of scenery failed to improve Lady Elizabeth's record in the paddocks for, as one visitor from the *Pall Mall Gazette* recorded, 'she fairly laid herself open to the reproach of barrenness and she may be regarded as a singular instance of unfortunate horseflesh.'

The gods of racing were cruel to Lady Elizabeth. Her contemporary Formosa won four Classics, yet she was Lady Elizabeth's inferior at two. Lady Elizabeth was comfortably six lengths better at two than her stable-mate Athena whom Formosa beat by three lengths in the Guineas. How fillies 'train on' from two to three poses one of the Turf's eternal conundrums. Formosa did; Lady Elizabeth clearly didn't. Although their generation has tended to be written down as a below average crop, it's not fanciful to suggest that had Lady Elizabeth been trained by someone like Mat Dawson or John Porter for an owner like Lord Falmouth or the Duke of Westminster, to name just two sets of alternative connections, she would've won any Classics for which they started her in the manner of a Wheel of Fortune or a Shotover.

The players moved on with their lives. After barely 18 months of widowhood, the 'Pocket Venus' married Sir George Chetwynd, adding weight to the adage 'horses for courses.' John Day lived on till 1882, his eyesight failing him toward the end; the Duke of Beaufort paid £100 for his old trainer to have an operation in an effort to stave off blindness but it was to no avail. Rous sailed on. 'It's a very odd thing,' he maintained, 'I lose my way now, going from Grafton Street to Berkeley Square, but I can still handicap.' As he entered his 80s, increasingly deaf in reality as he'd so often been to entreaty, some of his handicaps contained the odd 'blot'. But, as *Baily's* mused, finding an adequate replacement wouldn't be easy: 'His successor will be fortunate if he preserve to one half the extent of popularity which Admiral Rous has enjoyed among all classes of the racing community and which has rendered his name a household word.' The Admiral passed away in June 1877. It's been calculated that the 41 years service he gave the Turf had enriched the Jockey Club by £40,000. During that period he was, to quote the Duke of Beaufort, 'The Head of the Racing World.'

So ended the sordid drama of the 'Spider and the Fly'. The only person to emerge from it with reputation unscathed was George Fordham.

Buckstone

ELEVEN

CLASSIC HOODOOS

'Another dreadfully unlucky mount for Fordham, who cannot rid himself of the spell which seems to hang over him for the Derby and St Leger.'

That was the comment from *The Sporting Life* following Captivator's dismal performance in the Leger of 1870. But, in truth, it could have been printed after all too many of Fordham's experiences at Epsom and Doncaster. His record in the two premier Classics made grim reading. From 22 Derby rides he won just once – despite partnering five favourites. This miserable tale was replicated by 22 appearances in the St Leger yielding three seconds, two thirds and no victory at all – in spite of riding two favourites. Fordham could barely put a foot wrong at Newmarket where he triumphed in ten Guineas. But at Epsom and Doncaster he was hexed.

Baily's Magazine felt for him: 'Certainly Fordham has been unfortunate in the big races as he has been lucky in the minor ones; and as increase of age brings with it generally a corresponding amount of patience, we have no fear of the future for him in respect to the rich prizes of Doncaster and Epsom.'

Nevertheless, Fordham might be forgiven for wondering whether the 'hoodoos' would ever be lifted.

***

To begin with Fordham appeared destined to hit the bulls-eye at Doncaster. On his St Leger debut in 1857 he came third on the 8 to 1 chance Tournament, trained by Dick Drewitt. Tournament was travelling so well down the far straight that Fordham took a pull – only to discover he couldn't really get him properly going again. Four years later he occupied the same spot on Tom Parr's Kildonan. The following season of 1862 yielded his best opportunity thus far. He rode the 3 to1 favourite Buckstone for James Merry. Their principal rival was Tom Chaloner on The Marquis.

The Marquis and Buckstone had met in the Derby where the former, starting favourite on the strength of his victory in the Two Thousand Guineas, beat Buckstone by one and a half lengths for second place behind the rank outsider Caractacus. Although Buckstone was on the narrow side and lacked quality, he possessed a lovely smooth action that appeared more suited to Doncaster flat terrain and long straight. Despite the news that the colt's preparation had been hindered by him throwing a curb, the substitution of Fordham for Harry Grimshaw on Buckstone saw the two horses swap places in the market for the Leger. The afternoon did not begin auspiciously for Fordham: he came off second best in a match aboard a filly belonging to James Merry. This was one owner Victorian jockeys did not want to cross.

Viewed through the long lens of history James Merry appears as nothing less than a nasty piece or work. Although said to have been an ignorant and ill-informed man, he must have possessed a rich latent vein of common sense or he would never have prospered as he did. 'In Scotland "mechanical princes" are few and far between,' noted *Baily's Magazine*, 'but as a representative of their class Mr James Merry stands out in bold relief, taking as high a position in the community as he does this side of the border in the sporting world.' Merry's business, for instance, survived the failure of the Western Bank of Scotland where others crashed.

Merry's father was an itinerant Scottish pedlar who had the good fortune to stumble across rich sources of Lanarkshire coal. By the time he handed over the business to his son it was worth in excess of £1 million; and quickly augmented by the exploitation of local ironstone. Merry became the world's leading ironmaster, employing over 6,000 workers. Money certainly did nothing to soften James Merry. He was mean, hard and suspicious; as hard-natured as he was hard-featured. He much preferred cock-fighting (at one point he kept over a thousand cocks) to horse-racing – although nothing gave him greater pleasure than seeing one of his horses defeat something carrying the colours of a privileged aristocrat. If a man is measured by the company he keeps Merry came up exceedingly short. His closest associates were a wine merchant called Norman Buchanan who sponged off him remorselessly, and the retired prize-fighter Tass Parker who acted as his minder and enforcer. Not unsurprisingly he was never elected to the Jockey Club, though he was elected to Parliament for the Scottish seat of Falkirk Burghs. Merry's election had much to do with his butler who always accompanied him at the hustings on the distinct possibility his master would wind up in dire need of prompting. At one such rally Merry was asked about his position with regard to the Decalogue, but baffled by this reference to the Ten Commandments gave the answer 'I am for abolishing them all.' Much frowning and laughter ensued which his butler had his work cut out to quosh.

Merry, however, can claim to be Scotland's first Turf 'great'. His colours of 'black, yellow cap' first appeared in 1838 but his successes were attributable to the wisdom and judgement of others – namely his trainers. And of them there were several – men of the calibre of William Day, James Waugh, Mat Dawson and Robert Peck - because he distrusted each and every one of them. Yet his trainers provided him with a conveyor belt of big winners: a brace in the Derby, St Leger and Two Thousand Guineas; plus the Oaks. If reverses occurred when the money was down, excuses were sought and heads rolled. He was equally capricious toward jockeys, to the point of replacing Jem Goater on Lord of the Isles with Tom Aldcroft for the 1855 Two Thousand Guineas as the former was about to leave the weighing room in his silks. Although Aldcroft won that Classic by a neck, he was summarily accused of not trying after Lord of the Isles only finished third in the Derby; and, for good measure, Merry removed all his horses from William Day.

Consequently, Fordham must've felt Merry's hot breath on the back of his neck when bringing Buckstone to challenge The Marquis at the head of the straight. The pair immediately engaged in a sustained battle of wills. 'Never have we seen Fordham ride so desperately,' opined *Baily's*, 'for both private and public considerations urged him to beat his rival whose rise is enough to make any jockey jealous. Accordingly, he did all he knew; and it was clear which possessed the most patience would win.' *The Sporting Life* was similarly awed: 'To say that the two horses ran literally locked together is inadequately to express our meaning. The riding of Chaloner and Fordham was brilliant in the extreme for each, as if doubting the gameness of his horse, was afraid to move but sat in the saddle with hands and seat as firm as iron.' *The Morning Post* agreed: 'Head and head lay the two favourites, neither rider daring scarcely to move lest his steed should suffer.'

Just when Buckstone seemed to have got the upper hand, Chaloner drew one last effort from The Marquis and his mount proved the doughtier stayer. The crowd shouted 'dead heat!' But it was The Marquis's number 11 that was raised. The margin was given as a head. Fordham had no other option than face the music, and trust the future would offer another opportunity to land the St Leger.

Lady Luck had not finished toying with Fordham in the St Leger. His nadir came in 1868. Although Fordham had won three Classics on the wonderful filly Formosa, in the hours before the St Leger he got off her to ride Paul Jones, a horse belonging to his friend and ally George Hodgman. His decision was motivated as much by the colt's performance in a trial prior to the Leger as the adverse rumours of the filly's well-being. Thanks to that trial Fordham forfeited a Classic that would've broken his St Leger hoodoo.

Hodgman acquired Paul Jones as a yearling for 100 guineas. Like Formosa he was bred by James Cookson; by Buccaneer out of a Chanticleer mare, albeit his coat was brown not her dark chestnut. He was a colt of great bone, perhaps a trifle coarse, but one in whom his owner entertained great optimism. Paul Jones was still short of being cherry-ripe when Hodgman started him in the Mile Nursery at Goodwood which he won by a neck. At the commencement of the 1868 season Paul Jones was aimed at the Chester Cup; and after trialling impressively he carried £1,000 of Hodgman's money successfully at odds of 4 to 1. 'There have been equal certainties in racing, of course,' said the owner. 'I question, however, whether a greater has existed in connection with a handicap.' The Derby was a different proposition. He was sent off third best in the market behind Lady Elizabeth and Blue Gown and didn't feature. Paul Jones was a fine 'doer' and Hodgman thought him 'beefy'. He instructed his trainer, Balchin, to increase the colt's work load with a view to targeting the St Leger. To this end, Paul Jones was tried in late August with a three-year-old filly called Maesllwch that had won at York and finished third in the Yorkshire Oaks to Leonie; he gave her 2st 7lb and still beat her hollow. A form line to Formosa through the smart Leonie stated he'd a rattling chance of winning the St Leger. A confident Hodgman invested £1,000 to win £37,000: 'When I laid myself out for a coup I was not in the habit of practising self-delusion.'

Following The Earl's defection, Formosa became an increasingly firm favourite, her odds shortening to 3 to 1 by the eve of the race. At this point Fordham was still scheduled to partner her. But he was well aware of Paul Jones' trial – and must've been mightily impressed. Once rumours began circling about Formosa being lame he immediately abandoned the filly. Paul Jones' odds were slashed from 40 to 1 to 100 to 15. The ride on Formosa went to Tom Chaloner. When she appeared looking an absolute picture and as fit as a flea ('in the perfection of blooming condition' according to *The Times*), Fordham's heart must've sank.

It's always trotted out as a 'fact' that Fordham hated Epsom. If so he must've despised Doncaster because he confided in Sir John Astley that he distrusted Doncaster more than Epsom. The bend into the long home straight, he averred, was an ambush in waiting. He maintained that horses invariably swing wide at Doncaster, leaving gaps up the inner. He'd once seized such a gap only to see it closed in front of him by horses veering back toward the rail; he was repeatedly baulked and barely survived being brought down. Accordingly, as at Epsom, he preferred to be in front and free of trouble rounding that turn.

It was in this position that binoculars picked up Paul Jones. The Spy had led the field by six lengths down the back straight with both Formosa and Paul Jones toward the rear – the best place to be off such a fast pace. But Fordham pushed Paul Jones through the field and into the lead by the time the turn was reached and The Spy had weakened. Chaloner was more patient. Making up his ground steadily, he brought Formosa up to the leader's girths and waited. Fordham's thoughts can be imagined as he saw Formosa's chestnut head beside him. If those rumours of her health were groundless, he and Paul Jones were staring at defeat. Chaloner gave Formosa a kick in the belly 100 yards out and she cruised past Paul Jones to win her fourth Classic by two easy lengths. Chaloner was Fordham's Leger nemesis once again. 'Fordham in the last stride or two,' said *The Sportsman*, 'finding himself dead beaten, seemed to "chuck" up Paul Jones' head in disgust.'

Bell's Life crowed:

> We may note that the absurd rumour of Formosa being lame arose simply from the circumstances that in consequence of the ground being somewhat slippery after the rain on Tuesday, the trainer of the mare very wisely declined to gallop her round the course, and subsequently fancying she had trodden on and picked up a stone, he raised her foot to examine it. This was sufficient. Away went touts and would-be touts, and soon the news spread like wildfire that Formosa was lame, whereas all the time she was as sound as a bell.

Only a filly is eligible to win four Classics. Formosa was the first to achieve the feat. Just Sceptre (1902) would match her. And she was the first to achieve the Fillies Triple Crown. Fordham had missed making history. That realization, as much as anything, ensured he took defeat badly. And, true to character, he blamed himself. 'I thought I had the race safe and took matters a bit easy,' he told Hodgman. 'If I had, as I should have done, come clean away, I must have won in a canter. I have lost you the Leger and all that money. I shall never forgive myself.' The 'money' referred to was not only Hodgman's bet to win £37,000 and the winning stakes of £5,825, but also the potential sale of Paul Jones to an Austrian buyer for a further £5,000. 'I'm glad I've won,' William Graham told Hodgman, 'but my filly was amiss, and I went for yours!' The spirit merchant gave Hodgman an 18-gallon cask of whisky with which to drown his sorrows; doubtless Fordham would've resorted to some of 'Nicholson's London Gin' to do likewise.

Fordham partnered only one other favourite in the St Leger besides Buckstone: Lefevre's Drummond in 1872. By now the Leger crowds had grown out of all proportion thanks to 120 express trains and 90 day excursions bringing 35,000 strangers who'd exploited the advent of third-class railway tickets. Doncaster was hard-pressed to absorb them. 'The sporting capital of Yorkshire stands in need of many things - good hotels, reasonable lodgings and tender-hearted landlords and landladies,' lamented *The Times*, 'but we fear there is not much chance of any of the these benefits.' Drummond's form was nothing out of the ordinary. He'd won an uncompetitive Bognor Stakes at Goodwood and the three-runner Sussex Cup at Brighton. The chestnut's elevation to joint market leader at 11 to 4 was inspired by rumours of an outstanding trial back in Newmarket with his owner's decent six-year-old stayer Dutch Skater; and the fact that, in the dismissive words of *The Times*, 'the rest of the field might well deserve the terrible epithet of "rotten", which is so constantly heard on the Turf, as it is one of the worse ever known.' The one exception was easy to spot: the giant Prince Charlie, winner of the Two Thousand Guineas. When sent off favourite for the Derby, however, Prince Charlie's stamina was drained by Tattenham Corner – he'd go on to achieve fame as a sprinter and be immortalized in verse as 'The Prince of the T.Y.C.' And, just to ensure he'd no chance of showing his true form over a gruelling distance of ground like the Leger's, Prince Charlie had gone in his wind and become a 'roarer'. Somehow Prince Charlie's class and tenacity saw him hang on to the runner-up's spot, albeit five lengths behind Wenlock. As for Drummond, he was never seen with a chance and trailed in seventh.

Although Fordham had seven further cracks at the Leger, the neck defeat of Martyrdom one year after his rejection of Formosa was the nearest he came to the elusive victory. The colt belonged to Lord Calthorpe, an Army chum of Captain Machell. Following a poor effort in the July Stakes, he was united with Fordham in York's Prince of Wales's Stakes. His victory prompted Machell to back him at 25 to 1 for the Derby during the winter. The colt began his Classic campaign beaten a neck for third place in the Guineas when also heavily backed by Machell and Calthorpe. Although Fordham was enjoying something of a purple patch on the Bedford Cottage horses, he and Martyrdom failed to sparkle in the Derby won by Pretender. However, they made some amends at Ascot a fortnight later by upsetting the odds on the Derby runner-up Pero Gomez for the Prince of Wales's Stakes over the St Leger trip. Martyrdom's reversal of Epsom form perplexed a great many judges. But he was by a Leger winner, and this performance boosted his chances in Doncaster's longer Classic. Machell backed him accordingly.

And what a close call it was. Fordham appeared to be overhauling Pero Gomez inch by inch inside the final furlong. When the two horses were within 50 yards of the winning post it was clear that the prize was Martyrdom's if he could maintain this effort. But he faltered. Fordham sat down resolutely in a desperate attempt to coax something extra from his tiring mount. 'Had he seconded his jockey's efforts, Fordham would have won his first St Leger,' insisted *Baily's*, 'but though he nursed him with the most consummate tact it was to no avail.' Machell was not amused: he reckoned Fordham had lain too far out of his ground and given Martyrdom far too much to do.

On balance it seems whatever tactics Fordham deployed would've been to no avail – three words that just about sum up his St Leger experiences.

***

It's quite possible George Fordham was one of the few people of his time who viewed Derby Day as a trial rather than a treat. The Derby put his skills to a test that results seemed to suggest were somehow wanting. For a man acutely conscious of his reputation and morbidly sensitive to any criticism of it, such doubts must've fuelled increasing anxiety as he made his way to the arena his detractors believed came to fill him with dread. The 'legend' of Fordham's Derby hoodoo was born.

A Victorian Derby Day transcended sport. The St Leger drew crowds from every corner of Yorkshire, some intent on having a good time but the majority intent on watching a horse race. The reverse was more the case at the Derby. The race came second to the entertainment. A cross section of Britons from lords to louts flocked to Epsom Downs to celebrate the embodiment of 'Merrie Englande.'

Even that of those who looked upon the Derby as the sink of all iniquity were drawn to it inexorably.

This annual English carnival began well before cock-crow as London's populace began evacuating the city to congregate on Epsom Downs like, in the words of *The Times*, 'half a million gypsies'. Its writer continued: 'I do not envy the lungs of a man who can turn his back on London without rapture at the mere inhalation of the fresh country air. The road to the Derby is the best part of the Derby – it is what courtship is to marriage.'

While the brave tried the new-fangled option of the train, the road was everyman's ground. His Grace's four-in-hand had no right of precedence over the costermonger's donkey, the butcher's cart, the pony chaise, the hansom, omnibus or dog-cart. The whole endless caravan jogs and jostles along the 16 miles from London to Epsom on perfectly equal terms; the skill of the whip constituting the law of the road. Whistle-whetting halts at The Swan in Clapham, The Cock in Sutton and The Spread Eagle in Epsom itself served to punctuate the journey, enabling scores of envious pedestrians to chaff those better off over a tankard. So long as the sun shone these denizens from Belgravia to Bermondsey might blissfully rub shoulders, a throng divided by wealth, squalor, gentility, virtue and vice but this day united by a common bond of immorality. All eager to indulge their every whim. Not for nothing was Derby Day dubbed a 'National Saturnalia'.

The scene greeting Fordham on the Downs has been captured for posterity in the paintings and drawings of William Frith and Gustave Dore. It was one to take the breath away. The Downs resembled a vast ant-heap of humanity, its busy army of punters impersonating worker ants while the profusion of carts and carriages edged around more sedately in the manner of so many stray beetles.

In fact each person has his or her place, distinguishable by their dress code, a tell-tale sign of the English class system.

At the heart of the Downs is the gypsy encampment denoting the annual summer congregation of Romanies, tinkers and travellers from all over the British Isles. Washing-lines pegged-out with clothes are strung between the brightly-painted caravans; motley collections of ponies are tethered to stakes; goats, chickens and dogs roam at will. Groups of women, their pixie faces burnt nut-brown by many summers on the open road, their shiny plaited and pigtailed black hair just visible beneath vivid bandannas and headscarves, gold hoops swinging from one ear and a pink carnation behind the other, toil over a succession of large black cauldrons while their men folk play pitch n' toss and their children spin tops.

Surrounding this vibrant core is a melting pot made up of London's urban proletariat sporting flat caps and mufflers and rustics decked out in pleated smocks and knitted shawls. Pearlie kings and queens, their heavy, button-encrusted coats already bringing rivulets of sweat to their jolly red faces, sit at rows of trestle tables laden with food and drink. And on the other side of the green divide that is the track, blazers and cravats jostle for space with crinolines and parasols; until, finally, top hats and morning suits hold sway in the privileged sanctum of the Grand Stand.

What the likes of Frith and Dore cannot transmit, however, are the smells and sounds of Derby Day. The air is thick with the smells to tickle every palate. The aroma of rich fare wafts across the track from the distant Grand Stand. In one massive kitchen alone chefs are cooking 400 lobsters,130 legs of lamb, 65 saddles of lamb, 130 shoulders of lamb,150 ox tongues,100 sirloins of beef, 500 spring chickens and 350 pigeon pies. Closer to hand, stalls offering pie n' mash and jellied eels feed the working-class body while occasional banners declaring 'Behold the Lamb of God' offered mobile mission stations prepared to feed the soul.

Cutting through the gastronomic fug is a cacophony of noise familiar to Babel. There is no charge for spectators on the Downs and as far as the majority of its occupants are concerned racing comes a poor second in its order of priorities. The area is a raucous playground for the working classes to enjoy their unofficial holiday and it contains assorted ways and means of separating them from their money. Grinding hurdy-gurdies and shrill organ music accompanies the carousels enabling would-be jockeys the opportunity to sit a horse; touts, like 'Donkey Jimmy' fish for mug-punters with promises of 'an outsider to beat the field'; three-card tricksters entice the gauche with insidious patter; the proprietors of boxing booths bellow challenges to the foolhardy. Ventriloquists and fiddlers, negro tap-dancers and banjoists, acrobats and magicians readily entertain at the toss of a coin into a welcoming hat. There's even a gypsy whose speciality act is catching a rat with his teeth: his arms tied behind his back and the rat tied to a stake with room to move but not escape. Noise assaults the senses from every angle. Enough to make anyone's head spin. Perhaps even that of George Fordham.

Compared to other prominent jockeys of his era, Fordham's record in the Derby was poor; abysmal, even, judged by his otherwise high standards. John Wells and Henry Custance, for instance, won three; Frank Butler, Tom French and Charlie Maidment two. Like fellow champion jockey, Nat Flatman, however, Fordham would only ever manage one victory. The yardstick for George Fordham, as ever, is Fred Archer. To reprise: in 22 attempts Fordham won once and was placed twice despite partnering five favourites. Archer rode five Derby winners and three placed horses from 13 rides, four of which were favourites. Fordham's record in many ways mirrors that of his 20th century alter ego, Gordon Richards, who won his first and only Derby at his 28th and final attempt on what was the fifth favourite he'd partnered.

One possible explanation of this moderate record is that Fordham disliked taking the kind of risk which so often proved necessary during the hectic descent of Tattenham Hill. That the course was highly dangerous is beyond question: Tattenham Corner was regarded by Victorian jockeys as one of the worst bends to ride round – it was not only down a steep incline but on the side of one. In itself this posed Fordham no problems. After all, he did win five races for the Oaks. But the pace, number and generally poorer quality of the runners in the fillies' Classic seldom generated the tense hurly-burly of a Derby. In the 22 renewals of the Oaks in which Fordham rode, only two (1873 and 1883) had a bigger field than the comparable Derby and only three (1859, 1878 and 1881) were completed in a faster time.

Fordham's strategy in the Derby was to avoid trouble down the Hill by going clear - in the hope of keeping something up his sleeve for a successful exhibition of 'kidding' in the later stages. This was no simple ploy to execute in a Derby.

Fordham's first ride set the pattern. In 1857 he rode Dick Drewitt's Tournament, the 4 to 1 favourite in a field of 30. For Drewitt to have a Classic contender, let alone a Derby favourite, was unusual. The trainer's high hopes were dashed as soon as he came to saddle the colt. Tournament broke out into a 'black sweat'. When chaos ensued at the start poor Tournament's goose was cooked. 'I did think I was going to win on Tournament in Blink Bonny's year,' recalled Fordham years later, 'but there were about 40 false starts and Tournament made the lot. He was no sort of horse at all when they did get off at last.' The colt was soon in trouble as a result of a ferocious early gallop and was spent before Tattenham Corner. Had luck been on his side, Tournament might've landed Fordham a Derby and a Leger. But sprinting turned out to be his game; between Epsom and Doncaster he won the Stewards Cup at Goodwood.

In 1861 Fordham might have opened his Derby account 'but for a little hasty ebullition of temper' in the words of *Baily's*. The mount in question was Klarikoff, trained by John Scott for Lord St Vincent, who'd given Henry Padwick £5,000 for the colt with the Derby in mind. Klarikoff's only loss at two was in the New Stakes; Fordham nursed him to a comfortable victory in the Criterion – so often a precursor of Classic success. Yet if ever a horse was doomed it was Klarikoff. It seemed as if race officials had it in for him. After apparently running a 'dead heat' for the Two Thousand Guineas, the judge, John Clark, having declared there was not the difference of a race-card between him and Kettledrum, then awarded the race to the latter. And this after the colt had behaved like a mad horse giving rise to the suspicion he'd been 'nobbled'. Klarikoff then got left 30 yards at the start of the Derby owing to another exhibition of incompetence from starter McGeorge who confessed to not seeing him. Fordham was so enraged as a result of being in a good position for all the earlier false starts that he recovered his ground too zealously: he'd forced Klarikoff into second place by the top of Tattenham Hill. The horse tired to finish fifth. The absolute nadir of Klarikoff's fortunes was yet to come. Returning from Epsom to his Malton stables by rail the horse was burned to death when a spark from the engine set light to the van in which he was boxed. The colt wasn't insured and St Vincent received no compensation.

Typical chaos surrounding the start of a Derby.

Two years later Fordham took the mount on a different class of animal, a sure-fire prospect: Lord Clifden. Fordham had been instrumental in moulding this colt, a deep bay with black points by Newminster, bred by a Staffordshire wine merchant called Hind from his single broodmare named The Slave. The colt followed his elder sibling Lady Clifden, on whom Fordham would win the 1862 Stewards Cup, into training with Edwin Parr at Telscombe, near Lewes. 'The Sublime Edwin', as he was known throught racing, quickly recognized his potential. Lord Clifden had a perfect temper and the tremendous stride of his father who had used it to great effect when achieving his solitary success in the St Leger. The colt was tried before the Woodcote Stakes of 1862 with three others, two of them recent winners. As the Woodcote involved negotiating Tattenham Corner, this trial also involved taking one. Fordham brought Lord Clifden very wide, allowing the others to steal lengths off him up the inside. Only then did he give Lord Clifden the office. The colt sped away to put three easy lengths between himself and his pursuers: once the touts had run away to file their reports, in *Baily's* choice phrase, 'like an Irish cornet with an English heiress', 20 to 1 was the best price available for the 1863 Derby. 'Do you think I was riding that horse to win his trial?' Fordham replied when asked why he'd gone so wide on the bend. 'I tried to give him no chance to make a mistake in the Woodcote.' And so it proved. Lord Clifden was ten lengths adrift round Tattenham Corner but stormed up the straight to win the Woodcote in his own time. 'He is as fine a colt as we ever saw stripped and a real "clinker",' purred *Baily's*.

Lord Clifden had passed from Hind to Captain Christie (a pal of Fordham's who owned the terrifically fast Lady Clifden) for £4,000 plus a £1,000 contingency should he add the Derby; after the Woodcote he was sold once again, to Lord St Vincent for a reported £5,000 with the Derby contingency doubled. The colt's Derby odds of 20 to 1 were trimmed instantly to 12 to1. After the various catastrophes with Klarikoff, St Vincent was dying to own one good horse in his life and keener than ever to win the Derby. His title had passed from his uncle Admiral Sir John Jervis, who earned it from his renowned naval victory of 1797 over the Spanish; *Baily's* thought him 'firm in his friendships, liberal in his disposition, and a hater of all that low chicanery which is so much in vogue.' To a great many others, however, his reputation was that of a man reserved, selfish, indolent – and fickle when it came to his relations with trainers and jockeys.

In September Lord Clifden and Fordham added two races at Doncaster. First, the Champagne Stakes at odds of 5 to 4 on, after being practically left at the post. 'Fordham was at him nearly all the way,' reported *The Sporting Life*, 'but when the colt fairly got into his grand stride he bore down on the leaders and roused by Fordham he went on and won cleverly. Fordham declared that had not the horse been one of the most extraordinary he had ever ridden, he could not, considering the badness of his start, have won under any circumstances.' Despite a 7lb penalty, Lord Clifden then added a Sweepstakes in which he gave 10lb and a beating to the future Oaks winner Queen Bertha. *The Life* reckoned it had seen a potential Derby winner: 'Although Lord Clifden's performances have been picked to pieces by his carping opponents, it was agreed by all good and sound judges that no candidate was ever better entitled to his place in the Derby quotations.'

During the winter the colt was privately trained at his owner's Godmersham Park, near Canterbury, but he returned to Parr to commence his serious Classic preparations. While so doing, attempts were made to injure him by digging holes on the gallops and filling them with flints; the police also found various 'infernal spike machines' that would also have been hidden in the turf. And one morning the colt did slip up and injure himself. But Parr ensured the touts were kept in the dark about his well-being by letting a 'lookalike', called Bellman, take his place on the gallops. 'He has not been sick or sorry for a single day,' *The Life* duly assured its readers, 'and all who have seen him in Sussex declare that he goes over the ground like a deer.'

Fordham later explained all:

> He slipped up at Godmersham one day, lay there, he did, for ever so long. We all thought he was dead and that lamed him. The touts wrote that he went a wonderful gallop a few days before the Derby, but he did nothing of the sort, you know. I trotted him, cantered him half a mile or so, pulled up and did another trot, and that's what the touts made into a grand gallop.

The weather on Derby Day was atrocious. Rain fell in torrents. It failed to stop the Prince of Wales viewing his first Derby but Lord Clifden's retinue of guards found, in *Baily's* words, 'the path to the paddock to be of Crimea depth in mud that would require a company of sappers to make it passable.' The magazine continued: 'The preparations made for Lord Clifden were on a greater scale than the Clarendon for a German prince. Three gamekeepers formed his escort, under the command of an Irish gentleman strong enough to choke a "nobbler" as a cat does a mouse.' Then, piling more weight on Fordham's sensitive shoulders: 'Rumour speaks of the reward for both trainer and jockey if victory crowns their efforts as being on a munificent scale never before attempted.' There can be little doubt the pressure of riding the hot favourite got to Fordham as post-time neared. 'No one but me knows how good this horse is,' said the normally reticent jockey before he left the sanctuary of the weighing room.

One further concern to Fordham would be the start. He could hardly forget the farces blighting the Derby bids of Tournament and Klarikoff. False starts were a matter of routine in Victorian racing, and nowhere more so in the tense atmosphere of a Classic. Races could be settled at flag-fall. Matilda's narrow 1827 St Leger victory, for instance, resulted from being allowed an 80-yard head start. If the Derby field got away within an hour of the advertised time it was considered a job well done. McGeorge, who took over from William Hibburd as starter to the Jockey Club in 1860 (retaining the post for 24 years) was fussy and self-important, qualities some might suggest were a prerequisite for his job. The previous year had witnessed yet another debacle when three horses were left at the post - gaining him a severe reprimand from Admiral Rous.

McGeorge took no chances of any horse being left this time round. There were no fewer than 32 false starts in the teeming rain thanks to the repeated antics of Tambour Major before he let the field go. Lord Clifden had seemed to cope admirably, standing quietly while Fordham patted him reassuredly down the neck. Nevertheless, it's fair to say a great many of the 31 runners were in no fit state to give of their best thanks to the delay. Further chaos ensued when two horses came to grief on the descent to Tattenham Corner.

Somehow Fordham avoided the mayhem and led Macaroni into the straight. Having performed that miracle he then committed that most elementary of errors: he looked round for signs of danger. Macaroni's jockey was Mancunian Tom Chaloner, no mean exponent himself of artful jockeyship, having been tutored at Ashgill by the redoubtable Osborne family; 'an excellent specimen of the Manchester school whose subjects as soon as they are out of their egg-shells are taught to shift for themselves,' as *Baily's* wryly put it. 'A better jockey of his years never scaled: he is backed in the North like Fordham in the South. A duplicate of him would command any money.' Chaloner was a quiet unassuming man who adored his pets and set his parents up in a pub. More to the point, Chaloner was the 'Grim Reaper' who'd twice scythed down Fordham in the act of winning a St Leger. He and Macaroni had won the Two Thousand Guineas, encouraging the colt's owner, a former Liverpool banker of parsimonious reputation named Richard Naylor, to make bets enriching him by a further £100,000 (*£12 million*) should the Derby be added.

Man and horse seized their chance. Chaloner set about Macaroni. Lord Clifden's narrow advantage diminished as Fordham, awakened to the threat, transferred his whip from one hand to the other. The favourite faltered once, then, sensationally, once again: onlookers swore they saw him tread on a piece of orange peel. Chaloner forced Macaroni upsides. The pair drove for the line. They flew past the post as one two-headed beast. Fordham didn't think he'd held on. Judge Clark, said the only difference between them was that Lord Clifden's head was down and Macaroni's up as they flashed past. He gave the verdict to Macaroni. 'Macaroni was admirably ridden by Chaloner,' commented the *Pall Mall Gazette*, 'but Fordham rode Lord Clifden with no less judgement.'

Fordham was inconsolable. Any jockey who can retain philosophic calm after losing a Derby by less than a hand would be a master of composure. And Fordham was neither stranger to sentiment nor excessive sensitivity. Perhaps the tavern gossips were correct: he wasn't a Derby jockey. Perhaps he did lack the necessary 'bottle' to ride like a Dervish in this roughest of races on the most dangerous of racecourses.

The depth of Fordham's despair may be gauged by a story later written down by his friend, the owner and bookmaker George Hodgman. In expectation of celebrating Lord Clifden's victory, Fordham had been invited by Hodgman to dinner at his Carshalton home along with one of Fordham's best friends, John Mannington the vet. Fordham rode over from Epsom in the company of the steeplechase jockey Alfred Sait. As the pair trotted across Banstead Common they were met by Henry Oldaker, the Clerk of the Course at Harpenden, who knew Sait but had no intimate acquaintance with Fordham. Sait reported the following exchange.

'Well, Sait, I've often heard it said that Fordham pulled horses, but I wouldn't believe it. Now I am satisfied. I saw him with my own eyes deliberately pull Lord Clifden this afternoon.'

Sait tried tipping Oldaker the wink. But the message failed to get through.

'To do such a thing, and the horse favourite!' insisted Oldaker. 'It's shocking. I can't make out what the Stewards were about!'

Fordham's temper, usually so even, snapped with an almost audible twang. He vaulted from his hack and set about his accuser, forcing him into a prickly furze.

'Cheese it!' was Oldaker's quaint Victorian admonishment of choice. 'Here sir, you cheese it!'

'I'll cheese you!' retorted the aggrieved Fordham – before raining blows on Oldaker's head, back and shoulders with his whip until Sait came between them.

'Oldaker, you've asked for this,' said Sait. 'This is Fordham.'

'Beg my pardon!' demanded Fordham.

Oldaker did so instantly.

Fordham was still boiling with rage. 'Beg it again, you scoundrel!'

Sait advised Oldaker to ride away in the opposite direction - while he and Fordham continued to Carshalton. 'Don't speak to me,' said Fordham as he and Sait continued their journey at a funereal pace. 'But don't leave me. I'm cruelly hurt.'

Eventually Sait decided to ride on ahead to explain the reason for their delay to the dinner party.

'We were all very sorry,' wrote Hodgman of the incident, 'and a sadder man than Fordham was when he appeared I do not wish to see.'

Although the party had waited dinner for Fordham's arrival, the jockey excused himself. 'Thank you. But I don't want any dinner. I'm too upset.' He could not be persuaded to enter the dining room and sat outside on the stairs, sobbing his heart out.

Bell's Life offered commiserations:

> As all Fordham did was for the best, he has only to blame the fortunes of war and to reflect on the axiom relative to the glorious uncertainty of the English Turf. Whether if Fordham had waited longer with his horse he could have reversed the head is a problem we care not to attempt to solve for it is a dangerous attempt to pull a big horse out of his stride a short distance from home for fear of not again getting him into his action.

A considerably more colourful account of the finish came from beyond the trade papers. *The Spectator* wrote:

> At Tattenham Corner Lord Clifden was still ahead, and he came down the slope with a fleetness of foot that seemed to leave no chance for competitors. Only a yard or two from the winning post he was decidedly in advantage as he could be, and nothing seemed so certain as that he was the winner. Tremendous shouts arose from all points and Fordham, stirred up by them, called upon his horse. Near him was Macaroni, the primrose jacket of

the jockey slipping nearer in a line with Fordham's dark brown. These noble horses were being whipped as no cabman would whip a back, and spurred till the blood ran down their side. They dashed past almost frantically, and at that critical instant Lord Clifden seemed to slacken a little, and Fordham saw the primrose jacket a few inches before him. What a difference a few inches make! People who do not bet were sorry the favourite was beaten, he had run so beautifully and struggled so gallantly. Perhaps the false starts had worn him more than Macaroni; at any rate, that last second, that wont of two strides, lost Lord St Vincent some thousands, and made the day a black one for many others.

Fordham and Lord Clifden reappeared at Epsom for the Great Surry Foal Stakes over a mile on the Friday. The colt appeared stale and, despite Fordham giving him two short canters beforehand, 'looked stiff and disinclined to face the course' in the words of *The Sportsman*. In point of fact, despite his victory the Woodcote, Epsom was not a track that suited Lord Clifden's enormous stride. Sent off at the punitive odds of 10 to 1 on for what had been reduced to a two-horse race they scrambled to a head victory over Frederic Lagrange's Jarnicoton. An ignominious defeat had only been averted by the latter suffering a broken stirrup leather in the last few strides. Said *The Times*: 'The result showed that the favourite was not the horse which he has so long been considered.'

Thereafter Fordham lost the ride. Lord St Vincent was notoriously thin-skinned to any misrepresentation of his horses. There could be nothing lacking in Lord Clifden. Losing the Derby in such a manner had to be the jockey's fault. Fordham could be excused a chortle when the colt ran poorly in the Grand Prix de Paris in the hands of Tom Chaloner. Fordham's jollity was reported to St Vincent - which scuppered any hope of a recall for the St Leger. Doncaster's long flat straight would be more to Lord Clifden's liking that Epsom. And Fordham had to suffer the distant view of Lord Clifden and John Osborne winning the Leger from the saddle of the outsider Golden Pledge.

'Lord St Vincent thought I didn't do justice to him at Epsom, you know,' Fordham told a journalist later in life, 'but I think I did. He was as lame as a tree. I don't think he ever got right till the Leger. He was a bad baby sort of horse – couldn't start. When once he was set going he was a fine horse, no doubt. And afterwards, when they laid 4 to 1 on him in the Claret Stakes at Newmarket, I beat him on Rapid Rhone. I was delighted that time!'

How Fordham must've grown to hate the sight of Tom Chaloner. Besides besting him in three Classics, the Mancunian would later become first jockey to 'Old' Alec Taylor and, consequently, profit from Stirling Crawfurd's Classic winners Gang Forward (1873 Two Thousand Guineas) and Craig Millar (1875 St Leger) that Fordham might otherwise have partnered.

Fordham suffered two more Derby heartbreaks in the 1860s. In 1867 he rode Vauban. On the strength of his impressive victory in the Guineas the Duke of Beaufort's colt had been supported as a strong favourite for the Derby. His odds continued to tumble as Derby Day approached: good money was taken at 7 to 2, 100 to 30 and 7 to 4, and on the day itself he was only a 6 to 4 shot. While Vauban's odds contracted those of the horse who came to symbolize the 1867 Derby lengthened. That horse was Hermit who ran in the colours of Henry Chaplin, the squire of Blankney Hall, in Lincolnshire.

Hermit's victory in the Derby of 1867 has gone down in history as the Derby that 'broke the heart' of the Marquis of Hastings. The Hastings runner in the race had no chance of victory: Uncas would perform pace-making duties for Vauban. His bet in this Derby was *against* Hermit winning - purely because he believed Chaplin only began investing in thoroughbreds to needle him in retaliation for losing the hand of Lady Florence Paget. Chaplin, dubbed 'Magnifico' at Oxford on account of his style and zest for high living, was certainly rich enough to endorse the claim that he 'bought horses as though he were drunk and backed them as though he were mad.' For six months Hastings had accepted each and every bet with the alacrity of the arrogant – or a mug; should Hermit win this Derby he stood to lose £140,000 (almost *£17 million*). That prospect seemed frighteningly likely for Hermit had better form than Vauban at two, defeating him twice at Stockbridge. Throughout the winter he'd been trading consistently at a lower price than Vauban for the Derby. Indeed, such was his promise that his jockey, Henry Custance, broke the habit of a lifetime and put £25 on the colt at 20 to 1 for the Derby.

Was Hermit capable of reproducing his juvenile form? Machell and the colt's trainer, George Bloss, determined to find out. In a trial at Newmarket over a mile Machell set Hermit to give 10lb, worth just over three lengths, to his stablemate Knight of the Garter who'd finished just two lengths behind Vauban in the Guineas. Hermit thrashed him. Hermit had proved he was a live Derby contender. However, one week before the race Custance was riding Hermit in a gallop over the full Derby distance when the colt suddenly lurched and coughed, showering the jockey with blood. He'd burst a blood vessel. Trying to hide the news was hopeless. Hermit was nursed constantly, fed sparingly with hay, and covered with the lightest of rugs to keep his blood cool. Within two days he resumed light work. There was a slim chance the colt might make the Derby line-up after all. Slim became definite on the Monday. Bloss worked him round Tattenham Corner and reported to Chaplin: 'He bounded over the ground like a cricket ball. He wouldn't have blown a candle out at the end of the gallop. I think he is sure to win the Derby after all.'

Hermit's mishap and likely withdrawal caused Custance to accept an alternative mount. With the top jockeys committed, Machell chose to engage John Daley, the son of a Newmarket trainer. Daley was young, sound but unfashionable. He'd attended grammar school and suffered ribbing as 'the best educated jockey on the Turf.' His first winner came when he was just a ten-year-old weighing 3st 10lb; his lightness was exploited to ride winners of handicaps such as the Goodwood Stakes, Ascot Stakes and Stewards Cup. Riding a horse in the Derby was a gift from the gods for one such as he; as were the inducements. The 20-year-old was paid £100 to ride. But Machell promised a further £300 if Hermit was placed and £3,000 if he won. To the latter Chaplin pledged another £6,000.

Although the Press was describing this renewal as 'the year of mediocrities and misfortunes – never has there been a more indifferent lot', the epic undertones of the race were franked by weather of biblical proportions. The first day of the meeting on Tuesday heralded plunging temperatures and driving rain that caused *The Times* to suggest 'some outsider may yet drop from the clouds at Tattenham Corner'. On the Wednesday the cataracts of Heaven poured down on Epsom; by the afternoon the racecourse was reeling under the onslaught of sleet, snow and a piercingly raw wind that left a dull and dispirited crowd wondering if God had decreed a 'third winter'. Fine feathers drooped in ladies hat-bands; chignons came to tousled grief; muslin clung to soaked female limbs. The cheeks of gentlemen turned blue; hands were clapped; feet were stamped. Hermit was seen to 'shiver with the cold' while being saddled and might be backed at the peculiar odds of 1,000 to 15. Machell, who, unlike Chaplin, had hedged most of his earlier bets, helped himself to these generous odds and backed Hermit to win another £3,000.

Despite the elements John Day turned out Vauban looking a picture of health, his bright brown rump shining like a burnished conker. In a 30-horse field the market went 7 to 1 bar the favourite, who held steady at 6 to 4. McGeorge was his usual epitome of incompetence at the start: there were ten false starts spread over 45 minutes-worth of biting wind, sleet and snow. When McGeorge did finally get them away, Uncas came nowhere near fulfilling his role as pacemaker. Julius and Skysail led the cavalcade along the brow of Tattenham Hill, upwards of three lengths in advance of Vauban. Descending the Hill Julius dropped back beaten, and Fordham indulged the favourite with a 'pull' which gave the impression to watchers in the Grand Stand that Vauban was about to give the jockey the Classic victory he craved above all others. Crossing the road at the head of the straight Vauban had sailed into the lead pursued by Marksman and Van Amburgh; of Hermit there was no sign.

As soon as the cheers went up for Vauban and his jockey they were as quickly stilled. Fordham was seen to be hard at work on the favourite. Was the arch 'kidder' at it again? Was he fooling lesser jockeys into moving too early? Vauban faltered. Fordham wasn't 'kidding'.

> *With fruitless labour great Vauban*
> *The fav'rite in the Derby ran;*
> *George Fordham, with whip and spur,*
> *Could not on the fav'rite stir.*

The favourite was done. At the distance Marksman ranged alongside him, appearing all over the victor. Then, before binoculars could be wiped clear, Hermit appeared on the scene. Machell had instructed Daley to hold up Hermit with a view to making one long run in the straight. These orders were obeyed to the letter. As Marksman got the better of Vauban, Daley was seen making up ground hand over fist on Hermit. The chestnut put his breathing problems behind him and flew up to the former's quarters. Then, as the post loomed, Daley lifted him past Marksman to prevail by a neck. Vauban trailed five lengths back.

How much Chaplin won on Hermit's Derby is conjectural: anywhere between £140,000 and £160,000 (over *£19 million*). As for Machell, around £63,000 seems a fair assessment. Chaplin collected on two side bets: one with Sir Joseph Hawley of £50,000 that Hermit would beat his colt The Palmer; and another with James Merry of £10,000 that Hermit would beat Marksman. Hastings owed him £20,000. Chaplin, very generously in the circumstances, sent Hastings a note telling him he might settle when convenient. He gave Hermit's trainer, George Bloss, £5,000 – just reward for sleeping in the horse's box for some three months on a tiny iron bedstead during his lengthy preparation for the race. Daley must've thought he'd died and gone to heaven. From scratching a living he'd pocketed the best part of £10,000 that would sustain him for years. Then, two days later, he goes out on his only other mount at the meeting, Hippia, and wins the Oaks from the 'good thing' Achievement. He'd not only banished any money worries but also carved for himself a niche in Turf history as one of the select group of men to complete the Epsom Classic double in the same year.

All that remained were the reckonings and recriminations. Inevitably, when a hot favourite is overturned, some were aimed at the jockey. Joseph Enoch, Danebury's head man, told Fordham he'd ridden a bad race. He didn't think the jockey was well enough to give Vauban a proper ride, making far too much use of Vauban. Enoch had seemingly overlooked Epsom being about the worst course imaginable for a horse like Vauban whose stilty fore-legs were ill suited for running down Tattenham Hill. Fordham hardly needed this brickbat. He took the defeat badly – as he invariably did in big races.

Vauban found a new lease of life. Hermit won two uncompetitive races at Ascot, but he was upstaged by Vauban who won the Prince of Wales's by ten lengths from Achievement and two other St Leger candidates in Marksman and Julius before beating the filly again in a Triennial. Then he added the Goodwood Cup. Those successes over longer distances made the St Leger an obvious target - and seemed a straight fight between him and Hermit. But the path to Doncaster was not smooth. Vauban met defeat twice at York in late August, Achievement exacting 10-length revenge in the Great Yorkshire Stakes over the Leger trip. And the filly proceeded to put both the Guineas winner and the Derby winner in their place in the Leger: Hermit by a length and Vauban, back in fourth, by three. Fordham, however, was missing from Vauban's back. He'd other things on his mind. His three-year-old daughter Penelope was fighting for her life. He was at home in Slough and didn't resume riding until Newmarket on 24 September.

Little did Fordham, Day or Enoch know that an even greater body-blow would strike a Danebury favourite 12 months hence when the jockey's Derby torment continued with the downfall of Lady Elizabeth. This reverse was foreseeable. Fordham knew he was doomed as soon as he caught sight of the filly being saddled. Even so, the 1870s commenced with the worse blow of any Fordham endured at Epsom – because it was entirely unforeseen. As far as the racing fraternity, from stable lad to Press-man, was concerned this Derby was all over bar the shouting. It did not have to be won; it could only be lost. And Fordham lost it.

Mr James Merry owned a brilliant colt in the unbeaten Macgregor who was sent to post at 9 to 4 on – the shortest odds in the race's 90-year history. Macgregor finished fourth. Fordham's perceived 'failure' could not have come in the colours of a worse owner. Fordham had survived Merry's wrath following Buckstone's narrow defeat in the St Leger. But it might not hold a second time.

Merry was a fearless bettor when he thought he was on a 'good thing'. He'd already won a Derby, in 1861 with Thormanby. That victory netted Merry £85,000 (*£10.2 million*), and saw him leave Tattersall's on settling day with every pocket of overcoat, jacket and trousers - and even his top hat - stuffed with banknotes. But his overriding ambition was to win the Derby with a maiden, an unexposed 'dark' horse with whom he might cane the Ring. And in Macgregor he reckoned he had just the ammunition.

Macgregor was a short horse, standing a trifle high on the leg; his chief fault, he was terribly straight in front, would prove his undoing. The bay son of Macaroni had revealed prodigious ability as a yearling when James Waugh tried him over three furlongs in company with the yearling filly Sunshine and the four-year-old Miss Hayes. The older horse gave the youngsters just 12lb (instead of upwards of 42lb) but did not see which way Macgregor went despite the colt forfeiting a couple of lengths at the start. 'Well, he won damned easy anyhow,' said Waugh afterwards. One morning, however, Waugh noticed the suspensory ligament of Macgregor's off fore-leg was enlarged. It was the sign of things to come because the trainer could never give the colt a normal preparation thereafter. In part this accounted for Macgregor never seeing a racecourse as a two-year-old; he might've run at Ascot but for coughing and was sent to Newmarket for the Middle Park

Plate but ultimately left the way clear for his former trial companion Sunshine, who'd pretty much carried everything before her, winning the Woodcote, July and, under Fordham, the Champagne Stakes. Sunshine lost the Middle Park by a head; clearly, on Macgregor's home form with her he'd have won with bags to spare. Then Merry opted out of starting Macgregor in the Criterion, deciding to hide his shining light under a bushel for as long as possible.

At the commencement of the 1870 season Merry was still of the inclination to let Macgregor make his debut in the Derby and allow his galloping companion, Sunlight, who was a pound or two superior to Sunshine, to go for the Two Thousand Guineas. Waugh was not in favour. Macgregor was murdering Sunlight on the Russley gallops, and was currently on offer at the juicy odds of 40 to 1. Merry conceded; and sanctioned the participation of both colts at Newmarket. But Macgregor was a 'dark horse' no longer. By the off 100 to 30 was all that was on offer. Despite his jockey, the long-limbed John Daley, putting up a pound overweight, Macgregor made an exhibition of his field seldom equalled in the history of the Classics let alone a Two Thousand Guineas. 'It was the most complete case of hare and hounds I ever saw,' said Sydenham Dixon, 'and there can be no small doubt that he might have won by a hundred yards had there been any object in allowing him to do so.'

Eight days before the Derby Macgregor was sent to Bath for the Biennial Stakes over the Derby trip of one and a half miles. He was greeted at the railway station by a crowd of onlookers who followed him all the way to the course. Despite rumours stating Sunshine had just humbled him on the gallops only three dared oppose, including Fordham and his future Oaks winner Gamos. As Daley couldn't make the weight of 8st 7lb the ride on Macgregor went to Jemmy Grimshaw: his orders from Merry were 'Be sure and lie well up, and don't draw it fine.' One can visualize feathers spitting from Merry's mouth as running down the hill toward the home turn Grimshaw was some hundred yards behind Gamos. But as soon as Grimshaw let his mount stride out on meeting the rising ground the reaction was electric. Macgregor won by a dozen lengths. In the aftermath of the Derby, some suggested this performance had cost Macgregor the Classic. Yet two days before the Derby the colt displayed his well-being by crucifying his galloping companions; gossip insisted Macgregor was 21lb superior to Sunshine. And track evidence suggested he was a whopping three stone better than Gamos.

Merry had forfeited his chance to win the Derby with a maiden. His alternative was to make the novelty bet that Macgregor would win and The Cockney Boy would be last. Despite Macgregor's short odds the second half of the bet actually seemed the more cast iron. The Cockney Boy belonged to a Mr Rogers, a Hackney butcher, and was prepared on the marshes at Temple Mills near Lea Bridge by an East London veterinary surgeon with, allegedly, gallops against local pedestrians. His owner, dressed in check suit and blue birds-eye tie, gazed lovingly at his Pegasus in the parade while a snooty scribe from *The Sporting Life* saw only 'a coarse and untrained beast with cut knees and scarred all over, with a neck and behaviour like a country stallion.' In the race he was tailed off after a furlong, running all over the track before ploughing into a spectator and unshipping his jockey – and all before reaching the top of Tattenham Hill.

The trade papers were of one mind. According to *Bell's Life* it did not need the skill of a magician to see that on public performance and private trials the Derby was Macgregor's to lose: 'Everything points to Macgregor carrying the entire confidence of Mr Merry and his recent public form is so undeniably good that we look in vain for anything likely to elicit his overthrow.' *The Field* concurred, touting Macgregor as 'a sound horse with fine speed and rare staying power who we do not perceive can be beaten.' *The Observer* was of the opinion that 'Macgregor has spoiled the betting...the nearer we approach to the fatal hour, the less will there be said about the "rag, tag and bobtail" and on the day the "crack" will march down to the post the decided king of the castle, with nothing being said about his badly-shaped forelegs and shoulders.' *The Times*, likewise, chose to view Macgregor's conformation as no sort of hindrance to success: 'Macgregor is the be-all and end-all of every discussion. He stops the way to speculation, almost to the extinction of racing gossip in which the soul of racing man so much delights.' *Baily's Magazine* injected its ususal trace of humour: 'Never even in the Guards was promotion so rapid as Macgregor's elevation from an outsider to a premier for the Derby. He won the Guineas from beginning to end, finishing in front of his horses like a hare before a pack of harriers.'

Not even conditions underfoot as hard as a turnpike road were seen to be any encumbrance. In the view of the *'Sportings' Life*, *Gazette* and *Times* there could be no other winner but Macgregor: 'Extraordinary faith exists in the invincibility of Macgregor and it is almost looked upon as an indictable offence to impugn the correctness of his running in the Two Thousand Guineas,' opined the former. At the final Tattersalls call-over Macgregor's odds had tightened from 6 to 4 on to 7 to 4 on. And if Merry allowed Sunshine to start as well, the layers gave short odds to his horses finishing first and second. *The Morning Post* summed up Derby Day 1870 thus: 'Macgregor is said to have completely spoiled the Derby and many say they will not go and see it run on account of the apparent certainty it presents him.' One who did, however, was William Gladstone, making his first visit on a fact-finding mission for a forthcoming parliamentary Bill.

Here at last was a horse destined to change Fordham's luck. 'It seemed certain that at last Fordham would ride the winner of a race in which he had always been so curiously unfortunate,' Sir George Chetwynd wrote later on. But perhaps the gods were offended by this slice of 'luck' coming Fordham's way. There had appeared no reason to change Macgregor's jockey. Indeed, Fordham was down to partner the 100 to 1 shot Nobleman in Monday's list of probable runners, but his scratching was announced at teatime on the Tuesday – along with that of Sunshine and Sunlight. Fordham could not be left standing on the ground. The switch was made. Daley was sent a brief note to that effect; understandably, he was most aggrieved at having to stand down – as he was perfectly entitled to be. He'd ridden Merry's horses for some time and had done nothing wrong on Macgregor. And he'd pared himself down to make the weight. The excuse given was that as a result he was too 'weak'. *The Sportsman* sensed doom: 'The appearance of Fordham in the saddle caused much astonishment and those who believe in luck were not altogether well pleased at the sight.' Had the paper foreseen the stroll Fordham and Tom French, the rider of the Mat Dawson-trained Kingcraft, took on the morning of the race it might've been even less pleased. French spotted a horseshoe, picked it up and tossed it over his shoulder, exclaiming: 'George, I shall beat you today!'

As was his wont on Derby Day, Fordham sat out the first three races on the card. The inactivity brought him no peace. In the weighing room before the signal to mount, the habitually cheerful soul looked as glum as an undertaker's assistant and sat nervously biting his nails. Waugh tried to lift his spirits by extolling Macgregor's obvious chance. But the spectre of Lord Clifden loomed at Fordham's shoulder. 'You never know. There's no such thing as a certainty,' he mumbled. Indeed, there isn't and there wasn't.

The game is up for Macgregor (centre) who is already feeling the pinch at Tattenham Corner.

The favourite had frightened off all but 14 opponents (though one, Sarsfield, had still made the arduous crossing from Ireland) to produce the smallest field since Wild Dayrell beat 11 others in 1855. Macgregor was kept away from prying eyes by being saddled at Sherwood's and joining the others at Tattenham Corner – where earlier in the day staff had removed flints scattered on the grass in a perceived effort to bring about Macgregor's downfall. The colt's isolation failed to prevent his odds from at one point growing as cramped as 5 to 2 on before coming to rest at 9 to 4 on; the market went 11 to 1 bar the favourite.

After one failure, McGeorge got them away cleanly and Palmerston led them along the skyline to the top of Tattenham Hill. Fordham had Macgregor no further back than third all the way up the hill and down again to Tattenham Corner. Then, suddenly, those holding binoculars knew the worst. Fordham was already hard at work on Macgregor, 'the hopes of his supporters scattered to the four winds,' in the evocative words of *The Times*.

Chetywnd echoed the sentiments coursing through Fordham's many devotees: 'How impossible it seemed that Macgregor could be beaten, and the consternation which overwhelmed the plungers when, half the journey being completed, it was seen that Fordham was hard at work on him; Fordham who never began to ride till it was absolutely necessary. No one was a greater master of the art of "kidding" and for a moment layers of odds may have tried to comfort themselves with the belief he was not really beaten; but any such hopes must have been short-lived – the favourite had not a thousand to one chance.'

Kingcraft, the Guineas third but only 20 to 1 fifth-best in the market, swept into the lead and sealed victory in a matter of a half-dozen strides. At the line he, and the omniscient French, had four lengths to spare over Palmerston, who withstood Muster by a head. Macgregor was a further two lengths adrift. The one man allowed to smile was Johnny Daley, roundly congratulated on the fact that he'd narrowly avoided the landslide of criticism inevitably triggered by a 'hot-pot' being overturned.

The Sporting Life shed crocodile tears:

> The chagrin and annoyance of Macgregor's partisans can well be conceived and Fordham's statement is that he was going well enough until making the bend at Tattenham Corner, where he could not act at all. It was the same down Bath's hill, where Grimshaw had eased him.
>
> The defeat of Macgregor was a regular 'facer' for the public who did not expect the favourite would be compelled to give way to a horse he beat so far in the Two Thousand Guineas. The probability is that Macgregor was none the better for his visit to Bath and the hard ground at Epsom must have told against his fetlocks and pasterns.

By six o'clock the Downs began to empty; showers sending backers of the favourite back to London with tears on their cheeks to complement the falling rain. The crowd that had arrived in hopeful high spirits now departed in a mixture of good-humoured elation from victory and subdued silence from empty pockets. Either eventuality was lubricated by copious libation. The crocodile of pedestrians dodged the assorted convoy of carts, traps, chaises, waggonettes, hansoms, landaus, broughams, four-horse vans and omnibuses that exemplified the hierarchy of the road. Lurking in wait for the unwary would be the gangs of roughs and pickpockets armed with bags of flour to pelt and distract prior to wading among them and rifling their valuables.

Fordham had more to worry about than petty criminals. Merry was unlikely to take defeat in his stride – his mood blackened by someone stealing his watch and binoculars in the post-race confusion. Macgregor had made mincemeat of Kingcraft in the Guineas and the cantankerous owner would demand to know the reason why that exhibition hadn't been repeated. Recriminations would flow; accusations fly. No one would be harder on Fordham than Fordham himself. Had he made too much use of Macgregor? Had he kept him close to the lead in an effort to avoid trouble in running, as his critics averred about his ride on Sir Clifden? Fordham chewed on his disappointment but ultimately digested his doubts. 'The ground was as hard as the floor of a ballroom,' according to *Baily's*, 'and Macgregor did not look the same horse that ran at Bath, being dry in his coat and not going with the same freedom – he went up the Hill like a lamplighter up a ladder and Fordham was in difficulties like a man whose expenditure exceeds his income.'

Fordham reported to owner and trainer that one of Macgregor's forelegs had 'gone' at Tattenham Corner; he gained support from *The Times* which attributed Macgregor's defeat to 'his upright pasterns telling against him on the descent of Tattenham Hill.' But Waugh shook his head. During a stopover at Dorking railway station on the colt's journey back to Berkshire, he had him ridden over some cobbles to test Fordham's hypothesis. The horse coped admirably. The vet summoned to examine him, however, diagnosed 'slight fever in both fore-feet.' Waugh's blacksmith responded by calling the vet every name under the sun – not one of them repeatable.

Merry, naturally, had ideas of his own. Something nefarious must've occurred. He was adamant his colt had been 'got at'. Again Waugh disagreed. The former pugilist Tass Parker was one of three stationed in boxes adjacent to Macgregor on Derby eve specifically to ward off any attempts at foul play. On the Friday Merry's heavily backed Sunshine failed in the Oaks. Merry again cited foul play.

Once more Waugh demurred; the filly had gone in her wind. Waugh was finding Merry's imputations upon his ability wearisome. They'd started after the previous year's Chester Cup when he'd assured Merry he could back St Mungo as if he was unbeatable; but the jockey couldn't hold him and the horse injured himself running into the rails. If Sunshine had been trained properly, stated Merry, she'd have won every Classic – even though both owner and trainer knew she was patently touched in her wind and had, in any event, been fortunate to come back from a serious injury in the spring. The relationship between owner and trainer became as taut as piano wire. Waugh determined to bring matters to a head. He put Macgregor back into work as though there was nothing wrong with his legs. The colt broke down – never to race again. Waugh seized the opportunity to hand in his resignation.

Thus did James Merry receive some measure of come-uppance. A hard man he may've been, but Merry was no idiot. He'd lost a trainer; he wasn't about to lose Fordham. The jockey subsequently wore Merry's silks to success in the 1875 Vase aboard the Oaks and Leger winner Marie Stuart and the Gold Cup on his Derby winner Doncaster.

TWELVE

A LARGER HEARTED MAN

Whatever malevolence Fordham displayed in his harsh treatment of Archer as a jockey, he possessed many appealing characteristics as a human being. He was proud of his standing but never wore it with a cocksure air, preferring to leave that sort of thing to the latest 'feather' swollen-headed from sudden fame in a few handicaps. He was popular in private as in public life and could claim – though he'd never choose so to do – that he'd not an enemy in the world. The explanation was simple. 'I never came across a larger hearted man,' said Sir John Astley.

The man Astley grew to admire was blessed with cheerful brown eyes set in a round avuncular face. In later years that face was framed with a pair of luxuriant side whiskers as if by means of compensation for a thinning tonsure. His frame was that of a typical jockey: short and compact: 'the little man' as his close friend

Henry Custance affectionately called him. It was his good fortune to escape the desperate 'tyranny of the scales' imposed on Archer who was forced to dose himself with a noxious bespoke purgative known as 'Archer's mixture' to maintain a decent riding weight. However, unlike Archer's, his manner was somewhat unpolished and his conversation a mite uncultured, the inevitable outcome of his spare formal education – though he did sign his name in a handsome copper-plate.

The rather grave exterior displayed to strangers fled once Fordham was in the company of intimates, whereupon he became a jovial character exuding warmth and benevolence to his fellow man. With age and the years that brought the relentless spectre of Fred Archer, Fordham became more protective of his reputation and, to some, pushed that self-regard to the point of conceit. If his *Vanity Fair* caricature from 1881 is any guide there is certainly an air of the cocky bantam about that arms-crossed and braced-leg demeanour. He was, like many sportsmen, highly suspicious, and an old metal matchbox was his precious lucky mascot. Yet whilst it would be stretching matters to say he was moved to tears at the slightest provocation, that he wore his heart on his sleeve is fair comment. He was sensitive to a fault. 'Fordham was no stranger to sentiment,' wrote George Hodgman. 'The chief fault of that magnificent horseman was his excessive sensibility.'

Children and animals he found worthy of adoration. During Goodwood week, for instance, he loved nothing more than arranging races for the children of East Dean and distributing half-crowns to winners and losers alike. Fordham emphatically declined to meddle with politics and was never known to cast his vote in a general election. He also steered clear of conversations on horse-racing unless drawn out on the subject and a stranger could always find him ready to converse on any subject but his own particular business. No exception was made for members of his family. He did everything in his power to prevent his son having any involvement in the sport whatsoever; and once passed on this nugget of wisdom while holding up a finger on either hand: 'George, my lad, always remember this. Never let that finger know what that one does!'

Unlike the majority of his fellow jockeys Fordham seldom bet and was never averse to conveying such advice to others. A story was told to this effect in the *St James's Gazette* regarding a conversation overheard between Fordham and a 'gentleman' at Newmarket.

Gentleman: 'I want to put £5 on a safe thing for tomorrow. What shall I do?'

Fordham: 'Put the £5 note in your pocket, and get your wife to stitch up the pocket. That's the only safe thing to do at Newmarket.'

Fordham may have expressed reservations about racing, but never about the animal at its heart. He loved horses as animals rather than viewing them as mere fodder for the sport that gave him a living. Many a retired racehorse wound up as one of his hacks. One of them was the inveterate rogue Vici, capable of jumping over the rails at Nottingham when an odds on favourite one day and then running away with a decent handicap the following day. Fordham and Vici got on admirably until one morning the horse propped 200 yards from home. Try as Fordham might, the animal refused to budge, neither backwards nor forwards nor sideways. 'Stop where you are, then, you beast!' exclaimed Fordham, before removing the saddle and walking home. To the startled groom who asked where Vici was Fordham muttered: 'I don't know, and I don't care. I left him in the lane. You can either fetch him or you can leave him.' Fordham passed Vici on to Tom Cannon and even this exquisite horseman's patience was tried after Vici whipped round and thrust his backside through a bow window.

Fordham eschewed the high life that surrounded the Turf – although he accepted gratefully a photograph of the Prince of Wales which the future king presented to him after a particularly successful Goodwood (presenting one of himself in return). His holiday destination of choice was Southsea, where he preferred swimming in the baths rather than the briny and enjoyed boat trips round the Isle of Wight on an old boat named 'Heather Bell'. His regular pastimes of choice were those of the self-effacing rustic gentleman. He bred a few greyhounds for coursing, the best of which was called Silkworm. During the winter his first love was partnering one of his trusty equine pals - Levity, Pilgrim, Bobby, Woodburn or Babylon – to hounds; particularly with the Southdown Foxhounds and the Brighton Harriers during his time living on the south coast when, *Baily's* noted, 'he was invariably in the first flight at the finish of a run.' But not always safely; one nasty cropper while out with Mr Barchard's pack of harriers, for example, aggravated the damage to the knee injured by Miss Nipper. Another day out in 1879 very nearly ended in complete disaster when Bobby stepped in a rabbit hole and threw Fordham so violently to the ground as to cause concussion to the brain; and for a time Fordham's condition gave considerable alarm. Occasionally there'd be the bonus of an 'away' day with the Duke of Beaufort's Badminton, or else alongside Custance across his home country in east Leicestershire; though he never felt at ease chasing Reynard thereabouts as he did down in Sussex.

During the off season Fordham was also an avid football fan. His competitive spirit, however, seldom relaxed. He was wont to challenge Eli Elphick, 'The renowned sporting butcher', to various sporting matches, at £50 a-side, held on Brighton racecourse: for example, a flat race and a hurdle race. The 'sporting butcher', however, tended to put up a surrogate rather than ride himself; it made no difference – 'The Demon' invariably proved victorious. Fordham was an exceptionally able shot; and of an evening there was nothing he enjoyed better than billiards or whist, at which he was an expert – albeit an exceedingly slow one owing to the habit of consulting his book for direction. He was also a dab-hand on the dance floor – especially the three-handed reel – and took an instant love to the opera after being taken to a performance of William Vincent Wallace's *Maritana*.

Any free time during the summer was spent watching or playing his favourite game: cricket – a game at which he excelled. He was the regular captain of the Jockeys and Racing Officials XI that played the Sporting Press XI during the 'Sussex Fortnight', on the Sunday separating Goodwood from Brighton and Lewes. The matches were taken deadly seriously. When the Press XI received, in the words of *The Morning Post*, 'a sound castigation' in the 1867 fixture, played at the wonderfully named 'Dripping Pan' in Lewes, a re-match was arranged for the Kennington Oval. And the wily Press bolstered its XI with a 'pro' who happened to write the odd article. Nevertheless, despite contributing 78 of the Press XI's 167 runs, the 'ringer' was not the main attraction for the 1,000 spectators who paid to watch the game. 'Fordham was the "observed of all observers". Crowds of anxious admirers flocked round to get a good look at him. He was out for a duck in the first innings, but when his team were made to follow-on, he booked an unbeaten 34 in the second when the shouting and buzzing of the spectators was intense.'

On one score Fordham was intransigent: heaven forfend anyone, high born or low, who questioned his professional honesty, integrity or probity - as Lord Ribblesdale, William Day, Henry Oldaker and, in time, the Duchess of Montrose would testify. Captain James Octavius Machell, the orchestrator of Hermit's Derby success, was another who'd live to regret making hasty insinuations.

A parson's son, like Henry Chaplin, Machell had none of his Derby-winning owner's affability. He was six feet tall, slim, and very reserved to the point of being taciturn if he so chose. The military moustache, aquiline nose, beady eyes and bowler hat painted an accurate portrait of a vaguely sinister personality - diabolical even - forged in the white heat of public school and the Army. The young Machell had proved himself to be both an outstanding officer and athlete. While serving at the Curragh, for instance, he repeatedly won bets by executing the seemingly impossible parlour trick of making a stationary jump from the floor to the mantelpiece in Dublin's Morrison's Hotel. His physical prowess landed wagers as bizarre as a race over 100 yards along Newmarket's Bury road in which his opponent walked while Machell, with a start of 25 yards, had to hop. Thus did Machell learn to appreciate the value of 'handicapping'. Armed with such knowledge he funnelled his racecourse winnings into the purchase of racehorses, a pursuit that led him to hand in his papers. The Turf was his oyster.

Like Sir George Chetwynd and Sir John Astley he lived on his wits and the ability to exploit them for financial gain on the racecourse. If he wasn't pondering a coup he was executing one or attempting to thwart that of someone else. He quickly became an owner and racing manager not averse to exploiting his fine eye for a yearling by snapping up bargains and passing them on quickly to his many clients at a decent profit. He was a Machiavellian orchestrator of betting coups. Not for nothing did the bookmaking fraternity christen him 'Captain Mac-Hell'. A measure of his fearless gambling and uncanny shrewdness in matters of the Turf is demonstrated by the Will of this once penniless Army officer being proved at over £47,000 (*£2 million*). Regarded as 'the cleverest man in Newmarket', he was, however, more respected than loved. Whether genetic or acquired in pursuance of his war with the Ring, 'The Uncrowned King of Newmarket' was highly suspicious and hot-tempered, a combustible combination akin to a spark in a munitions factory. He enlisted Fordham's aid in his enterprises whenever he could, but Machell's acid-sharp tongue was always liable to burn a sensitive skin like Fordham's. Inevitably it led to what *The Sporting Life* described as 'the recent unpleasantness at Newmarket.'

In the spring of 1880 Machell planned to pull off a coup in a seller with Tulach Ard - against the wishes of Fordham who informed him the horse wasn't good enough. That, alone, was sufficient to rattle Machell, who didn't tolerate his judgement being questioned. The horse drifted in the betting and was beaten by a head. Machell fumed. In a tantrum he accused Fordham of not trying. Fordham immediately severed their relationship. 'That damned horse,' a repentant Machell later admitted, 'was no good and I lost the best jockey in the world.' Only a few years later Machell's nasty streak caused him to insult Fred Archer in a similarly thoughtless vein – a slur possibly contributing to the mental turmoil that led to Archer's suicide.

The singular occasion Fordham's own behaviour fell short of its customary impeccable level of honesty came when he rode for Sir John Astley in the Lewes Handicap and lost by a head to a horse belonging to Penelope Drewitt, now an impoverished widow. Her husband had died in October 1874. His last big win had come in the 1873 Royal

Hunt Cup when the 20 to 1 shot Winslow executed a well-planned 'job' in the hands of his former pupil. Winslow had been laid out for the race in masterly style. The four-year-old had only contested ten races in his life, securing half of them with Fordham's assistance. He'd not been seen out since winning the previous August, and the canny Drewitt gave all who asked about his chances beforehand a different answer. 'The clever people were so savage at having missed this long-waited for horse,' said *Baily's*, 'that they were driven to desperation.' Drewitt's widow kept the stable going with a handful of horses after his death, but the struggle to survive soon grew onerous. Any success made a difference. In matters like this Fordham's heart always overruled his head. He turned to Astley after dismounting at Lewes and said: 'Well, you know, Sir John, I ought to have won that race for you.' Astley assured him that was nonsense. 'Well, you know, Sir John, Mrs Drewitt has not been able to pay her rent and all through the race I could not help thinking of that damned rent, and, you know, I ought to have won.'

Astley adored Fordham the jockey as much as the man. This was hardly surprising since Astley was as affable and generous as Fordham. There were, ventured *Baily's Magazine*, 'few better-known faces among the busy haunts of men, none more popular with the many sets of society, one more gladly welcomed at warm corners.' Full of beard and rolling of gait, Astley was known to his countless friends on the Turf as 'The Mate'. Funds passed through the Astley coffers like tap water down a plug hole. At a pinch he'd ride a match himself, one notable occasion riding his own Drumhead at 16 stone to victory at Newmarket. In his pomp he'd also back himself in sprint races for he was lightning fast over 150 yards or more. Contrary to his soubriquet, Astley had been a soldier not a sailor, and had fought with the Scots Fusiler Guards in the Crimea, receiving a neck wound at the Alma that did nothing to prevent him fighting at Inkerman and Sebastopol. For a short while he served as an MP, a role totally unsuited to this blunt uncomplicated personality. On being asked by a heckler his opinion of the Liquor Bill he replied without demur: 'I don't know anything about the Bill, but mine was a damned sight too high the last time I paid it.'

Once Astley had taken a fancy to a jockey he would not hear anything against him. He'd back Fordham's mounts even against advice. Prior to the Derby of 1860, for example, Astley tried every trick in his extensive book to wheedle from Fordham details of the trial he'd ridden on Ten Broeck's colt Umpire. 'He left me as ignorant of his opinion of his mount, as if he didn't know there was such a horse,' wrote Astley. 'How many jockeys are there who would not tell a casual acquaintance in ten minutes all he knew about his Derby mount?'

Apart from the charitable lapse toward Mrs Drewitt, Fordham's honesty was unimpeachable. No one was allowed to doubt his integrity or undermine his reputation – although on occasion Fordham was an innocent participant in the sharp practices of others.

Shrewsbury's autumn meeting of 1862 was the scene of one such dodge. The track was one of those backwaters that seemed a gift from God for any Victorian 'plungers' intent on staging a coup or bookmakers intent on 'welshing'. One year the latter provoked a free-for-all in which a gang of Birmingham roughs – led by an ex convict nicknamed 'Hoppy' brandishing an umbrella with a spike at the end of it – charged the cheap stand armed with bricks; the missiles were as soon returned and one participant even took a door off its hinges and used it as a club.

It's safe to say that Shrewsbury was ripe for picking. George Hodgman described the particular piece of 'scrumping' in which

Fordham played a supporting role. The four principal participants were dead broke; they urged Hodgman to approach the Frail family, owners of the racecourse, with the suggestion of making up a small handicap over half a mile for gentleman riders – 'jockeys 5lb extra.' Hodgman was deputed to compile the weights, and duly entered four horses owned by his pals. They might place bets, and lay bets, on the outcome with impunity. Unfortunately, a fifth entrant was slipped in without their knowledge, a horse called Tom Sayers. Hodgman was assured Tom Sayers was 'a wretched bad horse' and couldn't possibly spoil the coup. But this set Hodgman thinking: there might be an upset; and the odds won't be generous about 'ours'. Then the brainwave struck him: 'We will go for Tom Sayers!'

Hodgman alerted the cabal's four riders to the plan, and 'bought' their compliance. Then he approached the owner of Tom Sayers to find out who he had in mind to ride his horse. Lo and behold Fordham had asked for the mount. 'That was enough,' wrote Hodgman in his memoirs. 'We knew George would try for all he was worth, and bad as was his horse we were determined he should win.' It was decided to put £1,000 on Tom Sayers. Hodgman took the commission to George Payne.

Though trumpeted by *Baily's Magazine* as the 'beau ideal of an English sportsman, investing all his actions with that chivalrous honour that has created for him not only an English but a European reputation,' no cutler would've regarded Payne as the sharpest blade in the box: he was known to back as many as two dozen horses in big handicaps and still miss the winner. Sent down from Oxford, he inherited a fortune of some £30,000 per annum on coming of age and promptly lost that much and more on the 1824 St Leger. The Ring, and especially the card table, saw to it that Payne subsequently ran through several fortunes. An eccentric life deserved an unusual demise. Payne hastened his own death by refusing to shield himself from the burning sun during the Lewes races of 1878. But throughout his 75 years he was cherished by his countless friends for his honour and incapacity for deceit. In consequence he was an admirable commission agent. His conversation with Hodgman went along the following lines:

'I want you to put me £1,000 on this race,' said Hodgman.

'What do you mean?' Payne replied. 'The thing's impossible. You couldn't get it on.'

'Oh, you'll be able to get anything on this cove,' laughed Hodgman. 'It's Tom Sayers.'

'Good gracious! He's not worth a thousand pence! He's a wretch!'

'It's all right. We've good men up. Nobody will know anything till they get past the post.'

At that moment Richard Ten Broeck appeared. 'I have asked Mr Payne to put me a thousand on Tom Sayers,' Hodgman told him.

'The American roared with laughter. Hodgman outlined the artifice. And Payne and Ten Broeck agreed to take £500 apiece into the Ring and get it placed.

The plot almost fell apart. The starter, out of Fordham's hearing, reminded the riders who was going to win the race. Tom Sayers wasn't listening. He refused to jump off at the first time of asking. But despite it being a 'proper' start his four opponents obligingly returned for a second effort. This time Fordham got him moving to the sound of the starter shrieking 'For heaven's sake, George, push the beast along. We're going for you! It's a man or a mouse today!'

Fordham was allowed to take the rails and the lead. The other four jockeys went out of their way to make things appear genuine, riding energetically one second and relaxing the next. Eventually Tom Sayers crawled home by three-quarters of a length. The rest finished in an authentic-looking bunch separated by necks. The owner of Tom Sayers was non-plussed to hear his horse had wound up favourite. When let in on the act Fordham broke into a chortle: 'I thought they were confoundedly kind to me. I ought to have been left on my beast a hundred yards!'

The syndicate's £1,000 brought in £2,500. The four riders received £75. The only men who didn't profit were the owner and rider of the winner. For some time afterwards Hodgman was frequently addressed by Fordham as 'Tom Sayers.'

It was more often the case that Fordham's honesty ensured he'd ride against his own money. Custance records a match at Newmarket in which he rode Trovatore (4 to 1 on) against Fordham on Lady Peel. On the way to post Fordham said to Custance: 'Yours is thought to be a certainty, isn't it? I have told a friend of mine to win me a bit on yours.' And yet, in a cliff-hanger finish, Lady Peel beat the favourite by a short head. 'Nor do I think I ever saw Fordham more pleased with himself although he had lost £20 by winning,' observed Custance.

Meanness was another human frailty Fordham had no time for. Skinflints would be paid in their own coin if the opportunity arose. In 1870 Fordham won the Goodwood Stakes on Paganini for Mr J Smith' – or 'Paganini Smith' as he was called because of the numerous victories won by that animal in his colours. Paganini was a very useful handicapper over a distance of ground. The five-year-old carried top weight of 8st 12lb and was conceding between 10 and 45lb to the other10 runners. Not unsurprisingly in mind of those concessions Paganini could be backed at around 7 to 1 for this gruelling marathon around the South Downs. Smith's confidence, however, was undiminished and he wanted to back Paganini accordingly. But before doing so, he walked round the Ring quietly asking the layers if Fordham had backed any horse to beat Paganini. He was assured in the negative. Fordham rode a peach of a race, preserving his horse's energy all the way. It was only in the last couple of furlongs that he joined issue with the leaders, a pair of featherweights. Paganini kept on in grand fashion to see them off by three parts of a length.

The present Fordham received for landing Smith's bets with such consummate skill was a miserly £5. As it happened, Fordham had little regard for money. He was apt to leave cash anywhere. This carefree attitude led one day to the theft of £20 from a waistcoat he'd carelessly left lying about and a 13 year-old stable lad suffering two months hard labour for the crime. But Smith's stinginess got his goat. Smith may not have been blessed with the financial resources of Ten Broeck, Beaufort, Lagrange or Lefevre, but £5 was an insult. Fordham bided his time. The following year Fordham rode against Paganini in the Newmarket Handicap. Approaching the finish Fordham sensed it would be a tight affair between Paganini, ridden by Jem Snowden, and himself on Idus. Moreover he thought Snowden's mount was going the better of the two. Without looking at Snowden he called: 'Jem, I'll save £5 with you?' Snowden stole a glance at Idus to ascertain how well he was travelling. This, of course, was what Fordham had angled for. Once Snowden was distracted, Fordham seized the initiative, got first run and won a short neck. 'It was a splendid piece of riding on Fordham's part for Idus was beaten half a mile from home,' reported *Baily's*. 'How he nursed him and brought him again to do Jem almost on the post ought to be told by his lips alone. Anyone but "The Demon" on Idus and it would have been Paganini's race.'

Foiling the mean Mr Smith gave him immense satisfaction. But he was not yet done with him. Now was the opportunity to hoist the skinflint on his own petard. Fordham passed the distinctly dyspeptic

Smith on the way back to unsaddle, and decided to vex him further. In a voice loud enough for his target to hear, he said to the boy leading him in: 'Look sharp! I think I am a bit short of weight.' The owner swallowed the bait and scurried gleefully into the weighing room to lodge an objection against Idus. Smith suffered the chagrin of seeing Fordham passed correctly - and find himself charged for making a frivolous objection. 'Quits!' said the smiling jockey as he passed the bemused Smith.

If one had to cite the principal character trait that distinguished Fordham from Archer it was a sense of humour. No one could ever assert that Archer and jollity were bedfellows. Fordham, on the other hand, was nothing if not convivial, and time in his company frequently plumbed hilarity. How he enjoyed playing pranks and practical jokes. Friend and foe suffered alike.

The prominent Brighton vet John Mannington was his frequent aider and abettor whenever Fordham put up at his place in Middle Street during the races. Once upon a time he'd been a decent gentleman rider on the Flat and got to know Fordham through riding a winner or two for Dick Drewitt. One of their pranks involved the local Brighton riding school and a new riding-master who was considered rather above himself. Mannington and Fordham decided to bring him down a peg or two. It was arranged for Fordham to enrol as a pupil. He was seated on a pony and, much to the riding-master's disgust, adopted every conceivable position he was expressly told to avoid. At last the instructor got Fordham to sit fairly straight so that he could trot up and down the school. 'Well, I think you have done enough for today,' the beetroot-faced tutor said patronizingly. 'You can tell your papa if you get on as well tomorrow as you have done today, you will be able to go out with the other pupils on Thursday on the cliff.' Fordham declined a return visit; and much laughter ensued at the prig's expense when eventually he saw his 'pupil' taming a bucking thoroughbred and was informed of his identity.

Another amusing 'adventure' enjoyed by Fordham and Mannington occurred at a little race meeting held on the sands at Littlehampton. Fordham took his diminutive hunting mare named Levity to run in one of the pony races. Professional jockeys were barred; but the youth riding Levity secured their heat by the rather 'professional' ploy of boring her opponent into the sea. Before the final was run, however, the question of Levity's height was raised. The measurement was taken on the sands. With the assistance of sundry taps from Fordham's whip on her shoulder the mare settled into the sand until she was finally passed. Justice was probably done because Levity lost her final – though not before a helpful onlooker had tipped over the Judge's box in an effort to improve her chances of snatching the decision. Subsequently invited to take drink at the Steward's house, Fordham proceeded to follow the party into the house with Levity in tow. The pair had almost reached the dining-room before being discovered

Fordham's second willing accomplice was Henry Custance – who was best man at Fordham's first wedding and godfather to his first born. The two jockeys were often taken for each other when in 'civvies'. One evening after riding in a trial for Hodgman at Carshalton they were taken to a little hostelry called The Greyhound where, to preserve their anonymity, Hodgman asked the publican to call the two men 'Simpson' and 'Wilson'. However, who should be sitting in the smoke-room but a Dr Shorthouse, the editor of *The Sporting Times*, whom Hodgman knew to be highly prejudiced about the riding of both Fordham and Custance. Hodgman decided to have some fun.

'Doctor,' said Hodgman, 'what do you think of Custance's riding now?'

'Custance!' bellowed the peppery gent. 'He be damned! He can't ride a bit! He hangs on. That's all he does.'

'Well, perhaps there is some truth in what you say,' said Hodgman, stirring the pot. 'But surely you will allow Fordham is better.'

'Oh, yes! He's a bit better. But, mind you, not much! Tom Chaloner can beat his head off!'

Somehow Fordham and Custance contained themselves. And set to gaining revenge over a game of cards. They won five shillings each from the good doctor and were as pleased as punch by so doing. The quartet arranged to meet for lunch back at The Greyhound the following day. Shorthouse arrived bearing a heavy stick with a top on it the size of a decent cauliflower. Brandishing it over the two jockeys, he snorted: 'Oh, Mr Simpson and Mr Wilson! I've found you out! I know who you are! But I haven't altered my opinion. Neither of you can ride!'

Fordham proved he could take a joke as well as play one by roaring with laughter.

A second jape arose while the pair were staying at Singleton during Goodwood week. Fordham had agreed to a single-wicket game of cricket with the bookmaker John Jackson for £5: he to play with a bat and Jackson to use a broomstick. Jackson shared Fordham's passion for cricket; and he'd already defeated a professional cricketer in another such contest. The bet was piffling; it was winning that counted. Bookmakers did not prosper from losing. And Jackson was one of the most successful of his time. Known throughout racing as 'Jock o' Oran' after the village near Catterick where he was raised the son of a sporting farmer, his career as a 'penciller' began with local coursing and pony racing. It didn't take him long to build the bank necessary to buy a horse or two – notably Saunterer and Tim Whiffler. Quick-witted and thoroughly unscrupulous, he boasted of having several jockeys in his pocket – and proved it when he was the mastermind behind the pulling of Blink Bonny, favourite for the 1857 St Leger. He rose to become the 'Emperor of the Ring' until his death at the age of 41 accelerated by, according to one obituary, 'inordinate habits of indulgence.'

For this gentleman's game Jackson reverted to type. Perhaps daunted by Fordham's reputation as a cricketer, the 'broomstick' he produced turned out to be a flattened hedge stake, about two feet high and up to two and a half inches wide; the nefarious bookie proceeded to smite Fordham's bowling all round the playing area. Defeat and the prospect of losing the bet to the blackguard appeared inevitable. Then Custance arrived.

'Do you call that a broomstick?' Custance asked Fordham.

'He would not play with anything else. What shall I do, Cus?'

Custance told him to bowl Jackson 'some nice easy ones for him to hit, but on no account to try to bowl him out.'

Jackson whacked a ball out of the ground into an adjacent orchard. He was completing his fourth run when Fordham cried 'Lost ball!'

A group of village boys quickly materialized. 'Now, my boys,' said Fordham, 'if you find the ball I will give you five shillings.'

'All right,' interjected Custance, you can offer ten.'

The ball was not found and, as dinner-time was approaching, the match was left for the day.

The next morning Jackson acquired a new ball and pressed for completion of the match.

'Oh no,' said Fordham. 'It was a one day's match. It's a draw. All bets are off.'

And then, just to rub it in, he added 'I don't like to encourage gambling.'

Jackson went away distinctly unamused. For it soon transpired that the 'lost' ball had been residing in Custance's pocket all along. The poor loser later challenged Custance about this sleight of hand. 'I sent it back to the same place where you got the broomstick from,' replied Custance, 'as I thought they ought to go together. And the next time you make a match with us, and try any of your games, just remember that two can play at them.'

A third jester with whom Fordham consorted was George French, an eccentric character known to one and all as 'Count Bolo'. He became clerk of the course at West Drayton, which lay on an island. In essence it was, like so many small tracks of the age, a vehicle for its owner to print money. Punters entered this 'welsher's paradise' at their peril. The wise knew what lay in store before reaching the track. The 'Count' would post 20 men on the bridge to exact payment to anyone who wished to cross. When a bill was put before Parliament to suppress suburban racecourses such as West Drayton, its Grand Stand, worth £200 at most but insured by French for £600, managed somehow to be razed to the ground. In reality 'Bolo' was probably one of Fordham's greatest enemies because Fordham, fond of a lark and easily led, would end up carousing and playing the fool long into the night instead of retiring to his bed.

Sometimes the biter was bit. On one of his many trips to ride in Paris he went into a hairdresser's. Being unable to speak the language, he acted out his desire for a haircut. The barber took him at his word – or lack of them – and left his head as bare as a cannon ball. On his next visit to the weighing room Fordham had to endure the joshing of Ned 'Mr Mellish' Smith, who was eager to know where he'd been doing 'time' or from which gaol he'd escaped. 'It's all very well for you to talk,' Fordham replied indignantly, 'but I'd like to know what you'd have done had you been in Paris and had your hair cut and been unable to tell them to stop.'

***

Fordham's greatest flaw lay inside a bottle. His drinking became the stuff of legend. A night's carousing in Lincoln was typical. An evening of whist and much liquid celebration in the company of 'Mr Mellish' and 'Brusher' Wells, following a well-supported win that afternoon, resulted in Fordham being carried to his bed like a babe-in-arms by a strapping chambermaid. Drink might be taken at any opportune moment. Cue the tale of Digby Grand – one not always retold entirely accurately.

Fordham and the ornery Digby Grand were made for each other. They were as much soul-mates as Fordham and Lady Elizabeth – just that theirs was a relationship fuelled by a mutual need for booze rather than affection. Digby Grand was trained by Henry Woolcott at Beckhampton for William Graham. He was named after the eponymous hero of George Whyte-Melville's book of 1853 that chronicled the feckless life of an adventurous, gambling Army officer and frequenter of fashionable society. The name proved apt. The colt's sire, Jackson's Saunterer, was a handsome black devil whose habit of throwing back his ears and whisking his tail betrayed temperament; and the son showed similar evidence of being an equine basket case. If it wasn't for the innate ability Digby Grand deigned to show on occasion it's fair to say his racing days would've been short-lived. There was no knowing when that latent talent would be demonstrated. With a cranky animal of this kind Fordham was the rider trainers turned to.

Digby Grand started his juvenile career in 1870 with three placed runs, in the third of which he'd been out-battled in a tight finish at Stockbridge. Fordham was duly put up at York. Unfortunately the pair came across a decent animal in Tullibardine. An hour later they were pulled out again for the Prince of Wales's Stakes which had cut up badly. Sent off 9 to 4 favourite in a four-runner field, Digby Grand broke his duck nicely by half a length. A further 'double event' followed at Newmarket. Digby Grand took his chance in the Middle Park – which was minimal and proved so. Two days later he was brought out again for a Prendergast Stakes that had been reduced to a match versus the filly Hannah, who'd also finished down the field in the Middle Park. Hannah received a pound and was shades of odds on to win. Things went smoothly for Fordham until the final few yards of the race when 'Digby Grand put his head back and gave unmistakable symptoms of wishing to cut it' in the words of *Baily's*. Somehow, Fordham's persuasion got him to the post a head in front. The Prendergast often signposted a Classic contender; as it did here. But it wasn't Digby Grand. It was Hannah who achieved Classic immortality by landing the Fillies Triple Crown.

At three the Fordham-Digby Grand partnership ran sixth in the Two Thousand Guineas and made much of the running in the Derby to be beaten only a head for third. 'Digby Grand succumbed the moment he was called upon,' scolded *The Morning Post*, 'and a rogue is never to be trusted especially over a distance of ground.' True to character, Digby Grand behaved like an angry mule when favourite for the three-runner York St Leger. 'He turned it up', in the words of the Press; and before the start of the St Leger proper he laid his ears back and defied Fordham's every entreaty to compete. Similar displays of mulishness were seen in both the Newmarket Derby and St Leger before the season closed.

Consequently, Fordham knew him to be, in the words of Sir George Chetwynd, 'a horse of very uncertain temper, and to have more up his sleeve than he cared to show us.' The following spring Digby revealed what was 'up his sleeve' by winning the 30-runner City and Suburban with Fred Webb off 7st 8lb - while Fordham looked on from the rear aboard the top weight Sabinus.

The next day Woolcott brought him out again for the Prince of Wales's Stakes over a mile. The 7lb penalty for winning the City and Sub raised his weight to 9st 13lb – so Fordham was back in the saddle. Digby was required to give up to four stone to his 14 opponents. The Ring believed the task was beyond him: the possibility he might consent to put his best foot forward on consecutive days was inconceivable. Fisherman (another of that name, not Tom Parr's stalwart) was made favourite; Digby Grand could be backed at 100 to 30. Few from Beckhampton bothered to support him. Clearly, Digby and George would need to be on top form this day.

As Fordham was adjusting the saddle preparatory to mounting he noticed Woolcott had a black bottle in his hand.

'What's that Harry?' he asked.

'A bottle of old port Mr Graham has sent to give Digby,' replied the trainer, who shared the owner's opinion that the horse needed a stimulant before a race if he was to pull out all the stops.

'Let's have a look at it,' said Fordham. Taking hold of the bottle, he took a long pull at its contents. Silently he handed the bottle to Woolcott, who followed suit.

Then Fordham regained possession of the bottle: 'I don't believe it would do him any good!' he muttered before raising the bottle to his lips for a second lengthy swig.

'I believe it's generally bad for them!' added Woolcott, taking another draught of his own.

Fordham looked to see if any remained - and quietly finished off the dregs.

At this point it's educative to read Tom Cannon's advice on how to get the best out of a 'rogue' for they have the ring of pure Fordham about them: 'One may try the effect, a quarter of an hour before his race, of giving half a bottle (not more) of port or sherry in order to make him run kindly. Though horses can take, comparatively, enormous quantities of certain drugs with impunity, still they cannot take drink much more than twice the amount that an ordinary man can without becoming intoxicated.'

Who was the tipsier of the pair is open to some debate; though it's doubtful whether a few slugs of port had much effect on a tippler like Fordham. Whatever the case, Fordham clambered aboard his shifty, faint-hearted partner to go out and win the race. After kicking Digby Grand under the flag to ensure they got away in line, he immediately took a pull and covered him up in the pack. Once into the straight Recorder (good enough to run fourth in the Grand Prix de Paris and in receipt of two stone from Digby Grand) burst to the lead. Fordham could be spotted doing nothing on Digby Grand, who was lobbing along as pleased as Punch. One 'cluck' at the distance from Fordham was enough to propel the old reprobate into the lead and a victory was secured 'very cleverly' by a length. The port had done the trick. And not just for Digby Grand. It had perked up Fordham no end. An hour later he went out no worse for wear to win the Great Met on Lefevre's Dutch Skater.

True to character, Digby Grand was beaten at odds on next time out. But that was at Newmarket. Epsom was his stamping ground. Back there for the Derby meeting he and Fordham won the Heathcote Plate over the track's lightning quick five furlongs turning the proverbial hand-springs. Epsom's quirky configuration certainly appealed to his quirky personality: it was the only track on which he won. He never won again. And the Press comment on his final run was a succinct 'seen figuring conspicuously in the rear.'

He and Fordham were the embodiment of Oscar Wilde's sentiment that 'work is the curse of the drinking classes.'

***

By the summer of 1875 Fordham's drinking had begun to get out of hand. His liver had taken a pounding and his immune system suffered in consequence. His lungs were showing signs of weakness and he was sometimes caught short of breath. He was a tired man.

In truth Fordham's heart did not always seem to be in his work any longer; at any rate not as consistently as of old. From 1872 there's a noticeable reluctance to start the season with visits to Lincoln and Liverpool. The 1875 season saw this trend gathering pace, manifesting itself in a score of 41 winners from just 141 rides (as opposed to the customary 300-odd), his lowest total in 20 years. After the now customary late start at the Craven Meeting, he missed Epsom's Spring Meeting, Chester and the whole of August, before ceasing on 15 October. Omitting August began as early as 1870. References are frequently made to his 'illness' or, as *The Sporting Life* phrased it, his 'domestic affliction' without specifying its precise nature. The combination of depression and dipsomania was the 'affliction' the *Life* was trying to avoid broaching.

And Fordham was no longer the 'kingpin' of old. In 1875 he now faced a rival he'd need to be on top form to repel. The Grays, Kenyons, Grimshaws and Constables were nothing special. They could be put in their place without undue exertion. But Archer was a different species of champion altogether. A champion with an insatiable appetite; a glutton who gorged on winners.

Occasionally 'The Demon' raked the coals. The flame would burst into glorious life. Levant's July Stakes was one such instance. Another memorable day came at Ascot when Doncaster won the Gold Cup. He was a sensitive animal who disliked rough handling and needed considerable humouring. And a sensitive horse demanded the assistance of the most sensitive jockey in the land. Doncaster and Fordham coasted throughout and cruised home by half a dozen lengths.

Fordham enjoyed the moment in the spotlight, doubtless conscious of the fact they were becoming rarer by the month. Then, out of the blue, he was handed the kind of opportunity 'The Demon' of yore would've relished: a ride in a match race at Newmarket. And this was not any old match. It was a match which the racing community had been demanding for some months.

The clamour to match the reigning Derby winner Galopin with the public favourite Lowlander had been building since Ascot. It would take place over the Rowley Mile for the substantial sum of 1,000 sovereigns a-side the day after the Cesarewitch; Admiral Rous set Galopin to carry 8st 2lb and the six-year-old Lowlander nine stone – 2lb more than weight-for-age. The usual partners of each horse were Morris and Parry respectively. When the owners were making the match everyone assumed Prince Batthyany held out for Galopin to carry the allotted weight in order to secure the services of Fordham. In truth, he asked for 8st 2lb as it was the lowest Jack Morris could do. Nobody blinked when the news broke that Fordham would partner Lowlander, and that should Morris not make the weight on Galopin he'd be taken off in favour of Fred Archer – Morris's overweight would be an encumbrance; Archer's overweight was 'out-weighed' by the mere presence of Archer. 'The interest in which this match was regarded was something extraordinary,' said *The Times*.

Even at this distance of time it's easy to appreciate the reason for Lowlander's public following. He was a gigantic chestnut of over 16 hands quite capable of carrying 14st to hounds. In fact, he'd winning form over hurdles, most recently at Liverpool. The previous season he'd justified favouritism in the Royal Hunt Cup by six lengths – some achievement in one of the calendar's most competitive handicaps. Not content with that success, he re-appeared on the Thursday and Friday to add handicaps over six furlongs and then ten furlongs (under the steadier of 10st 2lb), 'winning hands-down and astonishing us all.' Three successes in three days at diverse distances was a feat to be celebrated even by Victorian standards of equine versatility and stamped him as an outstanding animal. *Baily's* reckoned Lowlander had given Admiral Rous a headache: 'His future will be a puzzle to the Admiral; the ordeal of handicapping is a frightful one for a good horse and we fear that even Lowlander may not get through it.' The paper was correct. In the latest Hunt Cup, Lowlander was burdened with a 'stopping' weight of 9st 6lb; he led the far-side group for six furlongs and was then virtually pulled-up as the lightweights disputed the spoils. However, any idea that he just might be a back number at the age of six was promptly dispelled as he vanquished some noted speedsters in winning five races off the reel over shorter trips. Nevertheless, no one in the Press corps gave him a chance of beating the Derby winner at 2lb worse than weight-for-age even if, as some averred, it was a poor Derby; after all, he was just a handicapper. And he was essentially a sprinter not a miler. The early betting was even, but as the time approached for the pair to face the flag, the odds favoured Galopin at 6 to 4.

Galopin was a beautifully shaped thoroughbred of medium size of extreme nervous excitability – a defining trait he passed on to his son St Simon. He'd been a very fast juvenile who had won the New Stakes and been unluckily defeated in the Middle Park Stakes. His only outing before the Derby was a match over the Rowley Mile which he won by ten lengths. After winning the Derby he returned to sprinting to beat some smart juveniles in the Fern Hill Stakes at Ascot. Morris was a journeyman jockey and was never likely to concede the mount on his meal ticket: he made the 8st 2lb without difficulty.

The Press was in a ferment of excitement. 'In the opinion of many people this match is better worth a visit to Newmarket than all the other events of the week put together,' stated the *Pall Mall Gazette*. 'Had it not been for the great match,' observed *The Times*, 'the Great Eastern Railway need scarcely have run a special train from London. That was the sole item of interest, but still it was sufficient, and we must go back for some years to find a parallel case.' *The Sportsman* captured the words on everyone's lips as they made their way to the racecourse with its headlines: 'Who will win? Which do you fancy – the youngster or the old horse?'

Both horses were reported to be in fine fettle, though only those with powerful binoculars could so verify because they were saddled down at the Ditch Stables. Galopin was dwarfed by his opponent, but wasn't to be outdone in spirit. He delayed the start for a minute or two, seemingly keen to bite anything in sight. Here Fordham displayed his generous nature because he could easily have exploited Morris's deafness at the start and stolen a march, but he repeatedly forestalled the starter by shouting across to Morris that Lowlander would not move until Galopin had jumped off. 'How many jockeys,' asked Thormanby, 'would have been self-sacrificing enough to have done this!'

By common consent Lowlander still got the best of the start. But barely a neck separated the pair until the Bushes. There was no 'kidding' from Fordham this time. Either he couldn't hold the giant Lowlander or, more likely, he dared not let the Derby winner head him. At least that's what the correspondent from the *Pall Mall Gazette* thought: 'Fordham endeavoured to bring Lowlander along at such a pace that Galopin would be unable to overtake him.' At four furlongs or six Lowlander might well have prevailed. The scalding pace had certainly bottomed both horses by the time they raced into the Dip. But of the two it was Lowlander who'd shot his bolt. Not even the genius of Fordham could dredge up reserves of stamina that were not present. Galopin drew away up the hill to win by a length. The pair returned to the Birdcage to great cheering. Both were dead beat. Galopin, in the words of *The Sportsman,* 'looked as if he'd been dragged through a pond.'

This defeat hurt Fordham. His unrivalled knowledge of the Rowley Mile and his enviable reputation in matches had gained him this mount. The fact that he and Lowlander were set an impossible task cut no ice: two days later Galopin advertized his class by comfortably defeating the St Leger winner, Craig Millar, in the Newmarket Derby; the gulf between Classic horses and handicappers had, not for the first time, been demonstrated unequivocally. That failing did not lie at Fordham's door. But his reputation had taken a knock and his pride was hurt.

His nerve was also beginning to fail him. The fear of falling and being trampled under the hooves of a big field rode with him more often than ever. Any jockey who'd ridden for as long as Fordham had to come to terms with the prospect of falls. And, by and large, he had. But the memory of Miss Nipper never truly left him. There'd been other narrow squeaks that might've turned out calamitous. He'd been dropped twice at Ascot and knocked cold; the first accident costing him the winning ride on Buckstone in the 1863 Gold Cup. 'A filly of Mr Ten Broeck's called Curie got me down after we'd gone a furlong in the first race of the day,' Fordham explained to a visitor. 'That was a bad fall and I was dragged - thought I was done for that time, they did, and I couldn't ride for a long time; but it wasn't anything serious.' Three years later he was fortunate to walk away from another potential disaster. He was riding a promising two-year-old of Ten Broeck's called Fitzroy in a match against one ridden by Custance. Fifty yards from victory Fitzroy snapped a leg. Fordham had the speed of mind to pull both his feet out of the irons as the stricken animal hopped past the post but he couldn't bring himself to jump off as speedily as Custance recommended. 'Jump off!' Fordham cried. 'How about my knees?'

A fall at racing pace could be a killer; even a hefty kick might finish a career – as it had Nat Flatman's. Fate was fickle. Without warning clipped heels or crossed legs might catapult a jockey into the turf and leave him at the mercy of clubbing hooves. Fate might choose veteran or novice. A crash in the Liverpool Autumn Cup of 1881 would claim the life of young William Macdonald just as he'd begun getting on good horses like Corrie Roy and Foxhall to win top races like the Jockey Club Cup and the Cesarewitch. Fordham knew his next fall might just be one too many.

Confidence is everything in any sport. Fordham's had begun to falter. He admitted that after riding three losers in succession he felt he didn't ride with so much dash and confidence in the fourth. It wasn't as if he could go away and sharpen the tools of his trade on the gallops. This particular workman could not lay the blame for poor work on his tools. Technique was not the issue: not that Fordham could have consciously set about honing his technique since he barely knew its components – his was purely intuitive. Confidence in race-riding comes from making the right decision at the right time in race after race until the prospect of making an error never enters the jockey's consciousness. That connection had been broken. And whenever his 'nerves' were stretched as taut as violin strings and the black dog snapped at his ankles Fordham reached for the bottle. The ugly truth was that Fordham was operating under a vice that dare not speak its name: dipsomania.

It is a curious paradox that some Victorian jockeys did not eat enough while others drank too much. The unremitting struggle to meet low weights drove many a jockey to an early grave. This much was known and recognized: yet a Bill introduced in Parliament in 1860 to set the minimum weight at 6st 7lb was still defeated; and in the year of Fordham's first retirement in 1875, for example, the winner of the Lincoln and Cesarewitch carried 6 stone and the Cambridgeshire 5st 13lb. With their immune systems weakened by constant wasting, jockeys were susceptible to disease, and the weighing room was the perfect environment for spreading the most highly infectious of them – pulmonary tuberculosis or consumption. Samuel Kenyon and Ben Bray were taken at the age of 23; Harry Constable at 26; Tom French was 29; Tom Chaloner succumbed aged 46; wasting caught up with John Wells at the age of 39; Tom Chaloner died at 46.

Drinking to excess attacked the liver and further weakened the immune system. Fordham was treading a dangerous path; would he learn from the example of Jem Snowden?

When it came to drinking Fordham couldn't hold a candle – should it be a glass – to Snowden, a Tyke of gypsy descent and a wayward mind utterly uncorrupted by the three Rs. Snowden vowed he'd willingly give £5,000 to be able to stop drinking. But many trainers swore he was a better rider pie-eyed than most were stone-cold sober. Often he'd be seen going to post winking, blinking and half-laughing, imploring one of his fellow jockeys 'Just look arter us a bit, wilt thou?' Snowden's legs were hollow and when he hit the bottle hard he didn't ride at all. He once rolled up a week late for Chester races, remarking 'Things seem quiet for race time.' On being put right, he shouted incredulously: 'Then where the hell have I been for seven days!' Mindful of that farce it's no surprise to find Snowden rarely venturing far from his northern base. Whenever he did risk the journey south he proved his mettle by winning a Derby on Blair Athol and two renewals of the Oaks on Butterfly and Jenny Howlett. He should've won another Derby on Doncaster but on the morning of the race was found to be too drunk to ride and replaced by Fred Webb. The first time Fred Archer visited Stockton he was greeted by Snowden with a cheery 'they tell me thee can ride a bit, lad. Aal reet, maw lad, we'll see what thee's made on now.' Snowden pipped Archer after a furious battle. 'Noo, maw lad,' said Jem as they pulled up, 'thee can tell them i' the Sooth that there's mair jockeys in the world than thee. Tha cassn't ride for nuts!'

In his cups Snowden often displayed a waggish line in humour, delivered in a thick Yorkshire accent. While weighing out to partner an old plater named Aragon at Catterick he plonked himself on the scales and was handed the horse's blinkers. 'Naa, naa, tak it away!' he implored. 'Bleend horse and bleend jockey winnet dee!' All the paraphernalia was removed forthwith and Aragon won his race. On another occasion he was requested not to win by more than a neck in a seller because the connections wished to retain the animal cheaply. Snowden jumped the horse off like a bullet from a Martini-Henry to make every yard of the running and win by six lengths. The owner complained bitterly to a friend of Snowden's how he'd been put out of pocket, only to be receive the following rejoinder from the jockey via the intermediary: 'Thou tell him he ought to think himself lucky to win at all, as I saw five winning posts and didn't know which was the right one!' Snowden died flat broke at the age of 45.

Fordham had enough reason to seek solace in the bottle. The death of little Penelope in 1867 had been a body blow to this most sensitive of souls; and whenever an unsettling reverse occurred on the track, such as in the Lowlander match, the bottle called and drink was taken. Another season began to hold more dread than anticipation. His grip on reality became as precarious as a drop of rain on a blade of grass. Fordham could hold his booze better than Snowden: the Digby Grand episode demonstrated how it made no difference to his competence. But he did not wish to degenerate into the same shambling wreck and put at risk his peerless status among colleagues in the weighing room.

Why not retire? He'd accumulated enough money to enjoy a comfortable living for the rest of his life. Though some insisted he'd lost £60,000 (£7.2 million) thanks to Lefevre's investment advice, he knew better - his bank account was safely in the black. Riding fees alone amounted to over £2,000 (£240,000) per annum; 'presents' of £500 for winning a major race were routine; anonymous presents would arrive in envelopes containing £100 notes. In addition, he'd recently been the beneficiary of a revolutionary public testimonial initiated by Sir John Astley and Admiral Rous 'in recognition of his lengthy honourable public career' with subscriptions at three guineas a head. Inside the first month over 200 had subscribed: 'Fordham's universal popularity is certain to secure very extensive recognition from all classes of racing men.'

Thus, money was no obstacle. And racing had lost much of its attraction. He'd grown weary of the fickleness of fame: the greatest jockey one ride; old and useless after the next. He felt podgy, 8st 2lb being as low as he could manage. And he was too proud to play second fiddle to Archer.

Yes, why not retire? In the winter of 1875-76 this struck the 38-year-old Fordham as the considered judgement of a wise man. Without more ado he sold Beaufort House and moved to Brighton where the sea air, cricket of a summer and hunting with the Southdown of a winter promised a lifestyle free of stress and full of joy while he watched his children grow.

However, by the winter of 1877-78 the gloss had worn off this idyll and Fordham was seeking deeper and deeper refuge in the gin bottle.

The inscrutable gaze.

THIRTEEN

MISTER ARCHER

George Fordham's career can roughly be divided into two parts: pre-Archer and post-Archer. All 14 of Fordham's championships and two-thirds of his 16 Classics came before Archer opened his own accounts in 1874. At that point, the heights Archer would attain were unforeseen. In the *Sporting Times*, for instance, John Corlett opined: 'We do not mean to exalt him into a demi-god. Though he has won so many races, we cannot yet report him as being a really great horseman in the sense that Fordham is.' But what had been a period of virtually unchallenged supremacy for 'The Demon' descended into years of simmering rivalry with 'The Tinman' that often boiled over into open conflict. Archer's statistical pre-eminence in this latter period - especially his domination of the nation's principal Flat race - came to define Fordham's career and, in many eyes, relegate it to one of secondary importance.

This paints a false picture. There was little to choose between them. Both were multiple champions. Both left the stage setting a new British record for career wins. Both collected Classics like postage stamps. And both played by their own rules. Certainly Archer's maniacal attitude toward, and mastery of, Epsom's dangerous gradients unquestionably made him Fordham's superior round Epsom and contributed much to his string of Derby successes. Yet, by the same token, no jockey could hold a candle to 'The Demon' at Newmarket – not even 'The Tinman'. And whereas Epsom saw but six days racing each season, Newmarket boasted 25 in the spring and autumn (plus four on the July course) – which gave Fordham ample opportunities to prove the point. The scores in the two Newmarket Classics, for instance, favoured Fordham 10 to 6. The grudging respect in which Archer held his elder and nemesis was exemplified by a photograph of Fordham hanging opposite one of him above the mantelpiece in the drawing room of his Newmarket home.

The gods also bound the two champion jockeys together with tighter and bleaker knots. Both men were dogged by chronic health problems: Fordham fought lung disease, depression and dipsomania; Archer struggled with his weight and mental instability. Both were husbands and fathers scarred by the loss of a wife and an infant. And, as if to cement the synchronicity, they died within 11 months of each other.

It's not unfair to suggest that Archer's tragic demise while in his pomp has tended to colour the debate among Turf historians as to which man was the superior jockey. However, more weight should be given to the views expressed by contemporary voices. Victorian horsemen of every description who voiced an opinion were, virtually to a man, of one accord: George Fordham was in a class of his own.

Sir John Astley used Fordham whenever he could get him:

In my opinion Fordham was the best jockey I have ever known. Though not a first-rate horseman, he had wonderful hands, never abused a horse, and was an extraordinary judge of pace, was never flurried, and always knew to a nicety where the winning post was. And above all was a paragon of honesty.

A second eager patron was George Hodgman:

I always had a high – indeed, the highest – opinion of Fordham, whose superior, taking him all in all, has not appeared in my time. He would, when able, always ride for me; and, in turn, I was ever glad to hand him my colours. It is perhaps too late in the day to attempt to praise him. But no rider, neither of his own nor any other day, excelled him; and I question if his equal, all round, has been seen. Even the 'terrible Archer' acknowledged Fordham's unapproachable artistry, while he had a holy horror of his 'kidding'.

Tommy Heartfield rode against both Archer and Fordham:

Archer was a fine horseman, without a doubt, but I should certainly say not in the same class as Fordham. Everybody, when speaking of greatest jockeys, always used to put Fordham in a corner by himself and then they talked about the others. I never knew how he could make horses win races that nobody else could. Archer would win races with 10lb in hand and make it appear that he had got 21lb in hand. Fordham would win a race with 10lb in hand and make it appear he had got home by the skin of his teeth. That was the difference between the two men's riding.

As did Henry Custance, who won three Derbies:

In speaking of one whom I consider all round to be the finest jockey I ever saw or rode against, it is needless for me to say that I refer to my dear old friend George

Fordham. It is quite impossible for me to mention all the
fine races I have seen him ride.

John Osborne, who rode a dozen Classic winners in a career spanning
46 years from 1846 to 1892, did not demur:

> There's been a lot of good jockeys. Jem Robinson was a
> good jockey and so was Fred Archer. I am inclined to
> think Fordham was the best; you never quite knew where
> you had him. I should think he was a better jockey than
> Archer all round.

Fordham's standing among his fellow jockeys was complemented by
members of the training fraternity who had first-hand knowledge
of every crack jockey from Victorian deities like himself and Archer
through the Americans Sloan and Maher and the Australian
'wunderkind' Frank Wootton to Donoghue and Richards. Charles
Morton's 60-year career on the Turf, for example, bridged the 19th
and 20th centuries. He spent ten formative years with Tom Parr before
embarking on his own training career that led to him becoming the
leading trainer of 1908 and brought success in a dozen Classics, the
last in 1923.

> I read an article in a daily paper comparing Archer and
> Fordham with the present generation of jockeys in which
> the writer said that neither of the two men were anything
> like as good as Donoghue or Richards. I base my opinion
> not on hearsay, but simply personal experience.
>
> On the way back to town from Kempton one day
> I scrambled into a carriage where I found Mr Leopold
> de Rothschild. As the train was steaming out of the
> station Danny Maher joined us. During the journey
> the conversation turned to riding and 'Mr Leo' took the
> opportunity to congratulate Maher on a wonderful race
> he'd ridden that day, but he went on to say: 'With all due
> deference to you, the best jockey I have ever seen in my

life – you included – is Fordham.' And Danny quietly replied: 'So I have always believed.'

Mr de Rothschild was a man who had employed all sorts of jockeys to ride for him and he told Maher to his face that Fordham was the best he had ever seen.

Therefore I am not alone in my opinion. I think that I would rate Fordham a greater jockey than Archer. Not only was he mor skilful but he possessed the greater finishing power and one could count the number of races he threw away on the fingers of one hand. One could find no more interesting sight in the world than to see these two champions riding against each other. There used to be many matches and almost invariably Fordham and Archer were the jockeys chosen to ride. Some of these duels were tremendous, but certainly Fordham won the majority of them.

Both he and Archer were idolized by the public, Fordham representing the older school of jockeys and Archer the new. I think he was inclined to be slightly nervous towards the last two or three years of his riding career, but once on top of a horse all his old confidence returned to him and he would win as brilliantly as he had in the days of yore.

Richard Marsh was another champion trainer whose career spanned the centuries, from 1874 to 1924, and encompassed victory in 13 Classics:

For Fred Archer I had the greatest admiration as well as respect. He had some uncanny means, I thought, of imparting extra vitality to his horses. Yet, on the whole, I am inclined to name George Fordham as the greatest all-round jockey I have ever known. He was a master in judging pace in a tight fit, and no one knew where the winning post was better than he did. He would win a race by a head, and then carry 7lb more on the same horse and still win. You never knew after years of careful observation what he had in hand.

John Porter's career eclipsed even the aforementioned pair. His 43 years in the profession commenced with a degree from the 'University of Michel Grove' under the tutelege of John Bahram Day and saw him train over one thousand winners that included 23 Classics and featured no fewer than three winners of the Triple Crown plus one of the fillies equivalent. He went straight to the crux of the issue: 'Archer was an extremely "brainy" jockey, but not so finished a horseman as Fordham.'

The Press view was epitomized by *The Graphic*:

> Though lacking, perhaps, the extraordinary courage which made Archer such a splendid horseman on the Epsom course, Fordham was in other respects fully the equal of his more celebrated rival. Fordham's honesty was proverbial, moreover, and in this respect some of our younger jockeys would do well to imitate him.

And *The Sporting Times*:

> Fordham was generally able to get the better of Archer on the Newmarket course: he knew it like a book and all the ins and outs of it. Archer would look round, and there was Fordham, who was too clever for him. Whether or not Archer or Fordham was the better jockey, Fordham was the one one would prefer to have on a horse if one wanted him to win races later on. Archer was very handy with whip and spur, and often a horse he won a hard race on never did any more racing afterwards.

Further authoritative judgement came from *The Sportsman*:

> Fordham may properly be described as a jockey more fertile in resources than any of his contemporaries. Nobody could take a liberty with him in race riding, and probably the best of them who opposed him were at one time never comfortable until they had passed the post clearly in front of 'Old Fordham' as he used to be called long before he had reached the age at all justifying the expression. Fordham's errors in

judgement and oversights were few, and it may be written of him that he was one of the best and most honest of jockeys.

The opinion of one who knew what it took to be a master jockey and horseman received its due in *The Morning Post*:

> Since Jem Robinson's day no jockey past or present can compare with Fordham. And when repeated to him Robinson more than once admitted that 'Fordham is the best all-round jockey I ever saw' Fordham feelingly remarked: 'That's the highest compliment I could ever expect from such a great man.'

And most significantly of all, in what amounts to the final word on the debate, Archer's own mentor, Mat Dawson, concurred with the majority opinion. The dour Scot, trainer of no fewer than 28 Classic winners, of whom Archer rode exactly half, gave this unequivocal verdict:

> Taking him all round, I've never seen a better jockey than old George Fordham. He was the best of the jockeys that have come within my knowledge.

***

The difference in physique between these two great champions was pronounced: Archer taller than the average jockey, stooping and long-legged; Fordham squat, round-shouldered and short-legged. The contrast was mirrored in their personalities. They could not have been more different. One was genial and often apt to appear child-like if not actually childish in his behaviour; every child's favourite uncle. The other was somewhat dour and humourless by comparison, seemingly moulded with the role of mortician in mind. Fordham was the hail-fellow-well-met character never happier than with a glass in hand at the heart of the rowdiest group in the tap room – a scene and state of mind totally alien to Archer.

The demonic will to win of 'Mister Archer' caught in caricature.

These polar opposites manifested themselves on the racecourse. Though no one would argue that Archer lacked any affection for the thoroughbred racehorse, the distinct impression emerges that they were essentially a means to an end as far as he was concerned. As trite as it sounds, they enabled him to win races and make money. Long legs wrapped around them, spurs digging and whip cracking, winning was all that mattered to Archer. He gave no quarter – and expected none. Fordham's soft heart, by contrast, could be touched. Whip and spur were the last resort.

And Fordham's benevolence extended to the human as well as the equine. He held the welfare of his fellow jockeys in high regard and was always prepared to lend a helping hand – unless, of course, that jockey was Fred Archer. 'Never was there a fairer or more generous rider than Fordham,' said John Corlett, for so long the editor of *The Pink 'Un*. An incident in the 1864 Chesterfield Cup is worth repeating in this respect. Fordham was riding Lady Clifden. Half a mile from home they cannoned into her half brother Lord Clifden, causing the latter's saddle to slip round and John Osborne to be unshipped. The circumstances were dangerous in the extreme: the 25-runner field was just beginning to pick up speed. Rather than press on in an effort to win the race, as Fred Archer certainly would've done, Fordham instantly pulled up Lady Clifden in order to go to Osborne's assistance.

Fordham's largesse took many forms, and might come in or out of the saddle. He helped John Wells, for instance, win the 1859 Derby on Musjid. The colt's owner, Sir Joseph Hawley, stood to win £75,000, and certain bookmakers who stood to lose had paid two jockeys to make this outcome unlikely. The race, predictably, became a rough house. Wells was buffeted and pinned against the rails with nowhere to go but over them. Only some friendly assistance from Fordham allowed him to extricate his horse – and go on to win. In 1875 Fordham also got Jack Morris out of a hole on the favourite Galopin. As the hard of hearing Morris sensed victory and began easing down his mount, it was only the shouts of 'Go on, Deafie!' from Fordham that alerted him to the rapidly closing figure of Claremont. The revitalized favourite held on by a length.

The champion would often use his influence to gain a decent ride for others. In 1869 Fordham reckoned he knew a 'good thing' for the Cesarewitch. Having ridden in trials that suggested Hodgman's John Davis was a certainty for the race with just 6st 12lb on his back, he begged his friend to let him have the mount at a stone overweight. Hodgman said it would be an insult to Admiral Rous's handicapping to give Fordham the ride under such circumstances. Rather than sulk, Fordham suggested Sammy Mordan be given the chance to ride this certain winner in a big handicap. Mordan had been a lad at Drewitt's with Fordham. A good turn might give him a nice 'earner'. Hodgman told Mordan to sit quietly and let John Davis come home in his own time. But the jockey was always apt to get overexcited and forget his instructions. He also possessed a striking lisp. Fordham, riding Taraban, kept a fatherly eye on Mordan – and was astonished to see him pulling and sawing away at the horse while singing merrily to himself: 'Mittith Thammy Mordan's husband will win the Thetherwitch today. Mittith Thammy Mordan will have her thewing mathine tonight!' Fordham yelled: 'Let his head loose!' Mordan was somewhere other than Newmarket Heath that afternoon. He and John Davis were beaten into second after being held up in the pack and being struck into.

Another instance of Fordham's generosity toward his colleagues in the weighing room involved the afternoon he'd accepted an offer to ride three horses at Windsor instead of the stable's regular jockey.

Who should Fordham meet en route to the course but the said jockey, who, Fordham satisfied himself, had no knowledge of his being left 'on the ground' in favour of 'The Demon'. He fully expected to be riding the three horses himself. On arrival at Windsor, Fordham proceeded to keep well out of sight all afternoon. The stable jockey rode the horses and notched a treble. He was never made aware of the circumstances: neither his patron's duplicity nor Fordham's generosity. Fordham kept the names to himself. Fred Archer would not have conceived such a foolhardy act as foregoing a certain treble.

Nor was Fordham slow to give colleagues their due. In 1865 George Hodgman had a fancied contender for the Great Ebor at York in the form of Verdant, to be ridden by Tommy Heartfield. The horse Hodgman feared was Claremont, the mount of Fordham. He told the two jockeys he'd had 1,500 to 500 about Claremont and 800 to 100 about Verdant. After half a mile or so the pair drew away from the rest and slugged it out all the way through the last mile to the post. Verdant won by a head. 'I wish you had won,' Hodgman told Fordham, doubtless motivated by the size of his wager. 'So do I,' replied the beaten jockey. 'But that's the best boy I've seen for years. I did everything to beat him, but it was no good.'

Fordham's kindness frequently extended to the younger members of his profession to whom he invariably offered nuggets of sound advice. Young Edwin Martin's career was kick-started by a Cesarewitch success that may have eluded him had not Fordham appropriated his whip. In like vein, the emergence of so talented a jockey and horseman as Tom Cannon can be attributed in great part to Fordham. During his years as Danebury's principal rider he was both role model and mentor to the young Cannon – whom he referred to as 'My Boy' - and the measure of his success was Cannon's similarly silken gift with fillies and his absolute honesty. A pointed example of just how much

Fordham had taught his protégé came one day at Newmarket when a reporter watched a finish involving Cannon and Archer while standing beside Fordham at the rails.

> Fordham watched with his arms bent, as if imagining he was on the horse with Cannon.
>
> 'Sit still, Tom! Sit still! That's it! Good boy! Sit still! Sit still!'
>
> Then he clapped one hand into the palm of the other. 'Now then, Tom! Now then!'
>
> Sixty yards from the post, at that same instant, Tom Cannon makes the vigorous effort Fordham had requested and beats Archer by a head.
>
> Both men knew exactly when to move or else the verdict would have gone the other way.

No wonder *Baily's Magazine* was able to say with conviction: 'Among jockeys we can with truth say he has not a single enemy, for his kindness of heart always prompts him to make an excuse for deficiencies in their riding to which his attention has been called, adding "he could not have ridden him better myself."'

There was, of course, one jockey with whom Fordham was not on the best of terms. Extending the hand of friendship to Fred Archer was never on the agenda. Toward Archer a degree of malice was exercised at every opportunity – especially on the Rowley Mile. Only once did Fordham help Archer – and then only indirectly. In 1874 there was every chance Mat Dawson would put Fordham up on his Two Thousand Guineas prospect Atlantic. Fordham was likely tied to Ecossais for M Lefevre. With Fordham unavailable for Atlantic, Dawson entrusted the ride to the 17-year-old, and still a 'feather', Fred Archer who won the Guineas with almost three stone of lead in his saddlecloth. Ecossais was third. Archer had been given the opportunity to prove he was more than a 'feather'. He went on to land his first championship.

No champion concedes his title without a fight and Fordham was not about to accept lightly the loss of his crown. He was no longer at the head of the food chain; another predator now stalked the weighed room. The clash between the old and the new, the artist and the artisan was not long coming. Fordham was eager to put the new young champion in his rightful place.

In the Ascot Derby of 1875 he chose the grandest stage possible. Fordham was partnering Gilbert, a horse he knew raced best when another made the running for him while Archer was riding the Guineas and Oaks-winning filly Spinaway. A spot of 'kidding' was required. 'The Kidder' went straight to the head of affairs and dictated the pace for a while. Then he huffed and puffed – and dropped back on the home turn as if totally spent. Archer took the bait and went on, just as Fordham desired, and engaged in a battle for the lead with Earl of Dartrye. Needless to say, Gilbert suddenly perked up with someone to follow, caught hold of his bit and became a willing partner as Fordham commenced one of his trademark 'rushes'. Gilbert overhauled Spinaway and beat her by three parts of a length. Fordham smiled; Archer seethed.

Before his two-year 'sabbatical' in 1876 and 1877 Fordham had been obliged to watch the young tyro win back-to-back jockeys championships, the second of which saw Archer better his seasonal record of 166 by six. Then, during his absence, Archer raised the bar again to the unprecedented height of a double century with totals of 207 and 218. With 'The Demon' out of the equation the new champion quickly grew accustomed to getting his own way. Adulation went to his young head. He was heard to say at Manchester one day there was no Steward who dare suspend him. Other jockeys became frightened of his intimidation tactics. No one had the strength of character or the degree of skill at their fingertips to stand up to him. But then 'The Demon' came back. The old leading man was not ready to concede to the principal boy. He'd been out of the limelight for two years and obliged to read too many of Archer's rave reviews to put up with other than equal billing. He wasn't prepared to loiter in the wings. Centre stage under the spotlight was his reserve.

The fur soon began flying again. As the field circled down at the start of the 1879 Royal Hunt Cup, Archer's mount, Fiddlestring, had an altercation with Avontes, partnered by Fordham. To the amusement of all the jockeys within earshot, Archer began hectoring Fordham. 'The Demon' waited for the flow in invective to subside before hissing: 'You have taken a liberty with me, Mister Archer, and I will teach you to act differently. I may not do it now. I shall probably wait till you are on something that you fancy yourself about.' He paused for dramatic effect before ending with a hint of the mafioso: 'You must not take a liberty with George.'

It's doubtful whether the habitually inarticulate Fordham had ever strung together a more expressive clutch of sentences. Fordham smouldered like a Vesuvius aching to blow. The promised retribution erupted two days later. Archer was riding Silvio, his first Derby winner, in the inaugural running of the Hardwicke Stakes, for which the five-year-old was a raging 6 to 4 on favourite. Fordham was aboard Stirling Crawfurd's Lancastrian. With half a mile to run he drove the 100 to 8 long shot alongside Exeter and Phenix. John Osborne, riding Chippendale, was sat in behind the three leaders, upsides Archer and Silvio. He had a grand view of what happened once Archer decided to make his move on entering the straight.

'Pull on one side!' Osborne heard Archer bellow in expectation of being given free passage on the rails.

Osborne watched Fordham do nothing of the kind. Archer then attempted to come round the outside.

Then Fordham did pull out. 'I thought I saw some better ground in the middle of the course and made for it,' he afterwards explained innocently.

Archer was forced to yank Silvio wider still before he could ride a finish – while Chippendale was left to seize the sudden gap on the rail. Despite throwing everything at the Derby winner Archer failed by a head to catch Chippendale.

'In all that Fordham did there was not the slightest room for objection and yet he'd most assuredly prevented Archer from winning,' said Osborne.

The Press put the telescope to its blind eye. 'Had Silvio not been interfered with in his endeavours to get through,' observed *The Sportsman* without naming names, 'he would have secured this rich prize.' *The Times* chose to report the events with a cryptic reference to settling day at Tattersall's: 'One of those bits of Ascot ill-luck out of which what are called "Black Mondays" arise.'

Never was Archer so thoroughly paid with his own coin. 'I do not think Archer will ever take a liberty with George again,' said 'The Demon' as he dismounted.

The animus Fordham felt toward Archer followed him to the grave. Fordham did not attend Archer's funeral; and there's no evidence he even sent a wreath. Their feud probably continued on the fields of Elysium.

Sir Bevys

FOURTEEN

A GIFT FROM HEAVEN

When Sir George Chetwynd visited Fordham in early 1878 he found him in a sorry state 'owing to illness and nervousness caused by a failing against which he now manfully strove.' Chetwynd could not bring himself to call a spade a spade. Fordham had sunk close to becoming a hopeless alcoholic. The 40-year-old former champion looked and behaved like a man 20 years older.

Chetwynd decided sympathy was no way to rouse his friend from this torpor. 'What do you want to go on like this for?' he chided. 'You are not an old man! Why not come back and ride again?'

'Me?' was the startled cry from the husk that once was 'The Demon'. Fordham stared at Chetwynd and exclaimed: 'Why, if I tried to sit on a horse now I would fall off!'

Chetwynd persisted. At length Fordham was browbeaten into staying with Henry Woolcott at Beckhampton where he could 'dry out' and regain fitness by riding plenty of work. The ploy worked. The Spartan regime began to pay off. Those God-given hands of gossamer could never be lost, but gradually the muscles tightened again in thigh and calf. The surplus weight melted away. And the confidence returned. Bits of gossip concerning Fordham's possible resurrection began appearing in the Turf papers. 'The Demon' was on the verge of making a Lazarus-like return.

On the morning of Monday, 22 April 1878 he was spotted on Newmarket Heath riding Clemintine at exercise for Tom Jennings. The following day's trade papers confirmed he was the 'probable' rider of Pardon, a five-year-old trained by Jennings for Frederic Lagrange, in that afternoon's Bushes Handicap over the Ditch Mile. There was no more fitting location for Fordham's emotionally-charged reappearance than his beloved Newmarket. The measure of his efforts to get there shouted from the scales: he was riding 9lb lighter than when he'd departed two seasons earlier.

To avoid the ballyhoo, Fordham gained permission to mount Pardon half-way down the course. He rode down on his hack with Custance keeping him company. His resolve ebbed as he finally mounted Pardon and awaited the start.

'Cus, I wish I hadn't got up,' he lamented. 'Look at these kids; I don't know one of them.'

'My dear George,' Custance replied, intent on lifting his friend's spirits, 'don't you trouble about that. They will soon know you when you get upsides of them, especially at the finish!'

The one opponent Fordham did know was Fred Archer. And it was he who won the race. Fordham showed he'd lost none of his dash at the gate by getting Pardon away and clear. But it was only on sufferance. Advance and Archer sailed past to win by three lengths. It struck Custance that Fordham had not overexerted himself, which he attributed to his being weak and out of condition. But he remonstrated with him all the same. 'Why, you didn't have half a go!'

'You don't think I was going to let him beat me a neck the first time I rode,' replied Fordham, with a knowing wink, 'which he would have just done!'

'The Kidder' was back.

Custance hurriedly sought out Tom Jennings to report this exchange. He persuaded the trainer to run Pardon in the Bretby Plate over the shorter trip of six furlongs later that same afternoon. Jennings agreed. Starting at 4 to 1, Pardon beat the favourite by three-quarters of a length courtesy of one of Fordham's typical 'old fashioned rushes'. In *The Sportsman* the 'Special Commissioner', George Lowe, captured the mood of rising excitement: 'Each stride that Pardon made when he tackled Dunkery was answered by a cheer from the Ring.'

The moment elevated a mundane day's sport to something very special which those present were quick to appreciate. 'Except to contribute my mite of congratulation to George Fordham on his reappearance in the saddle and splendid horsemanship when riding Pardon,' commented 'Augur' (editor Charles Blake) in *The Sporting Life*, 'I shall pass over the first half of the card.' Custance was overjoyed: 'I never heard anyone receive a greater ovation than George Fordham did on his return to weigh in that day.' Charles Morton echoed Custance: 'Never in my life have I seen such a reception. The Duke of Wellington returning to England after the Battle of Waterloo had no more memorable ovation.' In *The Sportsman* 'Vigilant', now Henry Smurthwaite, was equally ecstatic:

> 'The Demon' is himself again and not yet done witching the world with his noble horsemanship!
> There was never a jockey more popular than Fordham, who has worn most of the silks and satins of the turf with

credit to himself and satisfaction to his employers, and the high esteem in which the master of the art of equitation is held was made abundantly manifest on his return into the winner's circle on Pardon. Winners and losers cheered alike; members of the Jockey Club vied with his brother professionals in their congratulations; and the bookmaker, as well as the backer, welcomed his return to busy life again, for assuredly in his time Fordham has been a friend to each. The air was rent with cheers and the height of the jockey's popularity was made patent on all hands. The sturdy little fellow was fairly overwhelmed by his reception. His services are certain to be much sought after, especially now he has broken the ice in such fine form.

Smurthwaite was right: those 'services' were quickly in demand. Shortly afterwards Fordham won his second race, on a mare of Sir George Chetwynd's called Calabria, at the Epsom spring meeting. 'Those of his many admires who had not been present at Newmarket,' reported Chetwynd, 'felt bound to express their pleasure at seeing this most able and honest horseman once more in the saddle, which no jockey has ever more adorned.' That old fires still burned brightly were confirmed at the next Newmarket meeting when 'The Demon' twice put one over Fred Archer. At Ascot Fordham made a vivid impression on the 18-year-old George Lambton who watched from the Trainers Stand as he won the Prince of Wales's Stakes on Glengarry:

> I was standing next to James Ryan, the trainer of Glengarry, and I remember that half-way up the hill there were four or five horses fighting out a desperate race. My eyes were glued on the green and gold colours carried by Glengarry as Ryan told me that he thought he could win, and I had a bet of £1 on the horse with him. I saw the green and gold jacket drop out. Ryan put his glasses down, saying, 'I'm beat,' and I thought it was all over. But not a bit of it, for then I saw my horse gradually creeping up again, and one dash close home put his head in front on the winning

post. This was my first lesson in the art of race-riding, and the first of many brilliant races I have seen George Fordham ride.

The Fordham magic was still there. And on any course, even a brand new one like Kempton Park where he won the inaugural race on 18 July. Not for no reason was Henry Hall Dixon heard to say while perusing the results one day: 'Fancy, Fordham, with all his knowledge and experience, and able to ride at 7st 5lb. It seems like a gift from Heaven.'

Fordham passed the 'gift' to a number of old patrons and friends. Sir John Astley, for one, was eager to exploit the gift that kept on giving. A Fordham-secured victory in a Newmarket nursery aboard Cromwell at 6 to 1 sent 'The Mate' home happy. William Stirling Crawfurd lost no time in once more securing the services of his former jockey on a retainer of £1,000; Fordham quickly repaid him by winning the Goodwood Stakes on Norwich. In the autumn Fordham rewarded his old patron with victory in the Newmarket St Leger courtesy of Sefton; and even a run of the mill success in a nursery over the Ditch Mile aboard the filly Out of Bounds was applauded by Chetwynd as 'consummate skill in the art of race-riding, as he won a head, sitting quite still, onlookers believing he'd won in a canter. But, he assured Mr Crawfurd, he could not have won an inch further.'

The victim of Fordham's larceny that autumn afternoon was an unheralded colt of Lionel de Rothschild's called Sir Bevys. His own moment would soon arrive.

***

Fordham finished the 1878 season with a commendable total of 58 winners and a winning ratio of one in four. But the New Year ushered in a personal tragedy to match the hammer blow of his daughter's death.

His wife had been fighting pulmonary tuberculosis for some 14 months in a sanatorium on the Isle of Wight where peace, rest and fresh sea air offered the only palliative care available. Penelope Fordham's inevitable capitulation to the disease came on 4 March 1879. She was only 40 years of age. Fordham was inconsolable. He was a widower with three children under the age of 12 to bring up on his own. All of a sudden the prospects of flogging his tired body through another season of purgatory seemed an ordeal too many.

Although he'd started the 1879 season with two wins from a handful of rides at Lincoln and Northampton in late March, he'd not been seen on course since 2 April. Events had conspired to overwhelm him. He couldn't shake off a severe chill caught while riding work at Manton prior to the Northampton meeting. And it was around this time that he took the skull-rattling fall from Bobby while out on the Sussex Downs; for some weeks the severe concussion that resulted caused doubts to be expressed about him ever making a complete recovery. On top of the emotional fall-out from the death of his wife, these blows to his physical well-being hit him hard. His breathing, in particular, was becoming laboured. With hindsight it's clear the disease that would eventually claim his life had begun to take hold.

Consumption, or pulmonary tuberculosis when the disease attacks the lungs, was the silent serial killer of Victorian England: a gradual enfeeblement and general wasting away of the body with mortality running as high as 500,000 a year. The disease was highly infectious, its deadly bacilli spread by coughing and sneezing and capable of lingering in air and dust. It particularly attacked those with weakened immune systems. Any person wasting in order to control their weight – such as a jockey. Anyone who imbibed too much alcohol – such as Fordham. Almost certainly Fordham had been infected by his late wife. Body and soul seemed damaged beyond repair. He withdrew from public scrutiny – driven by the need to drink himself into a happy stupor.

Until, one day in May, he was tracked down by John Wood, racing manager to Baron Lionel de Rothschild. Wood found the jockey in the parlour of a rustic tavern drinking gin and water, chatting and smoking with a band of regulars.

'The Baron would like you to come out of retirement and ride Sir Bevys in the Derby,' said Wood.

Fordham put down his glass. 'If they have got a horse that can win the Derby they ought to get someone who can ride it better than old George Fordham!'

His acolytes laughed on cue. Wood pressed him. But Fordham was adamant. The messenger departed.

The next day Fordham received a telegram from the Baron requesting his presence at New Court, the headquarters of the family bank in the City of London. Lionel de Rothschild was the eldest son of Baron Nathan Meyer de Rothschild, the founder of the English branch of one of Europe's most illustrious families, a friend of Wellington and the most influential banker in Europe. His sons carried on the de Rothschild tradition of assisting the British Government in raising seven-figure loans for such as the relief of famine in Ireland, the Crimean campaign and the purchase of shares in the Suez Canal Company. Not without justification did Disraeli describe the de Rothschilds as 'a family not more regarded for their riches than esteemed for their honour, integrity and public spirit.' Their wealth, power and prestige made them leaders of Victorian society; the character of the powerful Jew named Sidonia in Disraeli's 1844 novel *Coningsby* was allegedly based on Lionel de Rothschild.

His first winner came in a humble hunters' race at Gorhambury in 1842. In truth, Baron Lionel preferred hunting to racing, but the enormous success of his younger brother Meyer in the so-called 'Baron's Year' of 1871, that included a Derby (Favonius), the Fillies Triple Crown (Hannah) and a hefty gamble on Corisande in the Cesarewitch, inevitably ignited a degree of fraternal competition. Joseph Hayhoe became Lionel's trainer. George Fordham was his jockey. And he didn't want any other.

His meeting with the jockey at New Court was brief and to the point. Fordham made his case. 'If the colt is really so good, there are others who would do him more justice than I could.'

De Rothschild looked him in the eye. 'Look here, Fordham, you will permit me to know my own business.'

One can almost see the banker's gaze darkening: he was 70-years old and in constant pain from gout. 'You will go down to Newmarket,' he continued brusquely, 'and ride this horse a gallop or two. Then tell me what you think of him.'

Fordham knew he was on a hiding to nothing. De Rothschild's order brooked no contradiction. He did as he was bid.

On arriving in Newmarket he sought out his friend Sir George Chetwynd to tell him of de Rothschild's wishes. Chetwynd encouraged him to comply. Fordham duly reported to Hayhoe at Palace House Stables. Owner and trainer had thought their best chance of Classic honours in 1879 was with Gunnersbury who'd been placed in the Woodcote, July and Middle Park as a juvenile. But the colt had gone wrong; and 'Sir Boice', as Hayhoe's lads knew him, was unexpectedly elevated to the position of the Baron's first string. Hence the urgency to discover how much of a 'live' chance he possessed. The judgement in his forthcoming trial of a man like Fordham would be priceless.

On the face of it Sir Bevys had little to commend him. He was a smallish dark brown son of Favonius out of a stoutly bred mare called Lady Langden, which made him a half brother to Hampton – not the lowly Hampton of Fordham's youthful acquaintance but the winner of the Goodwood and Doncaster Cups and a successful sire. Some commentators, such as 'Skylark' in *The Illustrated Sporting & Dramatic News*, thought him 'rather cobby and at first sight he would certainly strike a casual observer as too short for a first rate Classic horse.' He was bred at Wytham, just outside Oxford, by Lord Norreys (who retained a half share in him) and was leased to de Rothschild who raced under the assumed name of 'Mr Acton' he derived from the location of his stud farm. Mindful of the many stones ultimately cast in the direction of Sir Bevys for his perceived lack of Derby-winning stature, it's worth mentioning that Norreys turned down an offer of £2,000 from M Lefevre for Lady Langden with Sir Bevys at foot. The colt struggled to break his maiden as a juvenile, eventually taking an Optional Selling Stakes at Newmarket in October from a filly claimed for £300. A fortnight later, on the same track, he ran well against the decent filly Out of Bounds in a one mile nursery to lose by a head in concession of 2lb. Nonetheless, Sir Bevys hardly attracted a second glance from the Press. In his two-page Derby preview 'Skylark'gave Sir Bevys just six lines, concluding: 'These performances do not read very grand; in fact he cannot be placed very high in the second class.' *The Times* was more emphatic: 'These performances were about equal to those of a selling plater.'

The trial Sir Bevys ran shortly before the Derby proved an eye-opener. It was over one and a half miles and he was asked to give 18lb to some fair middle-distance handicappers and fellow Derby candidate Squirrel, who'd won a couple of races for the Baron. He trounced them. De Rothschild – and Fordham – could go to Epsom with some crumbs of hope. The race had an open look to it, thanks, in the main, to the exclusion of Peter, the outstanding colt of the generation, owing to the death of his owner General Peel.

The appearance of Fordham's name in the list of runners and riders for the 100th Derby published at the start of the week caused many an eyebrow to rise. But he was down to partner Stirling Crawfurd's Lansdown (a four-time winner at two though out of his depth in the premier events) and not Sir Bevys: Dodge, MacDonald and Glover were the pilots mooted for the de Rothschild colt. However, Chetwynd had assured Fordham that Crawfurd's candidate had run poorly in his trials and would miss the Derby; there was no obstacle to him partnering Sir Bevys. A day later Lansdown was withdrawn. Twenty-four hours before the race Fordham's name appeared beside that of Sir Bevys – whose price instantly tumbled ten points to 25 to 1. That same morning Sir Bevys, with a boy in the saddle, was led by Squirrel over most of the Derby course at a 'capital pace' in the words of *The Sportsman*, 'and evidently liked the soft going, moving with great strength and courage through the dirty track which in some places was sadly cut up – it was one of the best gallops of the morning.' Sir Bevys's odds were clipped further to 20 to 1. The pundits, however, continued to scratch their heads. 'Never within my experience have I known so open a race for the great prize,' added the George Lowe. 'I am almost at my wit's end to name a horse that I consider most likely to win.' The paper's resident poet, however, had no such reservations:

> *The Corner reached to hug the rails*
> *Now Fordham tries his best,*
> *But Exeter and Rayon d'Or*
> *The fav'rite place contest.*

Over at *The Sporting Life* its editor, Charles Blake, had more optimistic words to say about Fordham's conveyance in the centenary renewal of the Blue Riband.

> Sir Bevys has not run this year. All that is known of him arises from the style in which he does his work and the weight he has been found to concede Squirrel, who has run very respectably this year, in a trial. Judged through his last year's running at the back-end with the smart filly Out of Bounds, Sir Bevys is fully entitled to take rank as a useful colt. He is a very evenly made, muscular colt, perhaps lacking a little in the length one associates with a high-class horse. At one time or another he has been backed for a lot of money and his breeding, by a Derby winner out of the dam of Hampton, is a combination which certainly ought to be productive of something above average if there is anything in the theory that 'like begets like'.

Sir Bevys would be Fordham's first mount for 55 days; and only his eleventh of the season. Thus, with the eternally reliable benefit of hindsight, it's permissible to fancy Fordham's Derby victory having been written in the stars.

Torrential thunderstorms throughout the Tuesday and the possibility of more rain to come failed to deter the Prince and Princess of Wales from attending this historic Derby. Nor would the extremely testing conditions in prospect negate the chances of the Fordham-Sir Bevys combination. Sir Bevys had big feet. The ground wouldn't hinder him and his stamina might just pay dividends. To the benefit of the crowd, if not Sir Bevys, the rain held off. As the field paraded in front of the enclosures, the Ring had settled on Guineas runner-up Cadogan as the 9 to 2 favourite to overturn the form with his Newmarket conqueror Charibert. The general lack of confidence surrounding any candidate was reflected by no fewer than 18 of the 23 runners (who included two French challengers in Saleador and

Zut - winner of the French Derby four days later) being sent off at odds of 100 to 7 or more.

For once McGeorge got the Derby field away to a beautiful start. Sir Bevys, however, couldn't lie up with the early pace and hadn't covered a quarter of a mile before he was being offered at 100 to 1. As Palmbearer and Caxtonian led round Tattenham Corner, Fordham could be spotted threading his way through the pack, skilfully plotting a course that avoided the most treacherous ground. Then there came the kind of moment that often determines success or failure in a Derby.

Fordham found his path blocked by the no-hoper Nutbush (singularly lacking the speed of his 1861 namesake), a stablemate of Palmbearer. Fordham shouted at the horse's rider, Willie Platt, to pull out of the way. For once in his Derby experience Fordham got the slice of luck he'd been so often denied. Platt thought Sir Bevys had no chance of catching his stable-mate so he complied: 'If I had not made room he would never have won.' It would've been no surprise to learn of Platt receiving a dressing down for his act of charity because on the basis of the staying power he'd shown by winning twice at Doncaster the previous week the connections of the Yorkshire-bred, owned, and trained Palmbearer had got odds of 200 to 1 about the 66 to 1 shot.

With Charibert (rumoured to be 'touched' in his wind) and Cadogan all at sea in the ground, the only targets for Sir Bevys to aim at were the two outsiders Palmbearer and Visconti. Sir Bevys, who was going stronger with every stride, tackled them one hundred yards from the winning post and running on as straight as a dart won cosily by three-quarters of a length and one length. That conditions were testing in the extreme was indicated by a winning time of over three minutes, the slowest in 24 years.

Fordham wins his single Derby.

A few years later Fordham furnished a journalist with his memory of the race. It was his customary modest, utterly unembellished summary:

> I daresay Sir Bevys wasn't a good horse, but the rest were very bad ones. They went a great pace at the start. I couldn't get near them going up the hill – couldn't get near them at all, and then had to pull out a long way to clear the crowd of horses coming round the corner. My horse was full of running then, and the others came back to me.

Few admitted backing the winner. One who did was Lord Rosebery, the owner of Visconti. He'd a bet of £13,000 to £200 on his own horse – plus a 'saver' on Sir Bevys. Another to profit was Poet Laureate Alfred Tennyson who'd taken £100 to £5 because, he explained, 'Sir Bevys was the hero of one of my early poems.' De Rothschild presented Fordham with a cheque for £20 and a pound of best tobacco. If truth be told it was the jockey who should have been thanking the owner for dragging him back into the saddle. Said Fordham to his patron: 'It strikes me, sir, that you know a lot more about me than I know about myself.' Six days after that exchange the Baron succumbed to gout. In his Will he left his jockey a bequest of £2,000 plus £300 per annum for the rest of his life.

The racing parish welcomed its favourite son with unbridled jubilation. 'That Fordham was greeted with the heaviest cheers of everyone on the course as he returned to scale need scarcely be said,' wrote Sir George Chetwynd, 'for his probity and honour were universally recognized and made him everywhere popular.' The winning horse, on the other hand, struggled for plaudits, the *Pall Mall Gazette* emphasizing 'it is probably not an exaggeration to say that the race was competed for by the worst field of horses which ever came to post for the Derby.'

The Sporting Life focused all its attention on the winning rider:

> Fickle fortune so willed it that outsiders should occupy the three leading places and that George Fordham, to whom the jade has hitherto been so unkind in the great race of the year, should at length be enabled to set the seal upon his fame as a jockey. Fordham has broken the long spell of ill-luck which has followed him through 18 Derbies, this result being in a great measure due to his magnificent horsemanship.
>
> It was good fortune Fordham had the mount for there can be no manner of doubt but that Mr Acton's colt was outpaced at first, and instead of biding his time, many a jockey would have commenced driving Sir Bevys along, thereby sealing his death warrant.
>
> When the cry went up that 'Fordham wins!' the great jockey was more thought of than the horse and his success is all the more notable and famous inasmuch that it is associated with the centenary of the race and the hundredth Derby will always be quoted when George Fordham's renown and ability as a horseman is the subject of discussion. He is the more to be congratulated on his success from the fact he had practically retired for two years from his duties in the saddle. No jockey was ever more deservedly popular.

The Morning Post was equally euphoric:

> Seldom, if ever, was the winner of the Derby received with more genuine and enthusiastic welcome. Those who have indulged in the hope and belief of Fordham winning the Derby must be glad the popular idol postponed his retirement from public life for a year or two, as the occasion here presented of attaining the height of his ambition might not have been realized.
>
> Carping critics who protested beforehand that the seniors nowadays think too much of their wives

and families whilst descending the hill to Tattenham Corner must think again. It has been Fordham's fate to suffer from this particular delusion, although no bolder horsemanship and no fairer or more honourable jockey ever wore a silk jacket. Now he has triumphantly dispelled that notion, thanks, in part, to the good offices of Sir George Chetwynd when it came to his knowledge that Mr Crawfurd would run nothing.

How much Fordham's patience, fine judgement of pace and artistic skills assisted toward Sir Bevys's triumph nobody speaks in more eloquent terms than the owner and trainer of the winner. If deficient in speed, Sir Bevys possesses wonderful stamina, in which important qualification nearly all his opponents proved themselves lamentably deficient. It is almost too absurd to imagine that anything that was behind Sir Bevys will turn the tables on him in the St Leger no matter what the ground may be.

Likewise *The Illustrated Sporting & Dramatic News*:

Many a time has the cup of Derby victory been dashed from the lips of the great horseman and doubtless it is all the sweeter for having been so long delayed. His reception with the 'mob' as well as at the hands of old friends among employers, jockeys and the general race going public was as enthusiastic as it was well deserved, and we take it the thunder of applause for once betokened the popularity of the rider rather than indicating the hero-worship often bestowed upon the victorious steed. The cheering crowd through which George Fordham made his triumphal progress to scale thought but little of the colours worn by their old favourite, nor of the horse which he bestrode, the demonstration being in favour of the jockey who had so long held a place in their affections.

The Baron's death de-faulted Sir Bevys's from his next target, the Grand Prix de Paris. Subsequently the colt developed into a 'whistler' and made no show in the St Leger (Fordham being obliged to partner Lansdown) for which he started joint favourite with the eventual winner Rayon d'Or. It also turned out to be his last appearance. After a career of just six races he retired to stud at a paltry fee of 10 guineas. Unlike his half-brother Hampton, Sir Bevys left no mark in the Stud Book; he died in 1896 disputing the tag as Victorian England's worse Derby winner with Sefton and Sir Visto. 'It is a curious example of the irony of fate,' wrote Sydenham Dixon, 'that George Fordham should have won his only Derby upon him, succeeding where he had failed when favoured with exceptional mounts as Lord Clifden and Macgregor.' Fordham would compete in the Derby a further three times but never came close to recording a second success.

That Fordham himself was a proud and happy man is underlined by an uncharacteristic exchange on the train carrying him back to London that evening. Who should climb into the same carriage but Henry Smurthwaite, alias 'Vigilant' of *The Sportsman*. The scribe was able to tell his readers in the next day's edition how the victorious jockey had forsaken his lifetime habit of not discussing racing; he'd happily relived his Derby triumph whilst recalling the circumstances he felt had prevented the likes of Lord Clifden, Vauban and Macgregor from lifting the Blue Riband in days gone by.

Fordham subsequently sat at home until Ascot, where he donned the colours of old patrons Graham, Bowes, Lagrange and Stirling Crawford. Ten rides for 'Craw' ended with victory on the last, Dalnaspidal II in Friday's Triennial. Fordham finished the season with a respectable total of 47 winners from 244 mounts.

It's safe to say the course of 1879 had subjected George Fordham to every human emotion. A year that had begun so gut-wrenchingly with the premature end of one marriage concluded with the joy of a second: and in between was the best wedding present of all - a Derby winner.

Fordham's bride at St Andrew's church Enfield on 15 November was his late wife's cousin, Lydia Selth. She was 35-years-old. Whether or not this was a marriage made on the 'rebound', it proved a happy, albeit short, one. The family settled in Brighton where it resided in a series of rented properties in New Steine, Brunswick Place and Norfolk Square. It was in the south coast town that May Lydia Fordham was born in early 1881; George Fordham's last child never married and died in Bath in 1951. Her mother remained attached to Brighton and died there at the age of 74 in 1918.

***

Another member of the Turf Establishment to benefit from Fordham's resurrection was the Duke of Beaufort. For a brief period the Duke, like Fordham, had been absent from the Turf - albeit for an entirely different reason. He had been drawing between £8,000 and £12,000 a year from royalties off his Monmouthshire properties until the Nant y Ghlow ironworks was forced to close. Either his hounds or his string of racehorses had to go. He opted to maintain Badminton's hounds. It says much for Beaufort's integrity that he'd survived at Danebury surrounded by reckless gamblers and shady characters like Padwick. By 1879, when he revived his Turf interests, John Day had been forced into retirement by a succession of bad debts and the onset of impaired sight. Beaufort sent his horses to join those of his cousin, Lord Calthorpe, at Bedford Cottage where Joseph Cannon now held the licence. Thus did Beaufort provide the conveyance for what came to be acknowledged as the fourth of Fordham's great quartet of rides: that aboard Petronel in the 1880 Two Thousand Guineas.

1st November 1879.

APPEARED PERSONALLY, *George Fordham*

M. { of *Uxbridge*, *in the County of Middlesex* of the *Parish*
a Widower,

and prayed a Licence for the Solemnization of Matrimony in
the *Parish* Church of *Enfield*
in the County of Middlesex
aforesaid,

M. { between *him* and *Lydia Selth*
of the *No 27 Tottenham Court Road*
in the said County, a *Spinster, of*
the age of twenty one years and upwards

and made Oath that he believeth that there is no Impediment of
Kindred or Alliance, or of any other lawful cause, nor any Suit commenced in any Ecclesiastical Court to bar or hinder the Proceed-
ing of the said Matrimony, according to the tenor of such Licence.

M. { And he further made oath, that he the said *Appeared*
Lydia Selth,

hath had *her* usual Place of abode within the said *Parish*
of *Enfield*
for the space of *Fifteen* days last past.

George Fordham

R. Robertson

Licence for Fordham's second marriage bearing his elegant signature.

Petronel was home-bred, by Musket out of Crytheia, one of the few mares Beaufort had not sold. Those seeking omens pointed to the fact that Cannon had never more than two or three of the Duke's horses in his care at any one time and yet the first winner he trained for his patron was another son of Crytheia called Brivan. Petronel stood barely 15.2 hands and his dark brown coat was so close to being black that he soon became known as 'The Duke's Little Black'. He made his debut in the highest class, the Middle Park, and fared accordingly; he finished in the pack. Next time out, however, he took the four-runner Troy Stakes by a neck from the Archer-ridden filly Strathardle. Charlie Wood was in the plate. Petronel was not regarded as Beaufort's number one Classic contender, however. That status rested with Belisarius until he met with a fatal accident during the winter. Petronel did not run again until the Guineas. He was reported to have wintered well and Fred Webb was to be his intended partner in what seemed a wide open Classic; betting in the subscription rooms was tame in the days leading up to the race. The death of the Marquis of Anglesey rendered void the nomination of Beaudesert, who'd won the Middle Park in the hands of Fordham; the Duke of Westminster's Bend Or, who'd scooped three of the other elite juvenile events, was being saved for the Derby; and Mask, the long-time winter favourite, had lost his prep race at the Craven Meeting. With no outstanding contender, favouritism was deputed to a horse who'd run no fewer than 11 times as a two-year-old for just five wins - Brotherhood, beaten by Bend Or at York, fourth in the Middle Park, and recently only third in the Craven Stakes.

'The race seems to lie between Brotherhood, who has the best of the public form,' calculated *The Times*, 'and the dark horses, the best of whom is believed to be Muncaster.' The latter was a fine upstanding 16.2 hands chesnut running for the Duke of Westminster instead of

Bend Or. However, there was another 'dark' horse about whom the Newmarket drums were beating. Petronel was quietly fancied by Cannon. Pretty soon 'The Tinman' was pressing the Duke for the ride. He was told the ride had been promised to Fordham should he not be required to honour his retainer with Stirling Crawfurd.

Archer's scheming would be foiled. By defeating Mask in the Column Stakes, Lord Falmouth's Merry-go-Round ensured his participation and Archer's presence on his back. But while 'The Tinman' posed no threat to Fred Webb's ride 'The Demon' did. At the last moment Stirling Crawfurd's outsider was scratched. And Fordham's name went up beside Petronel's.

The weather on Guineas day seemed a fitting comment on the quality of the 17-runner field: it was truly miserable, a biting easterly wind blasting the Heath that chilled both man and beast to the bone. Petronel stripped looking in the pink of condition, his quarters gleaming like billiard balls in the dull atmosphere. On looks alone his compact and strongly built frame gave him as good a chance as any, yet he was largely overlooked in the market and went off at the generous odds of 20 to 1. Those who placed more trust in coincidence than the formbook pointed to Petronel being number one on the card, like the Duke's Vauban 13 years earlier.

The field got away to an excellent start and immediately split into three: Brotherhood leading the far side group; M Lefevre's leggy representative Beauminet holding sway in the centre; while the near side tracked the 'rag' Napsbury. By the time they reached the Bushes the outcome appeared to rest between Muncaster and Beauminet, now racing side by side up the middle of the course. Suddenly Fordham brought up Petronel with one of those trademark 'rushes' with which he'd snatched so many races out of the fire on the Rowley Mile. Muncaster began to run 'green' as he met the rising ground out of the

Dip, and Beauminet tired. Petronel was gaining ground hand over fist up the stands side. The post beckoned. Beaufort believed Petronel had not got there first: 'Two strides further, and I should have won!' he told Sir George Chetwynd after Muncaster and Petronel had crossed the line divided by the width of the track. However, as he had on Sabinus, Fordham's inspired late run under the nose of the Judge was spotted and had stolen victory by a head. And, as when winning the same Classic on Formosa, Fordham achieved this feat of arms without aid of whip or spur.

The Sportsman set the tone:

> Quite like olden times it looked to see Fordham ride a winner in the colours of the Duke of Beaufort. Naturally the success was received with a cordial welcome on all sides.
>
> The finish was a wonderfully close and exciting one, Petronel winning in the hands of Fordham, who rode a beautiful race. It was a masterly exhibition on his part. The way in which he brought Petronel up to the girths of the leathering Muncaster and beat him reminded one of the day he won with Vauban. Indeed, "The Demon" was today seen to the greatest advantage, and there can be little doubt that the fine condition in which Cannon sent the colt to the post conduced greatly to his success.

These sentiments were universal. *The Times* echoed:

> Everybody was glad to see the once familiar 'blue and white hoops' carried to the front after so long an absence, and worn, too, by one whose younger days were so associated with the Duke and Danebury.
>
> Petronel won by sheer staying powers. It is doubtful if we have ever before witnessed a Guineas when a dark horse who never previously ran in public and a despised outsider whose two-year-old running was, to say the least, very indifferent, had the finish to themselves. So it was,

however; and a year which commenced with surprises seems likely to keep up its reputation.

Petronel was not engaged in either Derby or St Leger. Fordham subsequently won an Ascot Biennial and Doncaster's Great Yorkshire Handicap on him. But he abandoned Petronel in the Liverpool Autumn Cup for Prestonpans, whom John Porter trained for Frederick Gretton. This partner in the Bass brewery loved nothing better than a tilt at the Ring, and Fordham was booked well in advance for what was supposed to be Gretton's second string to Fernandez by his friend 'Lord Freddy' Swindell, who also happened to be Gretton's commission agent. This booking in itself was a tip that Prestonpans might wind up the stable 'selected' because Fordham was not fond of Liverpool owing to its tight bends and was usually reaching for pipe and slippers by the first week in November: what Fordham dreaded did come to pass in the following year's renewal when William Macdonald died after his mount was brought down. On the morning of the race Swindell informed Gretton the bets he desired about Fernandez couldn't be made – and Fernandez was withdrawn. Prestonpans had to give Petronel 3lb and could be backed at 11 to 2 so to do. He was generally regarded to be a non-stayer who'd find the Cup's one mile and three furlongs too far for him. But as the leaders hared off in front Fordham was content to watch and wait. 'Fordham rode a magnificent race,' said *The Times*. 'He waited with marvellous patience and, letting the leaders exhaust themselves, he came with one run and won by half a length, somewhat easily.' Unlike the Press, the public was unamused by Gretton's conduct. Fordham brought back Prestonpans, heavily backed by Gretton before the off, amid a cacophony of hisses and boos. Nor was Porter pleased: he ordered Gretton to remove all his horses from Kingsclere forthwith.

Fordham's association with the de Rothschild family continued with Lionel's son Leopold, who took first claim on his services in 1882. 'Mr Leo' was the most unselfish of men, and one who always wished to do good for others – which led him to being exploited by many in search of a 'hand-out'. He was never happy if his many friends had no share in any success gained by his horses. His relatively brief association with Fordham wasn't blessed with an absolutely tip-top performer: Nellie, out of Meyer de Rothschild's Oaks winner Hippia, being about the best. But it was her misfortune to be foaled in a vintage year for members of her sex: in 1882, for the single occasion in history, fillies won all five Classics. Fordham rode Nellie into third place behind St Marguerite in both the One Thousand Guineas and Geheimniss in the Oaks, while Shotover (Two Thousand Guineas and Derby) and Dutch Oven (St Leger) secured the other three Classics. If those rivals were insufficient Nellie also had the speedy Kermesse to contend with; indeed, it's conceivable that but for splitting both pasterns in the autumn of her juvenile season Kermesse would've proved the best of them all. Faced by this quintet Nellie fully deserved her few days in the sun, winning York's Prince of Wales's Stakes (from Dutch Oven) at two before adding the Newmarket St Leger and dead-heating with Kermesse for the Select Stakes (with Shotover back in third) in the autumn of 1882.

***

An even older association was rekindled when Richard Ten Broeck returned to England. The prodigal American's presence opened the way to Fordham getting on possibly the best horse he'd ever ridden. During a career that now spanned over 30 years Fordham had sat on some of the very finest thoroughbreds. Formosa and Thebais stood out among the many exceptional fillies. Colts of that standard with whom he enjoyed a regular association were fewer: Lord Clifden was probably the best of them; but he'd won on the likes of Thormanby, Doncaster and, recently in the St James Palace Stakes, Bend Or. Now Ten Broeck's faith in Fordham led to the jockey getting onto a colt possibly better than all of them: Foxhall.

Tobacco magnate Pierre Lorillard was the first American to own a Derby winner when Iroquois took the 1881 renewal (followed up by the St Leger). However, in many eyes, there was a superior American-bred three-year-old to Iroquois running in England during 1881. This was Foxhall who might conceivably have won the Triple Crown had he only been entered for the Classics. After the weights for the Cesarewitch set Iroquois the task of conceding 7lb to his American rival *The Times* opined: 'It is unlikely Iroquois would be able to beat Foxhall at level weights let alone giving him 7lb. Foxhall is universally looked upon as perhaps the best horse ever foaled.' His lucky owner was JR Keene.

Multimillionaire James Keene was not an American by birth but by manufacture. Born in London in 1838 he went to America with his parents at the age of 12 and grew up in Shasta, California. He sold milk, worked in a mill, taught school and edited a weekly newspaper. When he was 35 he bought some mules and went into the hauling business, supplying mines in Nevada. He made $10,000 in a year which he put to sterling use by purchasing a seat on the San Francisco stock exchange. Within three years he was worth $6 million. Keene moved east and his profits soared to $9 million in the first two years of arriving in New York, earning the white-whiskered businessman the soubriquet of the 'Silver Fox of Wall Street.' A contemporary wrote of him: 'A man of the plainest speech and the most absolute candour, he was probably the greatest Stock Exchange strategist that the world has yet seen.' Thoroughbreds became his passion and his only pastime. He developed a great eye for a horse and, as he had in business, soon exercised sound judgement in their management, spending every Sunday, summer or winter, at his stables studying and examining each of his animals in turn. 'He was proud of his horses,' commented *Horse & Hound*, 'and no animal of his was allowed to start unless he was as fit as he could be, and to do his best. Nor would he sanction manipulations for handicaps.'

Keene's horses followed Lorillard's to England. Chief among them was a two-year-old colt that he named after his son Foxhall. This offspring of King Alfonso (whom Keene purchased for 100 guineas at Newmarket Sales) traced back through Lexington to Diomed, the first winner of the Derby and subsequently sold to America. Placed in the care of 'Buck' Sherrard in Newmarket, the colt did not immediately distinguish himself, winning only two minor races at Newmarket as a juvenile in the hands of Charlie Wood. His first run in 1881 was in Epsom's City and Sub in which he went down by one length to the previous year's Derby winner Bend Or. Thereafter, Foxhall bloomed into, according to *The Times*, 'one of the best-looking three-year-olds trained at Newmarket.' He was then put aside until high summer when Keene decided to send him over to France for the Grand Prix de Paris.

The decision made enormous sense. It was the only opportunity for Foxhall to show his class against the current Classic generation at level weights; and the Grand Prix's first prize of £6,374 (*£½ million*) outstripped the Derby's. Foxhall had been partnered by Greaves at Epsom but someone with French experience would prove crucial. Keene consulted his friend and unofficial racing manager Ten Broeck. Fordham was engaged forthwith.

The Bois de Boulogne welcomed a wagon train of carriages making their way to Longchamp waving the stars and stripes. Nine stood their ground against Foxhall whose burgeoning reputation had made him 2 to 1 favourite. His principal opponent was known to Fordham. Tristan was a colt he'd ridden to many successes. He was a cantankerous so-and-so; some days he'd go and other days he wouldn't. He'd failed in both Guineas and Derby, but the previous Thursday he'd journeyed over to Longchamp to win the Prix de Deauville in good style. Adding spice to the mix this day was the presence of Archer on Tristan's back. The French had heard plenty about the bitter rivalry existing between the 'The Tinman' and 'The Demon'. Now they were about to watch it up close. Confidence in Archer's ability to tame Tristan saw his odds slashed from 14 to 1 to 5 to 1; the French Derby winner Albion was second favourite on 4s. The skies had turned dull and looked full of thunder – as had Tristan's temper. There was no proper parade ring at Longchamp and the crowd milled round Tristan like a swarm of wasps: he lashed out at anything or anybody that came too close.

A distance just short of two miles is a tough examination for a three-year-old in June but Fordham elected to make the running; Foxhall had plenty of stamina and guts. He'd need plenty of both. At the second attempt the field got away. Fordham drove the American horse straight into the lead in a determined effort to maximize his colt's attributes. Archer had no option but to wait. A sustained duel would've cut their throats and left others to prosper. After Dublin kept Foxhall company for the first mile or so, the American colt entered the final furlong looking to be a comfortable winner. But Archer was humouring Tristan. He waited until the last 50 yards and then brought him with a sustained challenge. The crowd roared to the duel. Archer whipped and spurred. As Fordham knew he would. Tristan clawed back the deficit. However, the wily George had kept a little something up his sleeve for just such an eventuality. He stopped 'clucking'; the fidgeting seamlessly metamorphosed into the strongest drive. Foxhall extended his neck. The two horses passed the post locked in combat like a pair of angry adders. And it was Foxhall's number 13 that went up in the frame.

'At one time it seemed as if Archer would be able to get M Lefevre's colt home,' reported the *Pall Mall Gazette*, 'but Fordham got the last ounce out of Foxhall and won a head.' *The Times* added: 'The Americans present loudly cheered the success of their champion, while there were a few hisses from people of other nationalities.' *The Sportsman* also drew attention to a victory that was 'apparently received with as much favour and enthusiasm as if the winner had belonged to a prominent member of the French Turf instead of to a representative of the mighty American republic. Our Yankee friends have every reason to be proud.' On the far side of the Atlantic in the hotels and clubs of New York the sole topic of conversation was 'the unbounded satisfaction that American colours have again come to the fore.' For securing the largest prize in his career Fordham received a present of £500.

Four days later Foxhall took his place at Ascot for the Gold Cup. He wasn't favourite. That privilege went to the previous year's St Leger victor, Robert the Devil. 'The Demon' versus 'The Devil' tag that would've been an advertizing executive's dream a century later, proved misleading in 1881. 'The Demon' got to 'The Devil's' tail a mile from home but got no further. Foxhall dropped away, 'a broken reed', according to *The Times*, to finish last of the quintet. Inevitably, the form of the Grand Prix was brought into question: in beating Tristan he'd probably not beaten much. More probably, the journey back and forth to France plus the terribly hard race against Tristan had, temporarily at least, got to the bottom of him.

Fordham's association with Foxhall here endeth. At the beginning of August Foxhall was transferred from Sherrard's care to William

Day, now training from Cholderton. The move to a trainer who'd slandered him over The Happy Land back in 1858 severed Fordham's connection with the horse. This was a pity because the horse quickly advertized his class, despite arriving at Cholderton lame in his hocks. He won the Grand Duke Michael Stakes at Newmarket in September; the following month he achieved the rare distinction of annexing both legs of the Autumn Double, the Cesarewitch and the Cambridgeshire. He took the former by 12 lengths ridden by William Macdonald, to whom Keene gave a present of £3,000; though the ill-fated youngster enjoyed precious little time in which to spend it. Jack Watts rode Foxhall in the second leg of the Autumn Double. The field was as competitive as ever. Bend Or (the 9 to 2 favourite) carried 9st 8lb of Fred Archer and lead – but wasn't even top weight; the dubious honour of humping ten stone went to Sir John Astley's Peter, winner of the Royal Hunt Cup and the Hardwicke Stakes. Petronel carried nine stone – the same as Foxhall, whose impost included 28lb in penalties. Fordham was aboard Tristan (7st 9lb). The race was a corker. Foxhall just got the better of the Oaks second Lucy Glitters and Tristan by a head and a neck. Fordham maintained he'd have won had not Lucy Glitters been leaning across him when Foxhall pounced. The winner shouldered 10lb more than any three-year-old had previously carried to victory in a race which always contained plenty of them. The following season Foxhall added the Ascot Gold Cup. The trophy was duly sent to Keene in New York, but he objected to paying the $1,000 duty demanded by the Customs. Given that he'd bet heavily on his horse and reputedly won £¼ million (*£20 million*), this does seem rather cheapskate on his part. Allegedly, Keene never bet again, saying: 'Any man who bets consistently is a sucker.'

Neither Keene nor Ten Broeck managed to emulate Lorillard's feat of winning an English Classic. But each of these Americans had left a warm and abiding impression. Ten Broeck returned to America in 1887. After the death of his first wife he'd married a rich Louisville widow. They settled in San Mateo, near San Francisco. Ten Broeck had grown more irascible with age and the onset of gout. So irritable and irritating did he become that his wife tried to have him declared insane. She failed; they divorced. On the morning of 1 August 1892 the 81-year-old Ten Broeck was found dead in his bed (arms neatly folded across his chest) at his tiny cottage, 'The Hermitage', forsaken and alone but 'no taint of dishonour upon his soul.' The body of George Fordham's great ally and friend was taken to Louisville for burial. Marse Watterson, publisher of the *Louisville Courier-Journal* paid tribute: 'The most intrepid gambler who ever backed a horse, bucked a tiger or bluffed on a pair of deuces.' Ten Broeck would've appreciated that sentiment, but even more so the exploits of the thoroughbred subsequently named in his honour whose triumphs included a famous match race against Mollie McCarty that became immortalized in song.

***

Christopher-Joachim Lefevre's colours had returned to the fray in 1880.

Fordham quickly rewarded his French patron with a French Classic: the 1880 Prix de Diane with Versigny. She was a leggy and rather narrow filly by Flageolet out of Verdure and, therefore, was a half sister to the Grand Prix de Paris victor Vermout. Lefevre had purchased the mare for 100,000 francs from Henri Delamarre after she'd run second to Mortemer in the Ascot Gold Cup. Versigny was lucky to enter training with Richard Carter Senior at Royallieu having been bitten by a venomous bug which necessitated weeks of care and convalescence. Thus, she was not considered ready to take her bow until the Grand Criterium at the back end of 1879; with Fordham in the saddle Versigny finished a creditable fourth. Her Classic season kicked off with wins in the Prix de Longchamp and Prix Hocquart prior to finishing second in the One Thousand Guineas under Fred Archer when she was still considered rather backward. Lefevre held her in high regard: 'She is very remarkable, in my opinion,' he informed a reporter before the Prix de Diane. With Archer unwilling to make the journey across the Channel (he had a low opinion of French racing, especially the conduct of French jockeys toward their English counterparts) Fordham became the obvious replacement. After riding work at Manton on the Saturday morning he headed for Dover. Eleven opposed his mount at Chantilly 'despite the favour in which Versigny was held'; the market went 7 to 1 bar the 6 to 4 favourite. Versigny proceeded to win in a canter by one and a half lengths. Indeed, she won so comfortably that 'save for its historical interest,' stated the *Pall Mall Gazette*, 'the Prix de Diane would not have attracted more attention than the other events in the programme.' The immediate cross-Channel trip for Epsom's equivalent received the expected outcome: a lacklustre display.

Fordham also partnered a beast as far removed from a sweet-tempered filly as might possibly be imagined, a steed fit for 'The Devil' let alone 'The Demon' – the idiosyncratic Tristan. A dark chestnut standing 16 hands by Hermit out of a Stockwell mare, he'd been such a sickly foal that, on the premise he was unlikely to survive, he was acquired by Lord Rosslyn for the sum of half a crown. Lefevre was obliged to outlay considerably more for him as a yearling. Tristan's association with Fordham began successfully in the Westminster Stakes at the Epsom Spring Meeting of 1880. The following afternoon a Fordham-deprived Tristan failed to give the 3lb sex allowance to Angelina by one and a half lengths. But a matter of days later the enigma that was Tristan began to assert itself. In a Breeders Plate at Newmarket he and Fordham totally reversed the form with Angelina; and the filly proved herself to be no slouch by going on to win the Woodcote and Acorn at the Epsom Derby meeting. *The Morning Post* reported: 'To the horror of the "plungers" the "glorious uncertainty" was again illustrated by Tristan, who'd finished well behind Angelina at Epsom. Whether attributable to the different course or change of jockey, we should not venture to decide. But the result was a "staggerer" for those learned authorities who make handicap books their special study. Fordham astonished everybody!'

Fordham and Tristan would go on to 'astonish' and, it must be said, infuriate, the racing public for a further three seasons. Fordham conjured 14 victories from this 'vile tempered' thoroughbred. Like the little girl in the nursery rhyme, when Tristan was bad he tended to be 'horrid'. Even with Fordham in the pigskin good days mixed freely with the bad. The former included the wonderful Ascot treble of 1882 in the Gold Vase, Biennial and Hardwicke; and the Epsom Gold Cup and the Ascot equivalent plus another Hardwicke the following season. The 1883 Gold Cup was a typically hairy affair. 'They tried to do me!' said Fordham afterwards. 'Webb was on Wallenstein. He went off with the lead and when he came to the turn where Tristan's stables were, he pulled up, you know, thinking mine would run out of the course. Tristan stopped too, and I had to holloa to the others who were just behind me, to keep clear of my heels, or he'd have been among them in no time.' The downright ugly was represented by the Goodwood Cup of 1882 when Tristan (at 7 to 2 on) effectively threw in the towel behind a mediocre maiden gelding called Friday who couldn't even register a win over fences. Eventually Fordham's patience with Tristan was exhausted. 'I didn't care much about riding him, and I let the long legged fellows, Archer and Webb, ride instead,' he explained. 'I can't afford to have horses pull me about! The long legged ones can get on and off easier. Tristan's a useful horse, he's not a wonder, and he was a troublesome horse, easy to get out of temper.'

Tristan continued to serve up the curate's egg until the day he retired the winner of 29 races. That the Duchess of Montrose was later moved to buy him for 20,000 guineas would've amused Fordham had he been alive. Nor would the news that Tristan ultimately killed himself by beating his head against the wall of his box in a fit of temper have come as any great shock.

Tristan was Lefevre's last truly outstanding horse. Dogged by failing health, the financier watched his seasonal returns plummet from over £20,000 in 1883 to not much more than £5,000 two years later. By the end of the decade his colours were gone from the Turf. As he became dogged by failing health, Chamant's horses were leased to Baron de Rothschild for a few years: among them was Heaume, winner of the 1890 Prix du Jockey Club. With his fortune melting away as rapidly as his health, Lefevre sold his estate and stud to M Albert Menier in 1892. Lefevre's 'checkered existance' ended on 27 June 1895 at the relatively young age of 60. It was a wonder he survived that long and died a free man.

**

The Fordham alchemy persisted throughout what was destined to be his swansong in 1883.

The magic, however, was limited. His body was feeling the pinch. Although travelling was a lot quicker and more comfortable than the early decades of his career (express trains could ferry him from Slough to Newmarket in less than three hours), he seldom felt up to the ordeal. He confined himself to the big meetings – Epsom and Doncaster for the Classics; his beloved Newmarket for all and sundry; and the great festivals of Ascot and Goodwood where he might stay for three or four days in the one place. Not for the first time York was missed; and he didn't ride at all between 3 August and 4 September. Fordham only took 261 mounts spread over just 66 days of racing. He only graced 13 racecourses, and Newmarket, naturally, accounted for half those race-days. Riding for Leopold de Rothschild (31 wins) and Christopher-Joachim Lefevre (15), was his priority. Nonetheless, his farewell campaign turned out to be very much a last hurrah with his score of 77 (a winning percentage of around 30%) featuring a six-timer at Newmarket on 24 April plus success in a Classic and prestigious events at the major meetings. Tristan, despite being as mulish as ever beforehand, took the Gold Cups at Epsom and Ascot; Ladislas the Ascot Derby and Jockey Club Cup; Wild Thyme the New Stakes, Chesterfield and Lavant; and the Scottish-bred Border Minstrel added the Goodwood Stakes.

Moreover, there was the *piece de resistance* that was the utter humiliation of Archer in the Brag-Reputation match at a rainy Newmarket on 10 May. What was but a minor event on the card became the day's big story. *The Sporting Life* put it into context perfectly:

> The match was one of those old fashioned and sporting affairs now so rarely seen on Newmarket Heath, yet which once were so frequent. The battle was a right royal one. That judgement in agreeing the weights had been

exercised was very plainly supported by the closeness of the betting with Brag having the slight call beforehand. But Reputation was favourite in running until Fordham showed he is still 'all there', especially in matches on Newmarket Heath, once more adding fresh laurels to the boundless wreath he has won on the course.

Newmarket was an appropriate setting for Fordham's sixteenth, and final, Classic victory, fittingly on a filly: Hauteur in the 1883 One Thousand Guineas. His seventh win remains the most by any jockey in the One Thousand Guineas. It also marked Fordham's second Classic for Lefevre.

Hauteur was a brown daughter of Rosicrucian who'd advertised her Classic potential by winning the Acorn, Champagne and Clearwell Stakes at two. Her victory in the Champagne Stakes was the definitive performance because she overcame a quartet of redoubtable colts in Galliard (winner of the Chesterfield and Prince of Wales's), Macheath (July Stakes), The Prince (Rous Memorial) and Chislehurst (Seaton Delaval Stakes). Hauteur was largely ignored at 10 to 1. Yet, as *The Times* commented, 'the filly cleverly bowled over all her opponents and came through to challenge Macheath and win a slashing race by a neck. The result was a blow for backers.' The strength of that form is to be gauged by Galliard going on to win the Two Thousand Guineas, with The Prince in third, before coming third in the Derby; and Chislehurst finishing second in the St Leger.

However, on Guineas morn most Newmarket 'experts' were behind Britomartis, another with smart credentials as a juvenile, representing the team of Lord Falmouth, Mat Dawson and Fred Archer. 'The question arises,' stated *The Sporting Life*, 'which has made the greater improvement in the meantime, and this is a ticklish point to decide.' There was no doubting which filly stole the eye: 'Hauteur has not grown much but would puzzle a Kentucky lawyer to find a better looking or trained filly than this hall-marked daughter of Rosicrucian.' The market sided with Hauteur at 9 to 4. Britomartis took the lead at the Bushes but soon wilted as Fordham drove Hauteur upsides and then clear. However, on meeting the rising ground, Hauteur began to look in distress and it took all of Fordham's guile to coax her home in what became a desperately tight finish with Malibran and Lovely.

The Times recorded Hauteur's success thus:

> By her brilliant, if not easy victory, Hauteur has confirmed her reputation as one of the best class animals among the two-year-olds of last season, and corroborated the fact that her Doncaster Champagne Stakes victory was by no means the fluke which some persons at the time persisted in asserting. The finish seemed likely to result in a surprise, but the favourite ran gamely and pulled her backers through. The three placed fillies ran a desperate race home ending in favour of Hauteur by a head from Malibran, a like distance to Lovely in third. Fordham has been in wonderful form all week and wound up today by winning two other races in addition to the One Thousand Guineas which brought his total to six.

Fordham had helped Hauteur to her finest hour. In nine further attempts spanning 1883 and 1884 she never won again.

***

While some old relationships flourished one of the oldest soured. The 'auld alliance' with Stirling Crawfurd soon sailed into stormy waters. A significant change in Crawfurd's private life led this reunion along a rockier coastline than was comfortable. In 1876 'Craw' had taken a new wife: Caroline, widow of the Duke of

Montrose. It's not unfair to say that in his new wife Crawfurd had acquired someone more than eager to grab the tiller. And someone ready to make Fordham walk the plank.

From the reams committed to print about the larger than life personality that was the Duchess of Montrose one builds a picture of a riddle wrapped up in an enigma. She could be generous of spirit one month and as toxic as a bag of snakes the next. She built a holiday home on the banks of Loch Lomond for the disadvantaged children of Glasgow and opened the Stableman's Institute in Newmarket where lads might read and relax. When Crawfurd died in 1883 she erected a church in his memory on Newmarket's Bury Road. But after the vicar she installed prayed for sunshine after a wet spell the Duchess scolded him: 'How dare you pray for fine weather when you know very well that my horse will need soft ground in the St Leger. I shall not allow you to preach in my church again.' It's a mark of this unpredictable woman that her threat fell by the wayside.

The Duchess was one of those people whom it can justifiably be said might start a donnybrook with the occupants of a funeral parlour. She displayed neither fear nor favour. Trainers, jockeys, owners, handicappers, reporters and servants were treated with the equal disdain – usually in language as salty as any sea dog's. She was even said to have hissed at the Queen at Ascot on one infamous occasion. One trait was constant: the blame for setback and disaster were always laid at someone else's door.

Captain Machell she soon got in her cross-hairs. At one time he managed her horses. But the friendship between two bull-headed individuals never held much hope of longevity. The subsequent insults and insinuations often provoked open warfare to the obvious entertainment of Newmarket's racing fraternity. The finest anecdote, whatever the bad taste, concerned Machell running over the Duchess's favourite dog in his hackney carriage: she swore she'd watched him bounce heavily on the seat directly above the axle to ensure the canine was suitably crushed.

The warning signs of a woman engaged at one's peril were there to see in the masculine cut of her clothes and a homburg hat invariably perched jauntily above a face adorned with too much war-paint for a woman of mature years. Once described as a young beauty, by the time of her marriage to Stirling Crawfurd, at the age of 58, her looks and her efforts either to mask of embellish them had left her looking more like an over-the-hill music hall artiste than a discreetly ageing aristocrat. With each advancing year her eyes were cast in the direction of progressively younger gentlemen – even extending to a ridiculous infatuation with Fred Archer. After Crawfurd's death she eventually snared one, hardly surprising given the money showered on the 24-year-old stripling she married at the grand age of 70.

She was known on the racecourse as 'Carrie Red' in snide allusion to the colour of her henna-dyed hair or 'Six Mile Bottom', after the village near Newmarket, by way of reference to her breadth of beam. This expansive derriere, however, would never smart from sitting on a fence. And the one thing no one doubted was that the Duchess of Montrose knew her onions when it came to racing.

Trainers might expect her interference as a matter of course. Only 'Grim Old Alec' Taylor defied her intimidation. One day the Duchess quizzed Taylor on the chances of a particular animal of hers and stood speechless as he replied: 'Damned to hell if I know Your Grace.' On another Taylor delivered the ultimate put-down: 'Your Grace, I have known two really clever women in my time. The first was my mother, who could train horses as well as my father. The second is my wife, who knows how to mind her own business.'

For an inveterate gambler like Carrie Red the enemy above all others – even worse than bookmakers, touts and the 'plungers' who stole her price – was the handicapper. Her horses always had too much weight. One such handicapper, the heavy-engined 20-stone Major Egerton, was accused of allotting them prodigious weights so he might ride them himself. Jockeys received similar treatment. Her favourites came and went. Huxtable was at one stage her lightweight jockey of choice – until he got beat on one fancy too many. 'Why on earth didn't you do as you were told and come along with the horse?' she raged. 'I am sorry, Your Grace,' mumbled Huxtable. 'But I should have had to come along without the horse.' On another occasion she discharged both barrels in the direction of the Robinsons (unrelated), her jockey Jack and the Judge, Charles: 'What with Robinson who cannot ride and Robinson who is apparently colour blind, I seem unlikely to win any races this year.'

It was always short odds that the hyper-sensitive Fordham would not put up with the Duchess's caprice for very long. Things went swimmingly to begin with: in 1880 Fordham handed Crawfurd the Stewards Cup (Elf King), Brighton Cup (Bay Archer) and Middle Park (St Louis). Better still, the following season he enjoyed Classic success with Crawfurd some 22 years after enjoying the first on Mayonaise.

The animal in question was another filly, a beautiful home-bred chestnut, by Hermit out of Devotion, named Thebais. Her first two outings were nothing special: a third at Stockbridge and down the field at Newmarket. Thereafter Thebais began to show that she just might turn into something special. Ten more races as a juvenile followed. She and Fordham won the lot. They included the Ham at Goodwood and the Criterion. Alec Taylor kept her away from prying eyes until the One Thousand Guineas the following May. She reappeared looking an absolute picture of a thoroughbred. Money was piled on her and she went off at 6 to 5 on. Fordham kept her close up behind in third until the Dip when the race was reduced to a match between her and Thora. Fordham tenderly pushed her to the post a neck in front. With most jockeys such a slender margin would've signposted an energy-sapping affair – and Thebais had clocked a race record time of 1minute 50 seconds suggestive of a torrid pace. But with Fordham it meant nothing of the kind. There were going to be other days. Thebais had proved her toughness with those dozen runs as a two-year-old but Fordham was mindful of how Lady Elizabeth had become soured by one gruelling race too many.

Thebais did not run again until the Oaks. The day was warm and the track dusty. The filly had kept her condition marvellously: 'Thebais has grown into one of the most handsome mares that ever trod the Turf,' stated *The Sportsman*. Again she started odds on; it was 8 to 1 bar. The only tiny element of uncertainty was created by the participation of Perplexite, the runner up in the French Oaks. 'It proved, however, that all apprehensions on this score were unnecessary,' reported *The Times*. 'The favourite waited until coming down the Hill, when she took command and justified the reliance that had been placed on her by cantering in a most easy winner by three lengths from Lucy Glitters. This makes Fordham's fifth win in the Oaks and his victory was exceedingly popular.'

Thebais enjoyed a regal progress through the summer meetings. She humiliated the future Park Hill winner Bal Gal (and Archer) by 15 lengths in the Nassau at Goodwood and did so again in the Yorkshire Oaks. Then, at Newmarket's First October Meeting she was beaten at 11 to 8 on. Fordham's record on the filly stood at an imposing 15 wins from 19 starts. But he never rode her again.

With Crawfurd cutting an increasingly bedraggled figure in face of the tempest that was his formidable wife, the link with Fordham was on borrowed time. Like many a mature lady the Duchess had developed an eye for younger men. 'The Tinman' not 'The Demon' was becoming the cynosure of Carrie Red's covetous eye. 'There's the coming Fordham,' she cooed after one of Archer's ferocious finishes. 'He'll teach George a bit before he's much older.' Craw attempted to calm the waters by informing Fordham he could pick and choose his mounts and only ride when he felt like it. But the Duchess wouldn't let go. Fordham was too old, she insisted; he was past it: 'He can no longer ride.' It's not hard to imagine Fordham hearing those words and muttering under his breath: 'You have taken a liberty with me, Your Grace.'

The inevitable parting of the ways came late in 1881. Fordham rode eight Crawfurd horses at Newmarket's Second October Meeting – and won on just the one. Among the vanquished was St Marguerite (a full sister to Thebais on whom he'd won the Chesterfield Stakes) in the Middle Park and Corrie Roy (at 5 to 4 on) in the Newmarket Oaks. The final defeat, on Young Duke, came at the hands of Charlie Wood riding Chetwynd's Exile II. The Duchess had seen enough. She'd seen the future. It might not always encompass Fred Archer but it could include Charlie Wood. Caustic comments were passed for all and sundry to hear. *The Sporting Times* reported cryptically: 'The Duchess of Montrose has requested Fordham to send in his cap and jacket. He did so instantly, for fear the Duchess might change her mind.' His reaction would prove as costly as it was inevitable because it denied him an eighth One Thousand Guineas courtesy of St Marguerite. 'The lady has conquered and Fordham's connection with Mr Crawfurd is severed,' observed *The World*.

'The Demon' could afford to bide his time to settle the Duchess, just as he did Archer. The Press was on his side and quickly pinpointed the vagaries of this meddlesome female interloper in the male 'club' that was the Turf. 'She gives orders to the jockeys,' reported *The Sporting Times*, 'and in not the most seemly manner, very soundly reprimanding them.' A doggerel mocked the couple thus:

> *Corrie Roy and Carrie Red*
> *Carrie Red and Corrie Roy*
> *One for the course and one for the bed:*
> *Isn't Craw a lucky boy?*

If revenge is a dish best served cold the plate Fordham served was gazpacho dotted with ice cubes. And it was perhaps the truest exhibition of vintage Fordham witnessed during this final chapter in his career.

It was saved for the Jockey Club Cup, run over the two miles two furlongs and 28 yards of the Cesarewitch course at his beloved Newmarket on 25 October 1883. The vehicle was Ladislas, a three-year-old bay colt owned by Lefevre. Charles Morton described Fordham's riding of Ladislas as 'the finest horsemanship I have ever seen. He had been riding for fully 30 years but he still remained the incomparable master of his craft. The people who were present at Newmarket that occasion witnessed an epic battle they never forgot to their dying day.'

Ladislas was decent colt but unexceptional. He wasn't much to look at, being somewhat on the wiry side. Bred, like Tristan, by Lord Rosslyn, he was by the stayer Hampton, a half brother to Sir Bevys. As a juvenile he'd proved himself superior in home trials to the subsequent Guineas winner Hauteur but on the track his career had been hit-and-miss. He and Fordham made all to win the Dewhurst (with future Derby winner St Blaise back in sixth) but weren't in the shake-up to Crawfurd's Macheath in the Middle Park. His Classic campaign had proved fruitless; yet he managed to win the Ascot Derby (again beating St Blaise) and Newmarket St Leger. Fordham had reached the conclusion that to get the best out of Ladislas he had to be switched off to the point of unconsciousness before being awoken for one short, sharp 'rush'. Fordham later confessed to having a soft spot for Ladislas: 'He was a good horse that day. He was coming on and just getting a good horse when racing was over. They tried him bad. They tried how to make him better, and made him worse. But he ran very game that time and stayed home well, you know.'

They had three opponents: 'If the field was a small one,' said *The Times*, 'it made up for the deficiency in numbers by its superior quality.' It's impossible to believe anything other than Fordham was going out to do everything in his considerable power to prevent one particular opponent from winning. Corrie Roy would run in the name and chocolate colours of Sir Frederic Johnstone, a fabulously rich and urbane member of the Jockey Club and highly respected. However, it was common knowledge the mare also waved the scarlet banner of the Duchess, and would be ridden by Fordham's successor, Charlie Wood. The five-year-old had won the race in 1881 and the Cesarewitch of 1882, plus four more prizes in 1883. The latter included the Goodwood Stakes 'in the commonest of canters' when conceding 17lb or more to her eight rivals; and the (Great) Ebor Handicap at York under top weight of 9st 12lb, likewise 'in a canter'. She was the 5 to 2 on favourite. The St Leger-winning filly of 1882, Dutch Oven, represented the Archer-Dawson-Lord Falmouth team; she numbered a Queen's Plate at Stockbridge among her three successes this year. The final runner was the tough four-year-old colt Faugh-a-Ballagh, frequently ridden by Fordham but today the mount of Fred Webb; he'd won the Alexandra Plate and four other races in 1883 for another former patron of Fordham's, the Duke of Beaufort. As the only three-year-old in the field Ladislas carried 7st 12lb; he received a stone from Corrie Roy, 18lb from the four-year-old Dutch Oven and 21lb from Faugh-a-Ballalgh. If those weight concessions were insufficient hardships to overcome, Ladislas's rivals also had to combat Fordham's peerless empathy with every dip, rise and blade of grass on the course.

Corrie Roy looked in the pink of condition and gave Charlie Wood nothing but satisfaction judging by the big smile he wore throughout the early stages. He thought he could leave the rest of them standing whenever he wanted. All the while Ladislas appeared to be toiling. 'Fordham grimaced and seemed to be flogging and spurring his horse for all he was worth,' according to the writer Arnold Binstead.' In reality Fordham had hardly touched Ladislas – nor did he till within six lengths of the post. 'Then he set to riding Ladislas in earnest and Wood tumbled to the fact that he'd been sold.' But it was too late and by the time Wood got his mare into full stride, the post had been passed and Ladislas had hung on. 'With the sole exception, perhaps, of Archer's finish on Melton for the Derby,' concluded Binstead, 'it was the finest piece of riding that I have ever seen.' Charles Morton swore he'd never seen anything like it in his life: 'Fordham gave them something to remember. He dropped down on Charlie Wood in the last 50 yards and beat him a head amid a turmoil of excitement. The redoubtable Charlie, never at a loss on such occasions, remarked to me after the race: "What do you think of that? You never know where he is on the course. He ought to be somewhere else!" – mentioning a place slightly warmer than Newmarket!'

The Sporting Life was no less in awe:

That Ladislas ran gamely and straight to the end there can be no doubt, but without in any way deprecating the merit of the horse's performance, the race in every way belonged to that erstwhile 'demon', and still princely horseman, Fordham, and it is not going one whit too far in praise of the performance to assert that almost countless are the examples 'George' in his time has given of his perfection in the art of horsemanship, he never exhibited it in a better light or rode a finer race in his life.

There is no record of any comments passed by the Duchess of Montrose, her face a picture of wintry detachment, as Fordham returned to a tumultuous acclaim redolent of Caesar driving his chariot into Rome after vanquishing the Gauls. Or, for that matter, any words that dropped from the jockey's lips as he passed by her en route to the weighing room. But one likes to think those brown eyes of his twinkled, the habitually friendly lips thinned and out of the corner of his mouth he hissed: 'You must not take a liberty with George.'

The Duchess was doubtless further irritated to learn that another of her arch enemies had also profited from Corrie Roy's defeat. Theodore 'Plunger' Walton was a Philadelphia hotelier and gambler who'd regularly plundered the prices on her horses. He'd done the same to Sir John Astley and, in the hearing of the entire Ring, was offered a sound thrashing by the baronet if he repeated the offence. Walton escaped this far larger opponent, though he was still forced to flee the country at the end of 1882 leaving accounts unsettled to the amount of £11,000. But like a bent nickel he turned up in Newmarket for the Jockey Club Cup. On the morning of the race he was strolling down the High Street with Binstead when he spotted a playing card on the pavement. He found it to be the seven of hearts. 'This is a dead straight tip to me,' he said, 'and I should play whatever is number seven on the card in the big race today.' Binstead assured Walton the Cup was virtually a walk-over for Corrie Roy who'd 'more likely be number one or two on the card.' The 'Plunger' wouldn't be moved: 'I can't help that. You play number seven, d'ya hear?' Number seven on the card was Ladislas. Walton began backing the colt for all he was worth. 'The Yank piled the stuff on,' reported Binstead, 'but it hardly affected the betting.'

Several 'jockeys in the Stand' blamed Wood for Corrie Roy's defeat. Chetwynd sprang to his jockey's defence – despite losing heavily on the race himself. 'Wood had to make all his own running and if he did not make the pace strong enough over such a long course, left out in the cold as he was by himself, three or four lengths in front, with a wholesome dread of Fordham waiting behind him, I do not think he was much to be blamed for being out-ridden by such a master of his art as Fordham.' And no blame should be directed at Corrie Roy. A month later she shouldered top weight of 9st 10lb to win the Manchester November Handicap by a head conceding 52lb to the runner up. The explanation for the partnership's defeat was simple: the genius of George Fordham.

Those who chronicled Fordham's career in the saddle were adamant it was defined by four great rides. However, it seems churlish for this performance on Ladislas not to be appended as a fifth.

***

Fordham's 77th and final winner of 1883 came, and wouldn't one know it, at the expense of Fred Archer. It gave him a share of third place in the list with Sam Loates and was number 2,587, and the last, of his career.

The race was the Brighton Cup on 31 October. His mount was de Rothschild's trusty five-year-old Brag on whom he'd already won five times during the season. Archer was aboard John Porter's crack filly Geheimniss, winner of the previous year's Oaks and four good races in 1883. She was a 2 to 1 on favourite. Brag received 18lb from the filly and Fordham made every pound worth double. Brag won by five lengths.

The 'gift' of Fordham's second coming had lasted six full seasons. But 1884 would prove a season too far. Fordham attended his beloved stamping ground of Newmarket Heath on Two Thousand Guineas afternoon. It had needed a herculean effort on his part to get there at all, so fast was his health failing. But he made an attempt to oblige old friend Mr John Foy by riding Scot Free in the Guineas. He found it was useless and he told Foy it would impair the colt's chances it he rode him because he was so weak he felt uncertain of keeping his seat in the saddle. Scot Free went out with Billy Platt (no more than a 'Butcher Boy' according to his detractors) to win the Classic by five lengths.

On 8 August Fordham's 'indifferent health' had improved sufficiently for him to make a belated appearance in the silks of Leopold de Rothschild aboard the two-year-old colt St Swithin in the five-furlong Great South of England Breeders Stakes at Lewes. The weather was, in the words of *The Sportsman*, 'broiling', and 'George, on mounting the colt came in for quite an ovation and was loudly cheered all the way to the post.' St Swithin made a race of it till half way before dropping away to finished fifth of six. Six days later, 14 August, he partnered another juvenile for 'Mr Leo': Aladdin in Windsor's Park Plate over six furlongs. They beat two home. 'The Kidder' passed the scales for the last time. The demonic fires had been doused for good. De Rothschild was a man renowned for his generosity and unconditional loyalty to those who served him. He marked the occasion with the presentation to his jockey of a handsome pipe in a case engraved with the legend 'Smoke flies away but friendship lasts.' Bookending that engraved on Smith's whip marking the start of his career, this sentiment signalling its end is a fitting summation of Fordham the man as well as Fordham the jockey. 'Mr Leo' replicated the generosity of his father toward the jockey they both admired by rewarding him with an annual pension of £1,000 paid in quarterly instalments of £250.

The Morning Post revealed what most had anticipated on 8 September:

> It was with no little pleasure we read of George Fordham's reappearance in the summer at Lewes and Windsor; but since then we have heard with unfeigned regret that the best all-round jockey and finest horseman the Turf has seen since Jem Robinson has abandoned all hope of ever riding again.

During this Indian summer Fordham added a further 428 winners to his tally – including his twelfth century (105 in 1880) and five more Classics, notably his Derby on Sir Bevys.

The retired gent.

FIFTEEN

IMMORTAL GEORGE

Fordham's greatness might be measured by statistics alone. He enjoyed 16 Classic victories, placing him joint seventh in the all-time list behind Lester Piggott - highlighted by that record total of seven in the One Thousand Guineas. Indeed, of the era's numerous great races, from the Lincolnshire Handicap through to the Shrewsbury Cup, the only one to elude him was the St Leger. He was champion jockey 14 times between 1855 and 1871, a total second only to Gordon Richards. He set seasonal records of 147 and 166 in 1860 and 1862 respectively; and rode 2,587 British winners altogether (plus a dozen or more in France and Ireland) that also established a new record. Despite the increasing proliferation of opportunities in 20th and 21st century racing provided by night racing and all-weather surfaces, he still retains tenth place on the all-time list behind Richards. And he rode seven winners from seven rides on one card (albeit 'losing' the dead heat in the run-off), a feat in this country beyond all bar Llanfranco Dettori.

In the summer of 1884 it was time to reminisce. Fordham welcomed a reporter from *The Illustrated Sporting & Dramatic News* into his Brighton residence overlooking Norfolk Square to look back on his riding career. The journalist found the jockey with a clear eye and healthy complexion, 'looking much better than he looked at Newmarket during Guineas week. Indeed, Fordham had been riding out in some comfort, even to the extent of partnering Leopold de Rothschild's Derby hope Talisman in a gallop; and, though the prospect didn't arise in the conversation, he was two months away from making his shock reappearance in the saddle at Lewes. Sat in his dining room, beneath portraits of some of his equine friends such as Hampton, Levity and Little David, Fordham produced the bible and the whip presented to him by the latter's owner way back in 1853 and read aloud the inscription he'd tried his best to follow throughout his career: 'Honesty is the best policy.'

Now was not the occasion to ask 'the Demon' about his struggle with alcohol or goad him into settling old scores with Lord St Vincent, CaptainMachell, 'Carrie Red' or Fred Archer. The conversation dwelt on happier times. It quickly turned to the great horses he'd ridden: who was the best?

> Well, it's hard to say, I've ridden so many. Perhaps Nutbush was the speediest of all. The old Admiral used to say so. She was a little mare, but carried wonderful weights, and went an extraordinary pace. Then there was Formosa, she was a fine mare. Then there was Lord Clifden. I've heard people say I beat Macaroni and won that Derby. Ah, but I did not! Lady Elizabeth? She lost her form and ran very badly.

What does he think of the present crop of young riders?

> Well, of course the young 'uns lose their heads when it comes to a finish, but so do the old ones, too, very often! They begin too soon, nowadays. They get to be jockeys all at once – I mean they are put up to ride a horse, and he carries them home, and then they don't win when it comes to real racing, and you hear about their 'bad luck'. It isn't bad luck, it's because they don't know how to ride – haven't learnt. I didn't become a jockey all at once, I can tell you, and in my young days we used to ride heats, which was good practice.

Who does he miss from not riding?

> Custance! He's a rum one, is Custance, you know. Mr Leopold de Rothschild is such a kind friend to me. I like him so much. He's always sending me something. Look at these magnificent grapes he's sent me just now.

Finally, the secret of riding his beloved Newmarket and judging its finishing line to a nicety?

> I always tried for the 'sheep track'. It was easier going on the track, if I could get there comfortably I think. I've often, as I've walked along those courses, stood and tried to find out just the line, and sometimes I've asked other people where they thought it was. It's not so easy to find the exact place to win as some people think. I've told men who've been with me to stand in the place and gone in the box and found they were a long way out. The best judges of racing are deceived about what's won when they stand near the winning post, you know. It's only the Judge himself, who's got them in line, that can tell. He's got a straight line, and can see what passes over it first.

And, on departure, the delicate question of what he regarded as the root cause of his present predicament: 'I expect it's the wasting that has weakened me.'

The damage done to Fordham's lungs was irreparable; the right lung in particular. The phrase 'galloping consumption' was no exaggeration in his case. That he lingered a further three years after hanging up his boots was a minor miracle. By the same token those extra years brought the torture of greater pain and a protracted death.

It was going to be a long dusk as the light died in George Fordham. But he could be in no doubt his sun was setting.

***

Fordham prepared for death in the familiar surroundings of Slough. The family moved into Villa Montrose, named with a sly nod to his one-time patroness; like Beaufort House, it was a prettily situated property in The Grove. Occasional relief sought amid fresh sea air. In September 1886 Fordham spent 10 days in Margate with his friend William Chalk, son of the local midwife who'd delivered his children; he complained of the weather being too cold but returned to Slough refreshed nevertheless. The following March he went to Bournemouth accompanied by his wife and daughters for a month. The visit was not an unqualified success; Bournemouth 'didn't agree with him.'

However, any relief was purely temporary – as his doctors had warned. He watched some football and cricket matches, enjoyed daily rides with 'Old Bill', as he referred to Chalk, in his pony and trap; and on several occasions attended the start and finish of meets of Sir Robert Harvey's Harriers and the Household Brigade Hounds. On 20 September 1887 he made was what to be his last public appearance, attending a cricket match between the Slough and Colnbrook fire brigades at the nearby Dolphin ground, again in the safe keeping of 'Old Bill'.

Villa Montrose

The final act commenced on the last day of September. A telegram is sent to his 21-year-old son George in Burton on Trent where he is employed by the brewery: the consumptive cough that wracked his father's wasted body had worsened and he is confined to bed under the auspices of his physician, Dr Brickwell. Put bluntly, Fordham was functioning on one lung; the other was almost entirely eaten away. On the first day of October the news is confirmed in print: 'His illness has acquired a serious aspect,' stated the *Pall Mall Gazette,* 'and the gravest apprehensions are entertained.' *The Sportsman* reported 'such a very severe and serious attack is attributed to taking an overdose of fruit salts.' A comfortable night's sleep and some milk and mutton broth left him breathing better and more cheerful, his mood buoyed by numerous inquiries for the latest information on his condition 'from all classes of society that testifies to the great esteem in which the grand horseman is held.' He is able to sit up in bed and writes a note to Chalk who undertakes the task of sitting with him through the nights. Brickwell reveals he'll never leave his bed again: 'He may lay for some time to come, but there is very little hope of his recovery.'

Bulletins are issued morning, noon and night; abbreviated reports of his condition syndicated in every provincial newspaper. Partial relief from periodic bouts of severe coughing comes only from a cocktail of milk and champagne. But, like Hamlet, 'The Demon' will not be granted the mercy of a swift 'shuffle off this mortal coil'. His will be that tableau of Victorian death beloved of cheap melodrama. He puts his affairs in order; he signs his Will; and a macabre death watch commences.

On Sunday, the ninth, the Fordhams gather round his bed, enabling him to distribute a number of specific mementos: gold and silver cups, goblets, claret jugs and plate accumulated during his career. This seemed to give him some measure of release. His voice grew stronger. On the Monday his son felt able to leave for Burton. That afternoon Fordham suffered a relapse. *The Sportsman* states he is 'very much worse, his cough is very distressing and he is at times very choked with phlegm. He remains conscious but no hopes are entertained. He is sinking fast.'

That same day *The Morning Post* prints the contents of a poignant pencil-written note from the dying champion: 'I should like to thank very much all kind enquiries after my health, as they have been far too many to write to; also to thank all nobleman and gentlemen for their long and honourable support.' Two such aristocrats, the Earl of Coventry and Lord Arthur Somerset, make the journey to Slough to pay their last respects.

On the Tuesday Fordham appeared to mount a defiant rally. It proves the false dawn gifted to many a dying man. His 'distressing cough' is alleviated by some bread-and-milk fortified with a dash of old port wine. How 'The Demon' must've relished the taste of this favourite tipple. Chalk sits up with him through the ensuing restless night which is punctuated by severe fits of coughing. Fordham sips a little milk and champagne. He asks Chalk which horse won the Cesarewitch, and one of his daughters reads him a description of the race from a newspaper.

At mid-day on the Wednesday, 12 October, Lydia Fordham and her two step-daughters Blanche and Nellie (George junior is unfortunately detained in Burton) sit beside their patriarch in anticipation of the inevitable. The lines on the face they know and love are now not so much drawn as incised to the bone. Death is working through him; driving life to the extremities. Even his voice sounds like ashes. They watch him eat some scalloped oysters washed down with a little brandy. At 6pm he sends for Chalk to join the vigil: 'I thought you would be with me in my last moments.' Those are his final words. He remains conscious till the end comes. Within ten minutes of death he's still able to sign two cheques; and swallow a tot of brandy like a condemned man mustering Dutch courage at the last stop before Tyburn Tree.

But there is no fight left in a body reduced to little more than a husk of its former self. Fordham closes his eyes and, one likes to think, stole a leaf from Stephen Dedalus's book by conjuring fleeting memories of 'vanished horses stood in homage...their meek necks poised in air...he saw their speeds...and shouted with the shouts of vanished crowds.' At 6.15 the white light of eternity beckons, and 'Immortal George' joins the other 'Immortals' in racing's Valhalla.

The official bulletin released at 7.20pm states: 'His final moments were most peaceable.' The official cause of death was given as: 'Exhaustion 20 days. Necrosis of right lung three years.'

***

Within the space of a year the Victorian Turf had bid farewell to its two most celebrated jockeys. The obituarists and tribute writers once more reached for their pens, led by the Turf's two principal trade papers:

The Sporting Life: Fordham was dearly loved, not only for his straightforward and bright career as a jockey, but also for his many other excellent qualities in private life. His truthfulness and honesty of purpose in all his dealings being such that it never left the slightest margin for anyone to place the least speck upon his well-known unblemished character. Fordham was the very happy illustration of a self-made man. He won his way to the top of the tree as much by his blameless character as his professional skill – on the wide course at Newmarket he had no equal in his best day. Throughout his lengthy career this prince of horsemen always bore an untarnished name. With the exception of, perhaps, John Osborne, no rider has been so long before the public, and his many achievements are matters of Turf history. For judgement of pace and 'kid' he was never equalled. Fordham's career was long and honourable and of unblemished splendour. We may say of him that 'After life's fitful fever he sleeps well.'

The Sportsman: Thus ends an honourable career on the Turf extending over 30 years during which time the faintest breath of suspicion never sullied his name. One of the best jockeys ever lifted into a saddle has passed away. This opinion was confirmed years ago by old experienced men who had understood the skill of Sam Chifney and James Robinson and other celebrities of long bygone days. The deep feeling of regret today throughout the country when the news of his death circulated will be keen, for Fordham was a man who, so far as his calling was concerned, led an almost blameless life. Many a young jockey had to thank him for sound and useful advice. Indeed, it was one of the finest traits of his character that he never attempted to take advantage of a youngster at the start, and it may safely be stated that he was one of the fairest riders that ever crossed a saddle. He was always the first to give encouragement to a beginner. He was implicitly trusted alike by his employers and the public, and the Turf can ill afford to lose him. His memory will long live fresh and green in the hearts of his friends.

Periodicals regularly carrying Turf content followed suit:

The Illustrated Sporting & Dramatic News (while advertizing the sale of postcards of Fordham at sixpence each): George Fordham bore a name which so long as racehorses are run on English turf will be held in high honour as that of a rider who was both jockey and sportsman, the two terms not being always applicable to the members of his craft. Fordham was a model jockey; certainly a jockey whose name will live in the annals of race riding.That all those who have testified to Fordham's skill should have felt compelled to praise his honesty is very much to the credit of the renowned horseman who has been taken from among us, but hardly compliments those who have survived. There must be many jockeys upon whom the praise could not justly be bestowed. Not even to his most intimate friend was he given to describe secrets, which he was wont to aver, were not his. "Kidding" was his chief characteristic; comparatively little mention has been made of his excellent hands, his marvellous knowledge of pace and his strength at the finish of a race.

Pall Mall Gazette: No jockey during the present century has been so esteemed and admired by all classes for his superb skills and unblemished integrity. He possessed every attribute: an equable temper; great patience; exquisite hands; unshaken nerves; consummate jockeyship; and a thorough comprehension of horses. Above all he possessed an honesty that has never during his long career been questioned.

Baily's Magazine: If rough and unpolished in his manner, Fordham, in relations of life, showed himself possessed of more valuable attributes; and his name will ever rank in the annals of the Turf with those of the highest artists in the saddle during the time he flourished.

National dailies joined in:

The Times: To many of those who have the experience and judgment required for making a comparison between the two, it will seem that the death of Fordham removes one who was an even more perfect master of his art than Archer. Certain it is that Fordham had such knowledge of pace and of distances as Archer had not yet acquired;

and if 'The Demon' did not win the Derby and the St Leger so often as Archer, frequenters of Newmarket will not readily forget some of his magnificent finishes. Fordham owed a great deal of his success to the fact that he rode with his head as well as his hands, and he was never seen to greater advantage than in one of those matches which Admiral Rous, Mr Ten Broeck and one or two others of the old school loved to make.

The Morning Post: No man who made race-riding a profession exhibited greater cleverness in deceiving opponents as to the merits of his mounts while he repeatedly exhibited a fertility of resource. And the faintest breath of suspicion never reached his proceedings.

Evening Standard: The death of George Fordham removes a jockey whose name will not soon be forgotten in the history of the Turf. It may be doubted whether a finer horseman ever sat in a saddle. With all his remarkable qualities as a horseman, Archer did not excel Fordham and probably did not equal him in the judgement and finesse by which victory is often secured against superior odds. During the years when his skill excited the warmest admiration of experts, Fordham's staunch integrity was no less conspicuous. It is noteworthy that a man who was never powerful should have had such perfect mastery over fractious and excitable horses. It was the head and not the muscle that made Fordham a great horseman.

Fordham's death was national news. Truncated versions of Fleet Street's many tributes appeared in provincial newspapers nationwide. No corner of the country was left in any doubt that a distinguished sportsman blessed with extraordinary gifts and reputation to match had passed away before his time.

Ralph Waldo Emerson might have had Fordham in mind when he penned the words: 'To earn the approbation of honest citizens and endure the betrayal of false friends; to have played ans laughed with enthusiasm and sung with exaltation. This is to have succeeded.'

***

After a spell of boisterous weather, Tuesday 18 October seemed tempered to the occasion of Fordham's funeral. There was not a breath of wind and the trees framing The Grove were half hidden by a softening haze which would have been fog but for the warm sunshine which held it in check and lit up Villa Montrose with a cheering light. It seemed as if nature herself had spread a mantle to deaden all sound, for the autumn leaves had fallen so thickly that even passing conveyances failed to raise more than a soothing rustle. Everything was suggestive of peace and rest, even down to the plaintive song of a robin chirruping from a tree top.

By noon the dining room of Villa Montrose overlooking the immaculately cropped lawn at the back of the house was completely filled with a collection of wreaths; those from the staff at Newmarket racecourse, the proprietors of *The Sportsman* and *The Sporting Life*, and Leopold de Rothschild, with a card saying 'A mark of sincere esteem and regard', epitomizing the breadth of Fordham's standing in the brotherhood of the Turf. Presiding over the table was a substantial cross composed of lilies, roses and ferns from his widow and children. Among the other floral tributes spread round the room were wreaths from Fordham's numerous friends among the ranks of owners, trainers and jockeys: 'Lord Freddy' Swindell, Captain Douglas Lane, Tom Jennings Junior, John Porter, James Dover, Jack Watts, Charlie Wood, John Osborne.

Mourners gather to view the cortege.

The cortege left Villa Montrose at 2 pm. The hearse, a handsome 'Washington Car', was drawn by four black Flemish horses plumed with sable feathers and adorned with heavy velvet trappings. Five mourning coaches followed, each drawn by a pair of full-maned and jet-black horses. Lydia Fordham and her three eldest children, George, Blanche and Nellie, rode in the first; Henry Custance was in the third; 'Lord Freddy' was among those in the fourth; Dr Brickwell, 'Old Bill and George Barrett (representing Tom Cannon) followed in the fifth. The glass sides of the car enabled onlookers a fine view of the wreaths and flowers adorning the coffin around the head of which were satin ribbons in the de Rothschild colours of blue and yellow. The procession made slow progress owing to the press of the crowd that fully vindicated the police presence, and the short journey to St Laurence's church where the Reverend H Saville Young, the rector of Slough and Upton, awaited its arrival, took 40 minutes to complete.

Fordham had requested his funeral be as private as possible and invitations extended were confined within rigid limits. Nevertheless, a vast crowd assembled amid the yew trees in the ancient churchyard to see him laid to rest, those who knew him and those who just came to pay their respects to a legendary jockey and the finest of sportsmen. A party of friends and admirers had packed a carriage on the Paddington train; local shopkeepers, workmen, apprentices and domestic servants either asked for leave or just took it anyway in order to mingle with countless retired gentlemen and even their Member of Parliament. It was evident Fordham's adopted home town of Slough had come to love him. Everyone present seemed to have known him and had a favourite Fordham anecdote to relate.

The coffin was carried into the 12th century church and placed on a bier in the nave while a tiny bell in the campanile overhead tolled the funeral dirge. At Fordham's express command the polished breast-plate on his coffin of English oak carried the legend:

It's not the race we ride,
'Tis the pace that kills.

After a short service the coffin was carried out to the mournful tones of the 'Dead March in Saul' from the church organ and borne to the plot Fordham had chosen near the pathway leading to the north door of the church which contained the remains of his infant daughter Penelope. The sides of the brick-lined grave were decorated with evergreens and wreaths. At the foot of the grave stood a rose bush with a single blood-red bloom half opened and drooping, nipped by the early frost, and symbolic of a life now passed away. In the words of the poet: 'Earth received an honoured guest.'

So many onlookers filed past the grave to steal one last glimpse of the coffin that fully two hours elapsed before the gravediggers and stonemasons could begin the completion of their tasks. This unusual epitaph on Fordham's coffin would be replicated on his tombstone. It seemed to encapsulate a lifetime of hard work. It spoke of brilliant feats of horsemanship; visions of bright silks flashing across greensward; of panting steeds thundering over the turf; of strained nerves and muscles; of bustle, anxiety and feverish excitement. Many of those present who saw the occupant of that highly polished coffin in his pomp could well appreciate the motto he chose to be remembered by.

Among the gathered members of the Press, however, there was a feeling that 'the Demon' had not received the unqualified show of respect from the Turf community that was his due. Charles Blake, editor of *The Sporting Life*, had this to say:

> At the graveside I looked around for the many friends that one would expected to have seen pay honour to George Fordham's last day upon earth but they were not there. Perhaps it is the fashion not to show outward sympathy by personal presence. However, I am too old fashioned,

in regretting the absence of many of those who were so closely identified with the famous jockey's career. There may have been others there that escaped my observation or information but I am only echoing the general feeling that there was a disappointment felt at the absence of many old friends whose presence could be counted upon.

I can only say that this was a kind of murmur and impression which ran through the minds of many of those present this afternoon and may naturally have brought forth the question 'Is life worth living for?'

Blake had a valid point. On the day of the funeral there was nothing other than run-of-the-mill mixed cards at Croydon, Shrewsbury and Newcastle to distract the Turf's leading lights. Prominent members of the Press turned out in force. Yet upon scanning the mourners for leading members of the Turf community the only principals Blake spotted were jockeys Custance and Barrett and trainers Porter and Dover. No-one, least of all 'The Demon', would've expected an appearance from the Duchess of Montrose or Captain Machell, hamstrung as their consciences must've been by their shabby behaviour toward him. Fordham had been predeceased by the Drewitts, Frederic Lagrange, Joseph Hayhoe, John Day and 'Mr Mellish'; Richard Ten Broeck was back in America and Christopher-Joachim Lefevre dare not set foot in the country. But the absence of friends and confederates like Hodgman, Chetwynd and Astley plus the likes of Alec Taylor, Joseph Cannon and Henry Woolcott from the ranks of trainers he'd served with distinction struck some as desperately disappointing. Even 'Mr Leo' stayed away, although in his case that decision likely as not resulted from a reluctance to subject the depth of his grief to public scrutiny. It's possible that by snubbing Archer's funeral Fordham may have disaffected some; but, if so, it's unlikely this would've escaped mention in the Turf Press.

The final resting place of 'Immortal George'.

Fordham's Will, signed a fortnight before his death, proved at £19,903 (*£1.6 million*) – considerably less than Archer's estate of £60,000 and due, by all accounts, to losses incurred from dubious investments following his initial retirement in 1875. His widow Lydia was bequeathed £5,000 and all his possession except those specified otherwise; his 21-year-old son George received £5,000 on attaining the age of 25; Blanche (aged 20) £3,000 in trust for her when 25 or on her marriage previously; a similar sum went to 18-year-old Nellie; and £2,000 to May (aged six); all four children to receive the interest thereof in the meantime.

***

Within the space of 11 months the two greatest jockeys of the Victorian age who'd opposed each other with such vehemence in life were reunited in death. Although it is fashionable to paint the past in roseate hues, the fact remains that the three decades 1860 to 1880 in Victorian England was a period particularly rich in superb jockeys, one standing comparison with any similarly lauded period in the 20th century. It's a moot point whether Donoghue and Richards or Piggott and Eddery dominated their contemporaries as much as Archer and Fordham did theirs. Comparisons, it's said, are odious – and pointless. The racing seat has been streamlined; race tactics diversified; the training of the thoroughbred itself fine-tuned. But when all due allowances have been made and caveats tabled one cannot escape the notion that greatness lies in the pages of history. Glory may be fleeting but the truth is never forgotten. Fordham's untouchable status is epitomized by the judgement of Sir Robert Sly, a Victorian patriarch of the Turf: 'I have seen two great jockeys in my time, Jem Robinson and George Fordham. But George was not only a great, he was an *honest* jockey.'

Fordham was the sort of loveable character who enlivened the fringes of a Dickensian novel. He was the Barkis or Micawber taken to heart by Victorian England; the diamond in its midst; one of their own. As a jockey he was a diamond in the rough, an instinctive genius incapable of analysing or explaining his alchemy beyond a mumbled equivalent of 'Barkis is willin.' As a man he was a flawed diamond. If for no other reason his fondness for a tipple placed him firmly in the camp of Wilkins Micawber. It was said he made just two mistakes in his life – one professional and one personal. He was guilty of looking round in Lord Clifden's Derby; and he acted naively in heeding the advice of M Lefevre on matters financial. The first charge he accepted; the second he denied. However, little was made of a single fact which clearly showed his enviable wisdom, namely that he steadfastly refused ever to vote in a parliamentary election.

Fordham's wife (who never remarried) always referred to her husband as 'Immortal George.' That's a grand sentiment. It may be biased. Yet it hardly brooks dissention. In the words of the younger Pliny: 'History ought never magnify matters of fact because worthy actions require nothing but truth.'

George Fordham, 'The Kidder' and 'The Demon' of the Victorian Turf, merits a lofty pedestal to himself for all eternity.

Weighed in and passed the scales, the last race run
Also weighed out to take the final flight:
And we who saw how straight he went and won,
Divine the verdict there, as here, 'all right.'

The feather weight was never feather-brained,
Had 'hands' and knees, almighty pluck and 'head'.
The fame be as 'The Kid' so swiftly gained,
Was his for life, and crowns the veteran dead.

Glued to the 'pigskin' in the 'plunging' days,
When many a fortune hung upon his skill,
Or won or lost, bestowed his mead of praise:
With 'Fordham up' the cynics' tongues were still!

Of all the members of a famous group,
We think of Fordham in his work and play,
His 'nursing', 'make believe', triumphant stoop –
Most brilliant horseman of a brilliant day!

Write then his epitaph, write one and all,
Who race for name and fame or simple self.
Faithful was Fordham, unto Fordham's call:
He rode for honour, riding for himself.
Byron Webber

APPENDIX ONE: CAREER
TOTAL OF WINNERS

Fordham's career total of winners has always been given as 2,587. This comprises 2,159 up to his two-year sabbatical of 1876 and 1877; followed by an additional 428 on his return between 1878 and 1884. The available sources of reference – *The Sporting Life*, *The Sportsman* and *Ruff's Guide to the Turf* – all agree on the latter figure of 428. That can be taken as accurate.

However, problems arise when examining available figures for the lengthier period leading up to Fordham's first retirement at the end of the 1875 season. Only *The Sporting Life* and *The Sportsman* offer any statistics for the whole period. At the time of his death both papers printed a list of totals per season. Although the two sets of figures tally for the initial nine seasons (1850 to 1858) they do not tally thereafter; nor does either list add up to the figure of 2,159 for the period 1850 to 1875 quoted by writers in both papers. Both fall short. The table in *The Life* came to just 2,118; *The Sportsman* made it 2,145. Those years at odds are 1859; 1860; 1861; 1864; 1865; 1866; 1867; 1868; 1870; 1873. Consequently, it's impossible to state definitively how many winners Fordham rode in those seasons.

Mindful of both aforementioned anomolies it's unwise to trust either table implicitly. The reasons are threefold. First: the haphazard nature of record-keeping during the early 19th century. Second: the demarcation between races held under Rules and races not under Rules may account for wins at some minor meetings being counted by one publication and not another. Third: sometimes a winning jockey is not credited; even the *Racing Calendar* does not always name the winning jockey in a walk-over or a match race.

Nonetheless, despite these misgivings, it would be remiss to exclude any sort of statistical summary. The appended table is derived from the *optimum* figure for each season as listed by the three sources (and are those referred to throughout the text). Even so, the *overall* career total based on these figures still falls *six* short of the accepted 2,587. The table should be viewed with that caveat in mind.

1850:	0	1863:	103*	1876: Did Not Ride		
1851:	1	1864:	137	1877: Did Not Ride		
1852:	0	1865:	150*	1878:	54	
1853:	4	1866:	112	1879:	47	
1854:	21	1867:	145*	1880:	105	
1855:	70*	1868:	111*	1881:	62	
1856:	108*	1869:	95*	1882:	79	
1857:	84*	1870:	46	1883:	77	
1858:	91*	1871:	86#	1884:	0	
1859:	118*	1872:	66			
1860:	147*+	1873:	88	* Leading Rider		
1861:	106*	1874:	57	# Joint Leading Rider		
1862:	166*+	1875:	41	+ Record Total		

APPENDIX TWO: CLASSIC RACES WON

ENGLAND

Two Thousand Guineas
1867 Vauban
1868 Formosa
1880 Petronel

Derby
1879 Sir Bevys

Oaks
1859 Summerside
1868 Formosa
1870 Gamos
1872 Reine
1881 Thebais

One Thousand Guineas
1859 Mayonaise
1861 Nemesis
1865 Siberia
1868 Formosa
1869 Scottish Queen
1881 Thebais
1883 Hauteur

FRANCE

Prix du Jockey Club
1861 Gabrielle d'Estrees
1868 Suzerain

Prix de Diane
1880 Versigny

APPENDIX THREE: OTHER MAJOR RACES WON

Ascot

Gold Cup: Lecturer (1867); Mortemer (1871); Henry (1872); Doncaster (1875); Tristan (1883)

Royal Hunt Cup: Chalice (1855); See-Saw (1869); Winslow (1873)

Alexandra Plate: Lecturer (1867); Doncaster (1875)

Ascot Stakes: Optimist (1861); Ishmael (1883)

Ascot Derby: The Earl (1868); Henry (1871); Atlantic (1874); Gilbert (1875); Ladislas (1883)

Gold Vase: Arsenal (1857); Sedbury (1858); Horror (1860); Marie Stuart (1875); Ambassadress (1881); Tristan (1882)

Coronation Stakes: Beechnut (1857); Athena (1868); Siberia (1965)

Hardwicke Stakes: Tristan (1882); Tristan (1883)

New Stakes: Zaidee (1856); Lady Elizabeth (1867); Belladrum (1868); Corisane (1870); Helmet (1871); Ecossais (1873); Wild Thyme (1883)

Prince of Wales's Stakes: Rustic (1866); Vauban (1867); Martyrdom (1869); Glengarry (1878)

St James's Palace Stakes: The Earl (1868); Dunbar (1869); Bend Or (1880)

Wokingham Stakes: Palmerston (1855); Suburban (1860)

Brighton

Brighton Cup: Adam (1856); Chevalier d'Industrie (1857); Tournament (1860); The Duke (1866); Bay Archer (1880); Brag (1883)

Champagne Stakes: Tournament (1857); Vulcan (1871)

Sussex Cup: Vulcan (1871)

Chantilly

Prix du Gros Chene: Alaric (1872)

Chester

Chester Cup: Epaminondas (1854); Knight of the Garter (1869)

Curragh
Challenge of the Kirwans: Altro (1858)
Kildare Handicap: Nuncio (1860)
Scurry Stakes: Sobieski (1860)
Stewards' Plate: Buckstone (1858)

Doncaster
Champagne Stakes: King of Diamonds (1859); The Marquis (1861); Lord Clifden (1862); Sunshine (1869); Hauteur (1882)
Doncaster Cup: Newcastle (1859); Ackworth (1865); Dutch Skater (1872)
Great Yorkshire Handicap: Prioress (1858); John Davis (1865)
Park Hill Stakes: Athena (1868); Toison d'Or (1869)
Portland Handicap: Welland (1863)

Epsom
City and Suburban Handicap: Adamas (1857)
Epsom Gold Cup: Tristan (1883)
Great Metropolitan Handicap: Captivator (1871); Dutch Skater (1872)
Woodcote Stakes: Lord Clifden (1862); Wild Thyme (1883)

Goodwood
Findon Stakes: Paris (1863); Mde de Figny (1875); Wandering Nun (1880)
Chesterfield Cup: Termagant (1856); Comquot (1857); Prince Plausible (1862); Drummond (1873)
Goodwood Derby: Longdown (1865)
Goodwood Cup: Baroncino (1855); Rogerthorpe (1856); Starke (1861); The Duke (1866); Doncaster (1875)
Goodwood Plate (Stakes): Gomera (1857); Paganini (1870); Taraban (1871); Freeman (1875); Norwich (1878); Fortissimo (1882)
Lavant Stakes: Mr Pitt (1863); Athena (1867); La Coureuse (1873); Mde de Figny (1875)
Molecomb Stakes: Marksman (1866)
Nassau Stakes: Beechnut (1857); Lady Atholstone (1871); Reconciliation (1879); Thebais (1881)
Stewards' Cup: Tournament (1857); Lady Clifden (1862); Elf King (1880)
Sussex Stakes: Jack in the Green (1865); Comte Alfred (1882)
Prince of Wales's Stakes: Mirliflur (1874)

Howth and Baldoyle
Flying Stakes: The Lamb (1860)

Huntingdon
Huntingdonshire Stakes: Field Marshal (1873)

Lewes
Lewes Handicap: Royal Sovereign (1860)
Sussex County Cup: Tournament (1857); Tournament (1858)

Lincoln
Brocklesby Stakes: Conquete (1879)
Lincolnshire Handicap: Saucebox (1855); Vigo (1860)

Liverpool
Liverpool Summer Cup: Pretty Boy (1856); Fairwater (1862)
Liverpool Autumn Cup: Prestonpans (1880)

Longchamp
Grand Prix de Paris: Fervacques (1867); The Earl (1868); Foxhall (1881)
Prix Gladiateur: Dutch Skater (1872)
Prix de la Ville de Paris: Cristal (1868)

Manchester
Manchester Cup: Saucebox (1855); Pretty Boy (1856)

Newmarket
Cambridgeshire: Little David (1853); Odd Trick (1857); See-Saw (1868); Sabinus (1871)
Cesarewitch: Prioress (1857)
Chesterfield Stakes: Cantine (1858); Ecossais (1873); St Marguerite (1881)
Clearwell Stakes: Scout (1858); Rustic (1865); Hannah (1870); Negro (1872); Feu d'Amour (1873); Hauteur (1882)
Craven Stakes: Blue Jacket (1857); Drummond (1874)
Dewhurst Stakes: Ladislas (1882)
Criterion Stakes: Beechnut (1856); The Happy Land (1857); Thormanby (1859); Klarikoff (1860); Flageolet (1872); Miss Toto (1873); Thebais (1880)
Grand Duke Michael Stakes: Athena (1868); Gamos (1870); Flageolet (1873); Novateur (1874); Hamako (1883)

Hopeful Stakes: Mr Pitt (1865); Athena (1867); Flageolet (1872); Wild Thyme (1883)

Jockey Club Cup: Flageolet (1873); Ladislas (1883)

July Stakes: Tolurno (1861); Robin Hood (1865); Lady Elizabeth (1867); Ecossais (1873); Levant (1875)

Middle Park Stakes: Beaudesert (1879); St Louis (1880)

Newmarket Oaks: Gomera (1865); Ischia (1866); Formosa (1868); Verdure (1871); La Coureuse (1874)

Prendergast Stakes: Preceptress (1860); The Marquis (1861); Jack in the Green (1865); Digby Grand (1870); Feu d'Amour (1873)

Newmarket St Leger: The Wizard (1860); Owain Glendwr (1867); Sefton (1878); Bay Archer (1879); Nellie (1882); Ladislas (1883

Northampton

Earl Spencer's Plate: Paris (1865)

Great Northamptonshire Stakes: Borderer (1858); Stampede (1862); Commandant (1881)

Shrewsbury

Shrewsbury Cup: St Giles (1857); Petra (1861); Spitzbergen (1881)

Stamford

Stamford Gold Cup: El Dorado (1854); Borderer (1858); Lecturer (1867)

Stockbridge

Hurstbourne Cup: Lecturer (1867)

Stockbridge Cup: The Clown (1864); Avontes (1879)

Warwick

Warwick Cup: Field Marshal (1873)

York

Gimcrack Stakes: The Earl (1867)

Great Ebor Handicap: Grand Inquisitor (1854); Rising Sun (1861)

Great Yorkshire Stakes: Oldminster (1861); Zetland (1862)

Prince of Wales's Stakes: Escape (1862); Martyrdom (1868); Digby Grand (1870); Nellie (1881)

York Cup: Windham (1866)

Yorkshire Oaks: Ines (1867); Toison d'Or (1869); Belfry (1880); Thebais (1881)

ACKNOWLEDGEMENTS

My thanks to Tim Cox and John Randall for sharing information on the puzzle shrouding Fordham's seasonal totals. And to Father Andrew Allen, Rector of Upton-cum-Chalvey, for providing the photograph of George Fordham's grave. All other illustrations are from the author's collection of contemporary newspapers and periodicals. Anyone wishing to claim copyright on any image is invited to contact the author.

SELECT BIBLIOGRAPHY

Ager *The Blood is Racing* (Charles Ager Publishing 2016)

Astley *Fifty Years of My Life* (Hurst & Blackett1894)

Binstead and Wells *A Pink 'un and a Pelican* (Bliss Sands & Co 1898)

Bird *Admiral Rous and the English Turf* (Putnam 1939)

Blyth *The Pocket Venus* (Weidenfeld & Nicolson 1966)

Cawthorne and Herod *Royal Ascot* (Treherne 1902)

Chetwynd *Racing Reminiscences and Experiences of the Turf* (Longman, Green & Co 1891)

Cook *A History of the English Turf* (Virtue & Co 1904)

Custance *Riding Recollections and Turf Stories* (Edward Arnold 1894)

Day *Racing Reminiscences of the Turf* (Richard Bentley 1896)

Day *Turf Celebrities I Have Known* (White & Co 1891)

Dixon *From Gladiateur to Persimmon* (Grant Richards 1901)

Dizikes *Sportsmen and Gamesmen* (University of Missouri Press 2002)

Fletcher *The History of the St Leger Stakes* (Hutchinson & Co 1926)

Hodgman *Sixty Years on the Turf* (Grant Richards 1908)

Humphris *The Life of Fred Archer* (Hutchinson & Co 1923)

Lambton *Men and Horses I Have Known* (Thornton Butterworth Ld 1924)

Marsh *A Trainer to Two Kings* (Cassell & Co 1925)

Mathieu *The Masters of Manton* (Write First Time 2010)

Mathieu *Beckhampton* (Racing Post Books 2015)

Mortimer *History of the Derby Stakes* (Cassell & Co 1961)

Morton *My Sixty Years of the Turf* (Hutchinson & Co 1930)

Onslow *Captain Mac-Hell* (Sporting Garland Press 1999)

Porter *John Porter of Kingsclere* (Grant Richards 1919)

Radcliffe *Ashgill: the Life & Times of John Osborne* (Sands & Co 1900)

Scott *Turf Memories of Sixty Years* (Hutchinson 1925)

Tanner *Great Jockeys of the Flat* (Guinness 1999)

Taunton *Famous Horses* (Sampson Low, Marston & Co 1901)

Thormanby *Kings of the Turf* (Hutchinson 1898)

Welcome *Fred Archer: His Life and Times* (Faber and Faber Ltd 1967)

Racing Calendar
Ruff's Guide to the Turf

Baily's Magazine of Sports and Pastimes
Bell's Life in London and Sporting Chronicle
Illustrated Sporting and Dramatic News
The Morning Post
The Pall Mall Gazette
The Sporting Chronicle
The Sporting Gazette
The Sporting Life
The Sporting Times
The Sportsman
The Times

INDEX

C

Cambridgeshire ix, 2, 11-13, 19, 56, 63, 73, 111-15, 195, 293, 343, 390
Camelia 162-3
Captain Arthur Annesley 179
Captain Christie 239
Captain Douglas Lane 20, 376
Captain Randolph Stewart 50
Captivator 223, 389
Cesarewitch 11-12, 28, 40, 52, 54, 56, 60, 62-3, 76, 110, 155, 174, 292-3, 308-9, 356-7
Ceylon 139
Chalice 29, 388
Challenge 65, 200, 389
Champagne Stakes 73, 78, 106, 158, 175, 240, 254, 349-50, 388-9
Charibert 325-6
Charles Blake 317, 325, 379
Charles Loates 177
Charles Morton 147, 302, 317, 356, 358
Charlie Wood 177, 334, 340, 355, 357-8, 376
Chester Cup ix, 8, 10, 16, 18, 41, 87, 173, 227, 262, 388
Chesterfield Cup 64-5, 185, 307, 389
Chesterfield Stakes 81, 203, 355, 390
Chippendale 312-13
Chislehurst 349
Christopher-Joachim Lefevre 119, 124, 134, 219, 344, 348, 380

City and Suburban Handicap 389
Clearwell Stakes 123, 349, 390
Clemintine 316
Colonel Edwyn Burnaby 50, 179
Cora 8
Corisande 322
Coroner 29, 62
Corrie Roy 292, 355-60
Cotherstone 109
Cristal 212, 390
Criterion Stakes 64, 390
Cromwell 319
Crucifix 83

D

Danny Maher 302
DD Palmer 46
Derby 34-6, 56-7, 68-70, 78, 107-10, 128-32, 185-6, 195-9, 210-18, 231-43, 246-57, 288-91, 321-7, 329-32, 337-41
Dewhurst Stakes 390
Diamond 166
Digby Grand 283-6, 295, 391
Don Juan 155
Doncaster 2, 17-18, 26-7, 56, 68-70, 72-3, 80, 86, 91, 131-2, 223-4, 228, 230-1, 288, 388-9
Doncaster Cup 26, 70, 131, 166, 389
Dr Brickwell 370, 378
Dr Shorthouse 279
Drumhead 272
Drummond 230-1, 389-90
Duc de Morny 138

J

Jack 'Deafie' Morris   174

James Cookson   80, 227

James Dover   161, 376

James Fordham   2

James Merry   39, 90, 159, 224-5, 251, 253, 262

James Waugh   159, 226, 253

Jem Adams   81

Jem Goater   177, 226

Jem Robinson   46, 302, 305, 362, 382

Jem Snowden   277, 293

Jenny Howlett   294

Jockey Club   14, 16, 30, 40, 50, 65, 72, 88, 122-3, 132-3, 136-9, 166, 182-4, 347-8, 356-7

Jockey Club Cup   133, 292, 348, 356, 359, 391

John Bahram Day   17, 28, 33-5, 38-40, 80, 146, 304

John Bowes   109

John Corlett   94, 299, 307

John Daley   205, 249, 254

John Day   33, 35, 38, 75, 81, 104, 190, 192, 194, 204, 207, 218-19, 250, 332, 380

John Gully   35, 38, 171, 192

John Jackson   84, 89, 171, 176, 280

John Mannington   244, 278

John Osborne   149, 247, 302, 307, 312, 373, 376

John Porter   78, 81, 146, 198, 203, 219, 304, 337, 361, 376

John Radcliffe   147

John Scott   34, 38, 109, 237

John Wells   21-2, 27-8, 30, 62, 71, 185, 235, 293, 307

Joseph Cannon   332, 380

Joseph Enoch   199, 251

Joseph Hayhoe   322, 380

Jouvence   14, 29

JR Keene   339

Julius   92, 94, 186, 205-6, 209, 250, 252

July Stakes   92, 158-9, 161, 203, 231, 288, 349, 391

K

Kaiser   132

Kangaroo   196

Kermesse   338

Kildare Handicap   389

Kildonan   224

Kingcraft   112, 128, 257, 259, 261

Kitchener   8, 16

Klarikoff   237, 240, 242, 390

L

Ladislas   158, 348, 356-60, 388, 390-1

Lady Clifden   239, 307, 389

Lady Coventry   81, 83, 86, 162, 203

Lady Elizabeth   81, 84-6, 107, 126, 159, 186, 188-90, 197-207, 209-19, 228, 252, 283, 354, 366, 388

Lady Florence Paget   190, 248

Lady Langden   323

Lancastrian   37, 69, 312

Lansdown   324, 331

Lecompte   48, 51-2, 57

Rustic 75, 388, 390

S

Sabinus 91, 111-15, 185, 285,
    336, 390
Sam Rogers 58-9, 173, 189
Sammy Mordan 308
Samuel Kenyon 102, 293
Saucebox 61-3, 390
Saunterer 89, 281, 283
Scottish Queen 78-9, 387
Scurry Stakes 65, 99, 389
Sedbury 64, 388
See-Saw 81, 106, 197, 388, 390
Shotover 219, 338
Siberia 75-7, 387-8
Silvio 312-13
Sir Bevys 314, 319, 321, 323-6,
    328-31, 356, 362, 387
Sir Charles Legard 185
Sir George Chetwynd 113, 125,
    146, 174-5, 219, 257, 270,
    285, 315, 318, 322, 328,
    330, 336
Sir John Astley 4, 125, 136, 173,
    228, 265, 270-1, 295, 300,
    319, 343, 359
Sir Lydston Newman 50, 56
Slane 9, 11
Sobieski 65, 389
Spinaway 311
Squirrel 323-5
St Hubert 39
St James's Palace Stakes 215, 388
St Marguerite 338, 355, 390
St Swithin 361
Stamford Cup 21
Starke 56-7, 148, 389

Sterling 111-13, 115, 175-6
Stewards Cup 10, 99, 237, 239,
    249, 353
Stockbridge Cup 128, 391
Summerside 71-3, 81, 387
Sunlight 254, 257
Sunshine 89-91, 253-7, 261-
    2, 389
Sussex Stakes 389
Suzerain 137-8, 213, 387
Sydenham Dixon 189, 202,
    254, 331

T

Tankesley 52-3, 56
Taraban 109-11, 308, 389
Tarragona 178-84, 215
Tass Parker 225, 261
Termagant 64, 389
Thebais 159, 338, 353-5, 387,
    389-90
Thomas Fordham 4, 72
Thora 354
Thormanby 15, 56, 121-2, 147,
    158, 253, 291, 339, 390
Tom Aldcroft 176, 226
Tom Ashmall 31, 74, 173
Tom Cannon 77, 86, 115, 149-50,
    174, 177, 196, 201, 212, 268,
    286, 309-10, 378
Tom Chaloner 82, 113, 138-9,
    173-5, 204, 224, 228, 242,
    246-7, 280, 293
Tom French 235, 257, 293
Tom Jennings 122, 129, 135, 174,
    316-17, 376
Tom McGeorge 82, 179

Printed in Great Britain
by Amazon